Reading Luther

Lutheran Theology
German Perspectives and Positions
Vol. 3

VELKD

LUTHERISCHER
WELTBUND
DEUTSCHES
NATIONALKOMITEE

Reading Luther

The Central Texts

Selected and annotated by Martin H. Jung

Published on behalf of the United Evangelical Lutheran Church of Germany (VELKD) with the German National Committee of the Lutheran World Federation (GNC/LWF) by Georg Raatz, Urs Mundt and Saskia Kredig

Translated by Neville Williamson

EVANGELISCHE VERLAGSANSTALT
Leipzig

Bibliographic information published by the Deutsche Nationalbibliothek
The Deutsche Nationalbibliothek lists this publication in the Deutsche Nationalbibliographie; detailed bibliographic data are available on the Internet at https://dnb.dnb.de.

First edition: © Vandenhoeck & Ruprecht GmbH & Co. KG, Martin H. Jung, Luther lesen, Göttingen 2016

This book is printed on age-resistant paper.

Cover: Kai-Michael Gustmann, Leipzig
Typesetting: Steffi Glauche, Leipzig
Printing and binding: CPI books GmbH

ISBN Print 978-3-374-06940-8 // eISBN (PDF) 978-3-374-06941-5
www.eva-leipzig.de

Foreword 2021

"The Reformation is a global citizen." That is how Martin Junge, General Secretary of the Lutheran World Federation (LWF), characterized the global dimension of the Reformation anniversary in 2017. And the mother country of the Lutheran Reformation is Germany. Its cradle stood in Wittenberg. The children of this global citizen, Lutherans as well as Protestants from all sorts of denominations all over the world, came to Germany in their thousands during the Reformation Decade as pilgrims visiting the memorial sites of the Reformation. The Luther Garden in Wittenberg, which was laid out on the initiative of the LWF, is a living testimony to the internationality of the Reformation, and it continues to grow.

But what does it mean to be a Lutheran today? For the formation of one's own Lutheran identity, it is helpful to reflect on its origins. What could be more natural than to read Martin Luther? Like Luther, the United Evangelical Church of Germany (VELKD) has adopted the humanist motto "ad fontes" (back to the sources) and published a selection of key texts from Luther's work in 2016 under the title "Luther lesen" (Reading Luther). They stand for important stages during the Reformation movement, whose international relevance became abundantly clear 500 years ago at the Diet of Worms. Luther had to answer to the Emperor, the man who said of himself that the sun never sets on his empire. And he delivered his speech (cf. pp. 124–127) in Latin, the lingua franca of the time, thus being able to address the scientific community throughout Europe. If Luther were alive today, he would be sure to write in English.

The international seminars of the LWF Center in Wittenberg frequently prove how greatly the participants from our partner churches value the opportunity to read Luther's texts and discuss them together. For many of them, it is the first time that they were able to deal directly with the original texts from Luther's hand. These experiences, coupled with the very positive reception of "Luther lesen" in Germany, led to our decision to have the book translated into English. The particular difference in comparison to other Luther editions is that the texts are short, accompanied in each case by an introductory commentary, so that the book is also suitable for private study. We have called our selection "The Central Texts" because we truly believe that the texts in this compilation are of prime importance. Nevertheless, we are conscious of the fact - which is emphasized by the title of our series "Lutheran Theology. German Perspectives and Positions" - that the texts were selected from a German perspective. In other countries, Lutheran Christians may well pose different questions with regard to Luther and consider other texts important. In addition, we hope that the selected texts will also inspire Protestants of other backgrounds, and indeed Christians of all denominations, to engage with Luther's thinking and make it fruitful for their own faith. "Reading Luther" contains such a wide and varied range of texts that it can help everyone to find an individual approach to Luther and his work, no matter where they live.

We believe that reading Luther's writings is eminently suitable for promoting Christian education. First of all in a historical sense, as an encouragement to determine our historical distance and position in relation to Luther's Reformation. Secondly, from a theological point of view, helping to clarify what it means to believe and live as a Lutheran. Thirdly, they speak to the heart, because Luther as an author almost always saw himself as a pastoral counselor, whose texts serve the examination and strengthening of conscience.

Our thanks go to all those who have helped to make the publication of "Reading Luther" possible. First, we are grateful to Fortress Press (Minneapolis) and the Philosophical Library (New York) for kindly allowing us to use the texts from their Luther editions, as well as Faithlife Corporation for supplying the texts from "Luther's Works". We also thank Mr. Neville Williamson for his dedicated translation work. Our thanks also go to the editors: Oberkirchenrat Dr. Georg Raatz from the church office of the VELKD for editorial support, former curate Urs Christian Mundt from the church office of the VELKD for project management and preparation of the manuscript, and Saskia Kredig of the GNC/LWF who, together with Florian Hübner (GNC/LWF), procured the texts. Professor Dr. Martin H. Jung helped to clarify many a tricky question. We are also thankful to him. Finally, we would also like to thank the Evangelische Verlagsanstalt in Leipzig for including "Reading Luther" in their program and Dr. Annette Weidhas together with Tilman Meckel for their support during the publication.

We join Gerhard Ulrich in wishing all readers a surprising and edifying, most certainly inspiring reading experience.

Hanover, Michael and All Angels 2021

Bishop Ralf Meister
Presiding Bishop of the United Evangelical Lutheran Church in Germany (VELKD)

Bishop Dr. hc. Frank Otfried July
Chairperson of the German National Committee of the Lutheran World Federation (GNC/LWF)

Foreword German edition 2016

In 2017 we celebrate the 500th anniversary of the Reformation. The Evangelical Church in Germany and its member churches have spent a whole decade preparing for this date, dedicating each year to one central theme of the Reformation. A wealth of literature has already been or is about to be published. Special studies and introductory books, as well as popular collections of quotations from Luther or anecdotes about him, are now on ample display in the bookstores. In addition, there are extensive editions of his works available for research. The large Weimar edition, which was begun in 1883 on the occasion of Luther's 400th birthday, today comprises 127 volumes with approximately 80,000 printed pages. Numerous other editions exist alongside it, making it difficult for the interested layperson to keep track. Where should you start, and how can you find your way through the masses of text?

The book in your hands is intended to provide orientation in this respect. It offers an anthology comprising a collection of the Reformer's central texts in *one single* volume. Pastors and other parish workers can refer to it when preparing confirmation classes or evening meetings. These texts are of great value to teachers of history or religion. But the book can also be recommended for reading in private. It is indeed only a selection, so that it naturally cannot represent the entirety of Luther's theology, but we can assure you, the reader, that you will gain a good and profound insight into Luther's life and thought.

Just as Luther insisted that Christians should read the Bible themselves, which still applies today, I would like to encourage you to read Luther's own texts. You will profit from the experience of his powerful, yet understandable language, with which he clearly and impressively formulates his concerns. But those aspects of Luther which are foreign or disturbing to us are not missing. The choice of texts expresses the tensions and ambivalences of his theology. At any event, you will be placed in a position to form your own judgment as to what fascinates you about Luther, or why it is simply a good thing that it all took place 500 years ago.

Luther comes alive in these texts: as a driving force of the modern age, but also as a man of his own time, involved in conflicts and debates, an outstandingly erudite theologian and philosopher who continues to fascinate and inspire down to this day. In these texts, we get to know him as a pious Christian with strong faith and doubts, as a person both tormented by fears and inspired by great hopes – and as someone whose texts are worth studying in order to go into more depth for a personal commemoration of the Reformation.

My thanks are due to all who have contributed to the success of this book. In particular, I would like to thank Prof. Dr. Martin H. Jung, who selected the Lutheran texts with a professional combination of deep expertise and pragmatism and translated some of them anew. His concise and informative text introductions guarantee a helpful guide for reading. I would also like to thank Oberkirchenrat Dr. Georg Raatz, who has supported the project from the beginning and provided editorial assistance from the VELKD church office. I would also like to thank the publishing house Vandenhoeck & Ruprecht for including the volume in its program, and Jörg Persch and Christoph Spill for their publishing support.

I hope that this book will be a source of profit to all its readers, and that they will allow themselves to be infected by Luther's own enthusiasm: that "a God means that from which we are to expect all good and to which we are to take refuge in all distress, so that to have a God is nothing else than to trust and believe Him from the [whole] heart" (Luther, Large Catechism).

Schwerin, Easter 2016

Bishop Gerhard Ulrich
Presiding Bishop of the United Evangelical Lutheran Church of Germany (VELKD)

Contents

Introduction

Prof. Dr. Martin H. Jung

Martin Luther – I always found him fascinating, but sometimes very unpleasant. I always found him inspiring, but sometimes I just didn't understand him.

Martin Luther - my first encounter with him came in 1969 at the age of 13, when I visited Wittenberg with Luther's home, the "Lutherhaus", and his tomb. In 1969/70, as part of my confirmation classes, I learned his Small Catechism off by heart and recited it. In the religious education at school, Luther did not play a role at that time - unlike Freud and Feuerbach. In 1976, as a volunteer with the *Aktion Sühnezeichen / Friedensdienste* (Action Reconciliation. Service for Peace) in Israel, I was confronted for the first time with Luther's hostility towards the Jews and thus got to know the "bad Luther". Further insights into Luther's sinister aspects followed. I learned that he had called for the farmers fighting for freedom and justice to be killed. I learned that, in contrast to myself and many other young Christians at that time, he considered Christianity to be compatible with military service. I learned that he had called for obedience to the authorities and declared that Christians were citizens of two different kingdoms, which meant that Jesus' ethical teaching only had limited validity in the world.

As a student, I found a new, positive approach to Luther with Michael Welker in Tübingen, as well as with Helmut Gollwitzer (1908–1993) and Friedrich-Wilhelm Marquardt (1928–2002) in Berlin. I discovered that Luther had linked religion to freedom and thus had a lasting influence on the history of religion in the modern age. I discovered how Luther had held the Bible in high esteem, but had nonetheless already practiced biblical criticism, factual criticism of the Bible, and did not hold it to be a textbook of world history and natural science. I discovered Luther's fascinating definition of God: "A God is what you trust with all your heart." I discovered the Luther who had propagated the universal priesthood, who had called for pastors to be elected by the congregations and had enhanced the role and reputation of women, who had advocated more and better education, demanded reform not just for the Church but also for society, who had considered sexuality to be a natural human need, who demanded toleration of the Jews and wanted to allow marriage between Jews and Christians and made sure that a translation of the Koran in Latin could be published for the first time. The modern, innovative Luther was and is admittedly sometimes also provocative. This applies especially to the sharp tone in which he points out the limits of political and economic power. Many passages sound as if they had been written for a modern audience.

My next Luther experience is connected with my first theological examinations in Tübingen in 1984. Heiko Augustinus Oberman (1930–2001) was one of the greatest 20th-century Luther researchers, but I had never had any classes with him. He asked me about Luther's justification of infant baptism – and I could not give him an answer. It was something I did not know at that time, but today I share Luther's argument: infant baptism shows that God accepts people who are not yet in a position to do anything for him. Viewed in this light, infant baptism stands for the central statement of the Reformation: the sinner is justified before God through faith alone, not through works.

It is also Luther's language which is fascinating. Luther was a master in formulating. His vivid and lively style of language, sometimes witty, sometimes coarse, makes it a pleasure to read his texts, even if the theology is not always easy to digest.

We still read Luther today - naturally and above all in the theological faculties and institutes, but also in local churches and sometimes privately at home. Luther would never have expected this. He himself did not think much of most of his works. He knew that they had been composed in a short time for a particular reason. He would have preferred them to have been quickly forgotten. He only wanted his catechisms and his book on the bondage of the human will to be preserved for posterity. It turned out differently. Even before Luther's death, his followers and successors began to collect and re-publish his writings. It was the start of a series of editions of Luther's works which has continued down to the present day.

Luther wanted Christians, including university professors, to study the Bible first and foremost. Protestantism developed a pronounced biblical piety and a theology that was to be seen as the interpretation of Holy Scripture. But later and indirectly, Luther also had an influence on Catholicism. Today, unlike in Luther's time, the Bible also enjoys a higher status in the Roman Catholic Church and in Catholic theological research.

Luther is one of the greatest theologians in the history of Christianity. He stands on an equal footing with St. Paul, with Augustine, Thomas Aquinas, Friedrich Schleiermacher and Karl Barth. The Protestant churches trace their origin to his reformatory ideas, and all the subsequent historical periods of Protestant churches and theology relate back to him and continue to do so today; for these reasons, Luther has an integrative function and provides confessional identity.

But how do we deal with Luther's darker aspects? Can Protestants still look in the eyes of their Catholic brothers and sisters or of Jews and Muslims after reading what Luther said about the pope, and about Mohammed, and his allegations against the Jews? And this also applies to Protestant fellow Christians – Zwinglians, Calvinists, Mennonites, Baptists, Schwenkfelders – who had to endure hardly any less polemical tirades from Luther.

Rome branded Luther a heretic; Luther demonized Rome. But the Roman Catholic Church of today is no longer the church that Luther fought against. The Protestant churches have also changed considerably since Luther's time. Whoever might feel attacked today should simply ignore many of Luther's polemics aimed at inner-church opponents.

Another thing: Luther was no saint, and did not want to be a saint. He confessed right up to the end that he was imperfect, that he was sinful. One of his last words was: "We are beggars", beggars before God, begging for forgiveness and grace. Luther relativized himself, and we may relativize him too. Whoever does not ignore Luther's dark sides – indeed, only someone who does not ignore Luther's dark sides – has the right to continue to invoke Luther, and may do so with a clear conscience.

There is no identity with an unblemished existence. If one should wish to back away from Luther on account of his imperfections, then one would also have to back away from Christianity itself, whose history abounds in dark episodes. Identity only exists in a broken form and must therefore always include self-criticism. The correct response to the broken history of this identity, as of all others, is not purism, but historical criticism.

Protestant Christians today are also disconcerted by a lot of what Luther wrote. Luther spoke frequently of the devil. For him the devil was a reality – just like God. Many Christians and many theologians would no longer agree with Luther today on this point. The concept of the devil as a person seems questionable to many. Nevertheless, one could agree with Luther that evil is greater than the sum of evil deeds, and more powerful. This is exactly what he wanted to express when he spoke of the devil. And there is a further consideration: when Luther describes people like the pope as being possessed by the devil, he distinguishes between the person and the power which is influencing them, thus allowing such people a chance to free themselves from this power.

Throughout his life, Luther expected that the world would soon come to an end. This is evident in his writings, but is another aspect which seems strange to us today, when we have a different attitude to life, despite all the crises of environment and climate. We lead our lives as if there were no end, as if we had all the time in the world – a world which would last forever. In defiance of all the findings of science, we tend to share the opinion of Aristotle, the "dead heathen" whom Luther opposed, who also regarded the world as everlasting. The Bible and Luther, however, remind us that our time and the time of this world are limited, thereby admonishing us to deal responsibly with our life and our world. This means that if Luther's work is correctly understood and translated, even the passages which seem foreign to us can prove to be up to date and worthwhile.

The texts I have selected are important, interesting and relevant for today. I took special care to include those texts that are often the subject of controversial discussion, such as Luther's writings on the Jews, and to bring out all facets of Luther, including his darker sides. The book is structured on the basis of the Reformer's biography. My research assistant Dr. Helen-Kathrin Treutler helped with the demanding work on and with the texts. I would also like to thank Dr. Georg Raatz from the church office of the VELKD for his attentive revision of the manuscript and many helpful suggestions. It was also he who had the idea for this book project and has contributed substantially to its realization.

Chronology

1483	Birth of Luther in Eisleben (10 November)
1497/98	Schoolboy in Magdeburg (cathedral school)
1498–1501	Schoolboy in Eisenach (St. George's parochial school)
1501	Student in Erfurt (basic studies)
1505	Graduation with a master's degree, start of law studies
	Thunderstorm experience and entry into a monastery
1507	Ordination to the priesthood, start of theological studies
1511/12	Journey to Rome*
1512	Luther appointed professor in Wittenberg
1517	95 Theses against indulgences: Beginning of the Reformation (31 October)
1518	Heidelberg Disputation
1519	Leipzig Disputation
1520	Luther is threatened with excommunication (papal bull, 15 June)
1521	Excommunication (3 January)
	Luther appears before the Emperor in Worms (17/18 April)

* New, generally accepted dating based on research by Hans Schneider (2011).

1521	The Emperor declares Luther an outlaw by imperial ban (25 May)
1521/22	Luther in Wartburg Castle, translation of the New Testament
1525	Peasants' War
	Luther marries Katharina von Bora
1529	Protestation of evangelical estaes of Empire at the Imperial Diet in Speyer
1530	Diet of Augsburg and the Augsburg Confession
1534	Completion of the Bible translation
1545	Beginning of the Council of Trent
1546	Luther dies in Eisleben (18 February)

Philipp Melanchthon on Luther's ancestry and birth

Only a few autobiographical anecdotes by Luther were passed down. The first biography of the Reformer was written by Philipp Melanchthon, his colleague and co-reformer in Wittenberg, who had worked alongside him since 1518. Melanchthon was also the first person to describe Luther's family background and birth, and this is the basis of all modern biographies of Luther. There is no doubt about the date of his birthday, but it is not certain whether the year was 1483; 1482 and 1484 are also possible. In the 15th century, births and baptisms were not yet registered in parish records. Melanchthon had spoken to Luther's mother and his brother, and with a student from Mansfeld as well. On several occasions, Luther himself had said that Eisleben was his birthplace. Nonetheless, it has been suggested that it might have been Mansfeld after all.

Philipp Melanchthon, Praefatio (1546):
Corpus Reformatorum, Vol.6, Halle/Saale 1839, col.155–170.
Translation: Neville Williamson.

The family bearing the surname Luther is ancient, belonging to the lower class and frequently to be found in the realm of the illustrious counts of Mansfeld. However, Martin Luther's parents first lived in the town of Eisleben, where Martin Luther was born. Later they moved to Mansfeld, where Martin's father Johannes Luther held various positions and was highly esteemed by all honest citizens on the grounds of his good reputation. His mother Margarita, wife of Johannes Luther, was not only endowed with all those good qualities which belong to a respectable married woman, but was also particularly marked by a radiant modesty, by fear of God and prayerfulness. Other respectable women saw in her a model of virtue.

I asked her on several occasions about the time of her son's birth, and she replied that she remembered exactly the date and the hour, while being uncertain of the year. But she assured me that Martin was born on 10 November in the night, after the eleventh hour. And the child had been given the name Martin, because the following day, on which the child was to enter the church by baptism, was dedicated to St. Martin. But as to Martin's age, his brother Jakob, a decent and respected man, said that the family believed he had been born in the year 1483 after Christ's birth. After Martin had reached school age, the parents educated their son at home, teaching him to know and fear God and to feel himself committed to further virtues.

As is customary among respectable people, they made sure that he learned to read and write. The father of Georg Oemler brought the boy to primary school when he was still very young. Since he is still alive, he can testify to the truth of our report.

The thunderstorm near Stotternheim: Luther becomes a monk (1505)

The Reformer was a monk. Many people overlook the fact that Luther lived in a monastery for twenty years. However, it was not his parents who decided that he should join a monastic order. In 1505 they had allowed him to start his law studies in Erfurt. But during the first semester, a thunderstorm changed his life, leading him to enter the cloister of the Order of Hermits of Saint Augustine in Erfurt. He remembered that this took place on 17 July, the feast day of St. Alexius, a respected and legendary saint and ascetic in Luther's time. Fearing for his life during the storm, Luther had promised Saint Anna, the grandmother of Jesus and patron saint of miners, that he would become a monk if he survived. He reminisced on this 34 years later, in 1539, in one of his so–called "table talks" in his home on 16 July, the eve of Alexius Day, and one of the visitors wrote the story down.

Martin Luther, Tischrede am 16. Juli 1539:
WA.TR, Vol. 4, p. 440, no. 4707.
Translation: Neville Williamson.

On St. Alexius Day, 16 July, he said: "Today is the anniversary of the day I entered the monastery in Erfurt." And he began to tell the story of how he had taken a vow when he had been on the road barely a fortnight beforehand, having been so terrified by a bolt of lightning not far from Erfurt that he shouted in horror: "Help, Saint Anna, I will become a monk!" … "Later I regretted my vow, and many advised me not to fulfill it. But I insisted, and on the eve of St. Alexius I invited my best friends to say farewell, so that they could accompany me to the monastery the following day. But when they tried to restrain me, I said: Today you see me for the last time. Then they accompanied me in tears. My father was also very angry about the vow, but I insisted on my decision. I never thought I would leave the monastery. I was wholly finished with the world."

The "Tower Experience": Luther becomes a Reformer

Ten years after the first dramatic change in Luther's life, ten years after entering the monastery, the monk became a reformer. Luther had been studying theology since 1505 and had become a professor of theology in Wittenberg in 1512. He gave lectures on the Psalms (1513–1515) and on the letters of Paul (1516–1518). He was struggling – both theologically and existentially – with the question of how to understand God's righteousness. Dealing with the Letter to the Romans (Romans 1:17), he found an answer that completely changed his understanding of theology, indeed his understanding of God. Luther only described this in detail once, thirty years later, in 1545, in a preface to a complete edition of his Latin writings. He had made this theological discovery related here in his study in the tower of the Augustinian monastery in Wittenberg, so that it was later often referred to as the "Tower Experience".

It has frequently been discussed when this breakthrough exactly happened. Luther's explanations are not explicit. Was it during the first series of lectures on the Psalms or only in connection with the second, which ben in 1519? Was it perhaps in 1518, that is, after the 95 Theses? Or was there no decisive turning point at all? Was it rather a process of recognition lasting months or years, which Luther later summarized into a narrative? The controversy among Luther researchers continues and will probably never end, because the answer is always dependent on the perspective of the interpreters.

There is much to be said for following the older Luther research and dating the "Tower Experience" to 1514 or thereabouts. It goes without saying that Luther did not anticipate the consequences of his discovery straightaway in all their aspects. It is certainly possible to experience both a sudden breakthrough and a longer cognitive process. Luther found authorization for his new teaching not only in the writings of Paul but also in those of the church father Augustine.

Martin Luther, Vorrede zum ersten Bande der Wittenberger Ausgabe der lateinischen Schriften (1545): WA, Vol. 54, pp. 176–187. Translation: AL, Vol. 4, pp. 500–502.

Meanwhile, that same year, I returned to interpreting the Psalms, building on the fact that I was more skillful after I had lectured on Saint Paul's epistles to the Romans, Galatians, and the epistle addressed to the Hebrews. Indeed, an extra ordinary passion for learning Paul had seized me in his epistle to the Romans. Up to that point it was not the cold blood around the heart that had blocked my path, but a single word in chapter 1 (Romans 1:17), "the righteousness of God is revealed in it." I hated that word "righteousness of God" because according to the usage and idiom of all the teachers I had been taught to understand it in terms of philosophy, that righteousness is a formal or active righteousness by which God is righteous and punishes sinners and the unrighteous.

Although I was living an irreproachable life as a monk, I felt that I was a sinner before God with an extremely distressed conscience. I could not have confidence that it could find peace through my performance of satisfactions. I did not love – I hated! – the righteous God who punishes sinners. Secretly, I expressed my anger with God, if not in the form of blasphemy, at least with intense grumbling. I said, "As if, indeed, it is not enough that miserable sinners, who are eternally ruined through original sin, are crushed by every kind of calamity by the law of the Decalogue, without having God add affliction to our affliction by the gospel and also by the gospel threatening us with his righteousness and wrath!" I raged with a savage conscience that was in turmoil. Nevertheless, I impertinently hammered on Paul over this passage, passionately wanting to know what Paul was after.

At last, by the mercy of God, as I was meditating day and night on what was holding this passage together – "the righteousness of God is revealed in it, as it is written: the righteous lives by faith" – there I began to understand that the righteousness of God is that by which the righteous person lives by the gift of God, namely, by faith. And this is the meaning: the righteousness of God is revealed by the gospel, namely, the passive righteousness with which the merciful God justifies us through faith, just as it is written: the righteous lives by faith. At this point I felt that I had been completely born again and had entered paradise itself through wide open doors. There a completely different face of the entire Scripture appeared to me. At that, I ran through the Scriptures as I had them in my memory, and I gathered together in other words parallel expressions, such as "work of God," (John 6:29) that is what God effects in us, "power of God," (1 Peter 4:11) by which he makes us powerful, "wisdom of God," (Luke 2:40) by which he makes us wise, "strength of God," "salvation of God," "glory of God."

Then, just as much as I had hated the word "righteousness of God," I now loved it and praised it as the sweetest of all words, and this passage of Paul became truly the gate of paradise. Afterward, in reading Augustine's *De spiritu et littera* I found that, contrary to what I had hoped, he, too, interpreted the righteousness of God in a similar way, as the righteousness with which God clothes us when he justifies us. Although he expressed these things imperfectly and did not explain everything … clearly, it was nevertheless reassuring that this idea – that God's righteousness is that by which we become righteous – had been taught earlier.

Into the public eye: Theses against indulgences (1517)

From 1515, the Church in Germany sold indulgences on a large scale. The proceeds were intended to finance the re–building of St. Peter's Basilica in Rome.

What is an indulgence? Indulgence means a remission or exemption. It means the remission of punishment for sins which had already been forgiven as far as the guilt was concerned. The Church distinguished between guilt and punishment. Those who committed a sin made themselves guilty. The guilt was forgiven by the priest in the name of God through the Sacrament of Penance, which entailed confession. But the forgiveness did not exempt the sinner from punishment. According to the Church, every sin also entailed a punishment. It was believed that many punishments could only be undergone in the afterlife, in purgatory, where they were imposed. Purgatory is not to be confused with hell. In hell, there was eternal punishment for sinners who had not confessed serious sins or whose sins had not been forgiven, as well as for notorious heretics. There was no escape. In purgatory, people were punished for a time, purified, as it were, so that they would then find entrance to heaven. Indulgence meant, above all, the remission of these "temporal" punishments for sins in this life, which would be executed in purgatory after death. The Church promised those who bought indulgences that they would not need to go to purgatory before passing into heaven.

Luther doubts whether purgatory even exists. He also denies the Church the right to interfere in God's punitive actions, which it based on the doctrine of the "treasures of the Church", meaning the merits of Christ and the saints. He also criticizes the fact that the sale of indulgences is obviously intended simply to earn money. And he emphasizes that repentance, understood biblically, is not an ecclesiastical ritual, but a life attitude. In 1517, Luther does not – yet – see the pope as the real culprit.

Luther developed his thoughts in 95 theses in Latin. The sentences are linguistically and theologically demanding because they were intended for scholars. Not all of them can be comprehended by today's readers. Luther was addressing the public, but initially only the academic and ecclesiastical public, who were supposed to debate his theses with him, not yet the public in general. As Melanchthon reported later, he is said to have "nailed" the theses on the door of All Saints' Church in Wittenberg on 31 October. This "Castle Church" served as an assembly hall for large events at the university. It also housed a large collection of relics of saints, which promised indulgence to those who visited and worshiped them. In any case, on 31 October, Luther sent his theses to various bishops and handed them out to friends. In a short time they were printed, possibly without Luther's initiative, in Latin and then in a German translation as well.

Luther's theses are reproduced in full below. Those which are most important and easier to understand are highlighted.

Martin Luther, Disputatio pro declaratione virtutis
indulgentiarum (1517): WA, Vol. 1, pp. 229–238.
Translation: AL, Vol. 1, pp. 34–46.

1. *Our Lord and Master Jesus Christ, in saying "Do penance …" (Matthew 4:17) wanted the entire life of the faithful to be one of penitence.*
2. *This phrase cannot be understood as referring to sacramental penance, that is, confession and satisfaction as administered by the clergy.*
3. Yet it does not mean solely inner penitence – indeed such inner penitence is nothing unless it outwardly produces various mortifications of the flesh.
4. And thus, penalty remains as long as hatred of self (that is, true inner penitence) remains, namely, until our entrance into the kingdom of heaven.

5. *The pope neither desires nor is able to remit any penalties except those imposed by his own discretion or that of the canons.*
6. *The pope cannot remit any guilt except by declaring and confirming its remission by God or, of course, by remitting guilt in [legal] cases reserved to himself. In showing contempt regarding such cases, the guilt would certainly remain.*
7. God remits the guilt of absolutely no one unless at the same time God subjects in all things the one humbled to God's vicar, the priest.
8. The penitential canons were imposed only on the living, and, according to the canons themselves, nothing should be imposed on those about to die.
9. Accordingly, the Holy Spirit through the pope acts in a kindly manner toward us in papal decrees by always exempting the moment of death and the case of necessity.
10. Those priests act ignorantly and wickedly who, in the case of the dying, reserve canonical penalties for one's time in purgatory.
11. Those "tares" about changing the canonical penalty into the penalty of purgatory certainly seem to have been "sown" while the bishops "were sleeping."
12. Formerly, canonical penalties were imposed not after, but before absolution, as tests of true contrition.
13. Through death, those about to die are absolved of all [such penalties] and are already dead as far as canon laws are concerned, in that by right they have release from them.
14. Imperfect purity or love on the part of the dying person necessarily brings with it great fear. The smaller the love, the greater the fear.

15. This fear or horror is enough by itself alone (to say nothing of other things) to constitute the penalty of purgatory, since it is very near the horror of despair.
16. It seems that hell, purgatory, and heaven differ from each other as much as despair, near despair, and assurance.
17. It seems necessary that, for souls in purgatory, as the horror decreases so love increases.
18. It neither seems proved - either by any logical arguments or by Scripture - that souls in purgatory are outside a state of merit, that is, unable to grow in love;
19. nor does it seem to be proved that these souls, at least not all of them, are certain and assured of their own salvation - even though we ourselves are completely certain about [their destiny].
20. *Therefore, the pope understands by the phrase "plenary remission of all penalties" not actually "all penalties" but only "penalties imposed by himself."*
21. *And so, those indulgence preachers err who say that through the pope's indulgences a person is released and saved from every penalty.*
22. On the contrary, to souls in purgatory he remits no penalty that they should have paid in this life according to canon law.
23. If any remission of all penalties whatsoever could be granted to anyone, it would certainly be granted only to the most perfect, that is, to the very fewest.
24. Because of this, most people are inevitably deceived by means of this indiscriminate and high-sounding promise of release from penalty.
25. *The kind of power that a pope has over purgatory in general corresponds to the power that any bishop or local priest has in particular in his diocese or parish.*

26. The pope does best in that he grants remission to souls [in purgatory] not by "the power of the keys," which he does not possess [here], but "by way of intercession."
27. *They "preach human opinions" who say that, as soon as a coin thrown into the money chest clinks, a soul flies out [of purgatory].*
28. It is certain that when a coin clinks in the money chest profits and avarice may well be increased, but the intercession of the church rests on God's choice alone.
29. Who knows whether all the souls in purgatory want to be redeemed, given what is recounted about St. Severinus and St. Paschasius?
30. No one is secure in the genuineness of one's own contrition – much less in having attained "plenary remission."
31. As rare as a person who is truly penitent, just so rare is someone who truly acquires indulgences; indeed, the latter is the rarest of all.
32. *Those who believe that they can be secure in their salvation through indulgence letters will be eternally damned along with their teachers.*
33. One must especially beware of those who say that those indulgences of the pope are "God's inestimable gift" by which a person is reconciled to God.
34. For these indulgent graces are only based on the penalties of sacramental satisfaction instituted by human beings.
35. *Those who teach that contrition is not necessary on the part of those who would rescue souls [from purgatory] or who would buy confessional privileges do not preach Christian views.*
36. *Any truly remorseful Christian has a right to full remission of guilt and penalty, even without indulgence letters.*
37. Any true Christian, living or dead, possesses a God-given

share in all the benefits of Christ and the church, even without indulgence letters.

38. Nevertheless, remission and participation [in these benefits] from the pope must by no means be despised, because – as I said – they are the declaration of divine remission.
39. It is extremely difficult, even for the most learned theologians, to lift up before the people the liberality of indulgences and the truth about contrition at one and the same time.
40. The "truth about contrition" seeks and loves penalties [for sins]; the "liberality of indulgences" relaxes penalties and at very least gives occasion for hating them.
41. Apostolic indulgences are to be preached with caution, so that the people do not mistakenly think that they are to be preferred to other good works of love.
42. Christians are to be taught that the pope does not intend the acquiring of indulgences to be compared in any way with works of mercy.
43. *Christians are to be taught that the one who gives to a poor person or lends to the needy does a better deed than if a person acquires indulgences,*
44. *because love grows through works of love and a person is made better; but through indulgences one is not made better but only freer from penalty [for sin].*
45. *Christians are to be taught that anyone who sees a destitute person and, while passing such a one by, gives money for indulgences does not buy [gracious] indulgence of the pope but God's wrath.*
46. *Christians are to be taught that, unless they have more than they need, they must set aside enough for their household and by no means squander it on indulgences.*

47. *Christians are to be taught that buying indulgences is a matter of free choice, not commanded.*
48. Christians are to be taught that the pope, while granting indulgences, needs and thus desires their devout prayer for him more than their money.
49. *Christians are to be taught that papal indulgences are useful [for them] only if they do not put their trust in them but are extremely harmful if they lose their fear of God because of them.*
50. *Christians are to be taught that if the pope knew the demands made by the indulgence preachers, he would rather that the Basilica of St. Peter were burned to ashes than that it be constructed using the skin, flesh, and bones of his sheep.*
51. Christians are to be taught that the pope ought to give and would want to give of his own wealth – even selling the Basilica of St. Peter if necessary – to those from whom certain declaimers of indulgences are wheedling money.
52. It is vain to trust in salvation by means of indulgence letters, even if the [indulgence] agent – or even the pope himself – were to offer his own soul as security for them.
53. People who forbid the preaching of the Word of God in some churches altogether in order that indulgences may be preached in others are enemies of Christ and the pope.
54. An injustice is done to the Word of God when, in the very same sermon, equal or more time is spent on indulgences than on the Word.
55. It is necessarily the pope's intent that if indulgences, which are a completely insignificant thing, are celebrated with one bell, one procession, and one ceremony, then the gospel, which is the greatest thing of all, should be

preached with a hundred bells, a hundred processions, and a hundred ceremonies.

56. The treasures of the church, from which the pope distributes indulgences, are not sufficiently discussed or known among Christ's people.
57. That [these treasures] are not transient worldly riches is certainly clear, because many of the [indulgence] declaimers do not so much freely distribute such riches as only collect them.
58. Nor are they the merits of Christ and the saints, because, even without the pope, these merits always work grace for the inner person and cross, death, and hell for the outer person.
59. St. Laurence said that the poor of the church were the treasures of the church, but he spoke according to the usage of the word "treasure" in his own time.
60. Not without cause, we say that the keys of the church (given by the merits of Christ) are that treasure.
61. For it is clear that the pope's power only suffices for the remission of [ecclesiastical] penalties and for [legal] actions.
62. *The true treasure of the church is the most holy gospel of the glory and grace of God.*
63. But this treasure is deservedly the most hated, because it makes "the first last."
64. In contrast, the treasure of indulgences is deservedly the most acceptable, because it makes "the last first."
65. Therefore, the treasures of the gospel are nets with which they formerly fished for men of wealth.
66. *The treasures of indulgences are nets with which they now fish for the wealth of men.*

67. Indulgences, which the declaimers shout about as the greatest "graces," are indeed understood as such - insofar as they promote profits.
68. Yet they are in truth the least of all when compared to the grace of God and the goodness of the cross.
69. Bishops and parish priests are bound to admit agents of the Apostolic indulgences with all reverence.
70. But all of them are much more bound to strain eyes and ears intently, so that these [agents] do not preach their own daydreams in place of the pope's commission.
71. Let the one who speaks against the truth of the Apostolic indulgences be anathema and accursed,
72. but let the one who guards against the arbitrary and unbridled words used by declaimers of indulgences be blessed.
73. Just as the pope justly thunders against those who, in whatever way they can, contrive to harm the sale of indulgences,
74. much more so does he intend to thunder against those who, under the pretext of indulgences, contrive to harm holy love and the truth.
75. To imagine that papal indulgences are so great that they could absolve a person even for doing the impossible by violating the mother of God is insanity.
76. On the contrary, we have said that papal indulgences cannot take away the very least of venial sins, as far as guilt is concerned.
77. That it is said that even St. Peter, if he were now pope, could not grant greater graces is blasphemy against St. Peter and the pope.
78. On the contrary, we say that even the present pope, or any pope whatsoever, possesses greater graces - namely, the

gospel, "deeds of power, gifts of healing ..." - as in 1 Corinthians 12:28.

79. *To say that the cross, emblazoned with the papal coat-of-arms and erected [in the church where indulgences are preached], is of equal worth to the cross of Christ is blasphemy.*
80. *The bishops, parish priests, and theologians who allow such sermons free course among the people will have to answer for this.*
81. *This unbridled preaching makes it difficult even for learned men to defend the reverence due the pope from slander or from the truly sharp questions of the laity:*
82. *Namely, "Why does the pope not empty purgatory for the sake of the holiest love and the direst need of souls as a matter of the highest justice, given that he redeems countless souls for filthy lucre to build the Basilica [of St. Peter] as a completely trivial matter?"*
83. Again, "Why continue funeral and anniversary Masses for the dead instead of returning or permitting the withdrawal of the endowments founded for them, since it is against the law to pray for those already redeemed?"
84. *Again, "What is this new piety of God and the pope that, for the sake of money, they permit someone who is impious and an enemy to redeem [from purgatory] a pious, God-pleasing soul and yet do not, for the sake of the need of that very pious and beloved soul, redeem it purely out of love?"*
85. Again, "Why are the penitential canons - long since abrogated and dead in actual fact and through disuse - nevertheless now bought off with money through granting indulgences, as if they were very much alive?"
86. *Again, "Why does the pope, whose riches today are more substantial than the richest Crassus*[1]*, not simply construct*

the Basilica of St. Peter with his own money rather than with the money of the poor faithful?"

87. Again, "What exactly does the pope 'remit' or 'allow participation in' when it comes to those who through perfect contrition have a right to full remission and a share [in the church's benefits]?"
88. Again, "Could any greater good come to the church than if the pope were to bestow these remissions and participation to each of the faithful a hundred times a day, as he now does but once?"
89. "Since, rather than money, the pope seeks the salvation of souls through indulgences, why does he now suspend the documents and indulgences previously granted, although they have equal efficacy?"
90. To suppress these very pointed arguments of the laity by force alone and not to resolve them by providing reasons is to expose the church and the pope to ridicule by their enemies and to make Christians miserable.
91. Therefore, if indulgences were preached according to the spirit and intention of the pope, all of these [objections] would be easily resolved - indeed, they would not exist.
92. *And thus, away with all those prophets who say to Christ's people, "Peace, peace," (Jeremiah 6:14) and there is no peace!*
93. *May it go well for all of those prophets who say to Christ's people, "Cross, cross," and there is no cross!*
94. *Christians must be encouraged diligently to follow Christ, their head, through penalties, death, and hell,*

---

[1] Ancient Roman politician, famed for his wealth.

95. *and in this way they may be confident of "entering heaven through many tribulations" rather than through the [false] security of peace.*

New theses: The Leipzig Disputation

His indulgence theses of 1517 were intended by Luther to instigate a disputation at his university, a form of academic debate common at the time. Although this never took place, Luther did dispute with members of his order in Heidelberg in 1518 and with the great Catholic theologian Johann Eck from Ingolstadt in Leipzig in 1519. Luther's theses for the Leipzig Disputation repeated what he had written earlier, but finished with even stronger criticism of the Church. Luther branded his opponents as "sophists" and "theologists", meaning bad philosophers and bad theologians, while he himself referred to decisions of the Council of Nicaea, which had met in 325 and was generally recognized.

Following the church father Augustine, Luther developed a very strict, serious doctrine of sin that corresponded to his experiences as a monk. He branded the counter position as Pelagianism, linking it to a 4th-century doctrine connected with the theologian Pelagius, among others, which had been condemned at various synods. He believed that he was even in agreement with Aristotle in this respect, who was highly revered by his opponents. But Luther contrasted a person's radical recognition of their sin with God's radical readiness to forgive. He rejected the Church's practice of reserving the forgiveness of specific sins for higher dignitaries. Every priest was obliged to forgive anyone who was ready to repent.

During the Disputation itself, Eck drew Luther even further out of his reserve, and Luther declared that popes and councils could be in error, and frequently had been. At the Council of Constance in 1415, some of Johann Hus' thoughts had been wrongly condemned. In Constance, the theologian Hus from Prague had been declared a heretic and burned at the stake.

Martin Luther, Die Thesen zur Leipziger Disputation (1519):
WA, Vol. 2, pp. 160 f.
Translation: LW, Vol. 31, pp. 317–318.

Martin Luther will defend the following theses against new and old errors at the University of Leipzig.

1. Every man sins daily, but he also repents daily according to Christ's teaching, "Repent" (Matthew 4:17), possibly with the exception of a person who has just been made righteous and who does not need repentance, although the heavenly vinedresser daily prunes the fruit-bearing vines (John 15:1–2).
2. To deny that man sins even when doing good; that venial sin is pardonable, not according to its nature, but by the mercy of God; or that sin remains in the child after baptism; that is equivalent to crushing Paul and Christ under foot.
3. He who maintains that a good work and penance begin with the hatred of sins and prior to the love of righteousness and that one no longer sins in doing good work, him we number among the Pelagian heretics; but we also prove that this is a silly interpretation of his holy Aristotle.
4. God changes an eternal punishment into a temporary one, that is, the punishment of carrying the cross. Canons or priests have no power to burden one with the cross or to remove it, although, deceived by harmful flatterers, they presume that they can do this.
5. Every priest must absolve the penitent of punishment and guilt. If he does not, he sins. So does a higher prelate if he reserves secret matters without good reason, though the usage of the church, that is, of flatterers, opposes this.

6. Perhaps the souls in purgatory do render satisfaction for their sins. It is brazen rashness, however, to assert that God demands more of a dying person than a willingness to die since in no way can this assertion be proven.
7. He who babbles about the free will being the master of good or evil deeds shows he does not know what faith, contrition, or free will are; nor does he know who imagines that one is not justified alone by faith in the Word, or that faith is not lost in every mortal sin.
8. It is contrary to truth and reason to state that those who die unwillingly are deficient in love and must therefore suffer the horror of purgatory, but only if truth and reason are the same as the opinions of the would-be theologians.
9. We are familiar with the assertion of would-be theologians that the souls in purgatory are certain of their salvation and that grace is no longer increased in them; but we marvel at these very learned men that they can offer the uneducated no cogent reason for this their conviction.
10. It is certain that the merit of Christ is the treasure of the church and that this treasure is enhanced by the merits of the saints; but no one except a filthy flatterer or one who strays from the truth and embraces certain false practices and usages of the church pretends that the merits of Christ are the treasure of indulgences.
11. To say that indulgences are a blessing for a Christian is insane, for they are in truth a hindrance to a good work; and a Christian must reject indulgences because of their abuse, for the Lord says, "I, I am He who blots out your transgressions for my own sake" (Isaiah 43:25), not for the sake of money.
12. Completely unlearned sophists and pestiferous flatterers dream that the pope can remit every punishment owed for

sins in this and the future life and that indulgences are helpful to those who are not guilty. But they cannot prove this with so much as a gesture.

13. The very callous decrees of the Roman pontiffs which have appeared in the last four hundred years prove that the Roman church is superior to all others. Against them stand the history of eleven hundred years, the test of divine Scripture, and the decree of the Council of Nicaea, the most sacred of all councils.

Luther demands reforms: "To the Christian Nobility" (1520)

Of all his writings, Luther's reform program addressed to the nobles and published in 1520 proved to have the greatest effect on the course of the history of the Reformation. Luther described a church which had built walls around itself to protect it from reforms. These walls consist of three central doctrines which Luther depicts and subsequently refutes: 1. There is spiritual authority and secular authority, whereby the spiritual state is superior to the worldly jurisdiction. 2. Only the priesthood, in particular the pope, is entitled and competent to interpret the Bible. 3. Only the pope can summon and chair a church assembly, a council. Luther, on the other hand, declares that all Christians have a spiritual status and are priests. With his doctrine of "the priesthood of all believers," as it was later known, he encouraged the nobility, the secular authorities, to reform the Church, but also said that every single Christian should take church affairs into their own hands in their own parish. In the second part of his pamphlet, Luther presented 44 proposals for reform concerning the Church, politics and society. There was hardly any aspect of life which he failed to mention, and he was not reticent in his demands for social changes.

Luther's "Nobility Tract", as the work is known in short, was published in August 1520 and soon reprinted in fifteen editions. Tens of thousands of copies were distributed not just in Germany but all over Europe. To this day, it remains one of Luther's most frequently read texts.

In 1520, Luther experienced his greatest journalistic successes and the dissemination of pictures of him began. After the first Luther picture, which was never published in print, Lucas Cranach created a second, more pleasing one in 1520, which was printed in many variations. It shows the monk, dignified, in a niche with the Holy Scripture in his hand. Cranach thus wanted to show Luther to the curious people as a theological teacher, preacher and monk whose teachings were firmly based on the Holy Scriptures.

Martin Luther, An den christlichen Adel deutscher Nation (1520):
WA, Vol. 6, pp. 381–469.
Translation: AL, Vol. 1, pp. 380–463.

Three walls that protect the church from reforms

The Romanists have very cleverly built three walls around themselves. Hitherto they have protected themselves by these walls in such a way that no one has been able to reform them. As a result, the whole of Christendom has fallen horribly.

In the first place, when secular authority has been used against them, they have made decrees and declared that secular authority has no jurisdiction over them, but that, on the contrary, spiritual authority is above secular authority. In the second place, when the attempt is made to reprove them with the Scriptures, they raise the objection that only the pope may interpret the Scriptures. In the third place, if threatened with a council, their story is that no one may summon a council but the pope.

In this way they have cunningly stolen our three rods from us, so that they may go unpunished. They have ensconced themselves within the safe stronghold of these three walls so that they can practice all the knavery and wickedness that we see today. Even when they have been compelled to hold a council, they have weakened its power in advance by putting the princes under oath to let them remain as they were. In addition, they have given the pope full authority over all decisions of a council, so that it is all the same whether there are many councils or no councils. They only deceive us with puppet shows and sham fights. They fear terribly for their skin in a really free council! They have so intimidated kings and princes with this technique that they believe it would be an offense against God not to be obedient to the Romanists in all their knavish and ghoulish deceits.

May God help us and give us just one of those trumpets with which the walls of Jericho were knocked down (Joshua 6:20) to blow down these walls of straw and paper as well and set free the Christian rods for the punishment of sin, [as well as] bring to light the craft and deceit of the devil, to the end that through punishment we may reform ourselves and once more attain God's favor.

Attack on the first wall: The distinction between clergy and laity

Luther shows that, as a result of the universal priesthood in Christianity, there is no basic difference between clergy and laity, but only a pragmatic distribution of the work to be done. Referring to recognized church fathers of the 4th and 5th centuries, Augustine, Ambrose and Cyprian, he makes it clear that bishops were elected by the people. He vigorously rejects the Roman view that the clergy – even with respect to worldly matters – were superior to the laity and thus above the secular authorities. On the contrary, Luther grants the authorities the right to intervene in and reform the Church. He is against church jurisdiction – the so-called Canon Law – which prevents this.

Let us begin by attacking the first wall. It is pure invention that pope, bishop, priests, and monks are called the spiritual estate while princes, lords, artisans, and farmers are called the secular estate. This is indeed a piece of deceit and hypocrisy. Yet no one need be intimidated by it, and for this reason: all Christians are truly of spiritual status, and there is no difference among them except that of office. Paul says in 1 Corinthians 12:12–13 that we are all one body, yet every member has its own work by which it serves the others. This is because we all have one baptism, one gospel, one faith, and are all Christians alike; for baptism, gospel, and faith alone make us spiritual and a Christian people. But if a pope or bishop anoints, tonsures, ordains, consecrates, and prescribes garb different from that of the laity, he can perhaps thereby create a hypocrite or an anointed priestling[2], but he can never make anyone into a Christian or into a spiritual person by so doing. Accordingly, we are all consecrated priests through baptism, as St. Peter says in 1 Peter 2:9, "You are a royal priesthood and a priestly realm." And the Apocalypse says, "Thou hast made us to be priests and kings by thy blood" (Revelation 5:9–10). For if we had no higher consecration than that which pope or bishop gives, such consecration by pope or bishop would never make a priest, and no one could say Mass or preach a sermon or give absolution.

Therefore, when a bishop consecrates it is nothing else than that in the place and in the name of the whole community, all members of which have the same power, he selects one person and charges him with exercising this power on behalf of the others. It is just as if ten brothers, all the sons and equal heirs of a king, were to choose one of their number to rule the inheritance for them: even though they are all kings and of equal

---

2 The original text reads »Ölgötze«, literally »anointed idol«. This is an expression equivalent to »stuffed dummy«, somebody who is merely visible but not active. It contains an allusion to the anointment of priests with oil and also to the disciples who slept in Gethsemane at the foot of the Mount of Olives (in German *Ölberg* »oil mountain«).

power, one of them is charged with the responsibility of ruling. To put it still more clearly: suppose a group of earnest Christian laypeople were taken prisoner and set down in a desert without an episcopally ordained priest among them. And suppose they were to come to a common mind there and then in the desert and elect one of their number, whether he were married or not, and charge him to baptize, say Mass, pronounce absolution, and preach the gospel. Such a man would be as truly a priest as if he had been ordained by all the bishops and popes in the world. This is why in cases of necessity anyone can baptize and give absolution. This would be impossible if we were not all priests. Through canon law the Romanists have almost destroyed and made unknown the wondrous grace and authority of baptism and Christian status. In times gone by, Christians used to choose their bishops and priests in this way from among their own number, and they were confirmed in their office by the other bishops without all the fuss that goes on nowadays. St. Augustine, Ambrose, and Cyprian each became [a bishop in this way].

Since those who exercise secular authority have been baptized with the same baptism, and have the same faith and the same gospel as the rest of us, we must admit that they are priests and bishops, and we must regard their office as one that has a proper place in the Christian community and is useful to it. For whoever has crawled out of the water of baptism can boast that he is already a consecrated priest, bishop, and pope, even though it is not seemly that just anybody should exercise such an office. Because we are all priests of equal standing, no one must push himself forward and take it upon himself, without our consent and election, to do that for which we all have equal authority. For no one dare take upon himself what is common to all without the authority and consent of the community. And should it happen that someone chosen for such office were deposed for abuse of it, he would then be exactly what he was before. Therefore, a priest in Christendom is nothing else but an officeholder. As long as he holds office, he takes precedence; where he is deposed, he is a peasant or a townsman like anybody else. Indeed, a priest is never a priest when he is deposed. But now the Romanists have invented *characteres indelebiles*[3] and blather that a deposed priest is nevertheless something different from a mere layman. They fancy that a priest can never be anything other than a priest, or ever become a layman. All this is just contrived talk and human law.

It follows from this that there is no true, basic difference between laymen and priests, princes and bishops, or (as they say) between spiritual and secular, except that of office and work, and not that of status. For they are all of spiritual status, all are truly priests, bishops, and popes. But they do not all have the same work to do, just as priests and monks do not all have exactly the same work. This is the teaching of St. Paul in Romans 12:4–5 and 1 Corinthians 12:12 and in 1 Peter 2:9, as I have said above, namely, that we are all one body of Christ the Head, and all members one of another. Christ has neither two bodies nor two kinds of body, one secular and the other spiritual. There is but one head and one body.

---

3 According to church dogma, with the understanding of consecration to the priesthood as a sacrament, the prevalent opinion was that a man's ordination to holy orders effected in him a lasting and permanent change, comparable to baptism, which can also not be reversed.

Therefore, just as those who are now called "spiritual," that is, priests, bishops, or popes, are neither different from other Christians nor superior to them, except that they are charged with the administration of the word of God and the sacraments, which is their work and office, so it is with secular government, which has the sword and rod in hand to punish the wicked and protect the good. A cobbler, a blacksmith, a peasant - each has the work and office of his trade, and yet they are all alike consecrated priests and bishops, and everyone should benefit and serve everyone else by means of their own work or office, so that in this way many kinds of work may be done for the bodily and spiritual welfare of the community, just as all the members of the body serve one another (1 Corinthians 12:14–26).

Now consider how Christian the decree is which says that the secular power is not above the "spiritual estate" and has no right to punish it. That is as much as to say that the hand should not help the eye when it suffers pain. Is it not unnatural, not to mention un-Christian, that one member should not help another and prevent its destruction? In fact, the more honorable the member, the more the others ought to help. I say therefore that since secular authority is ordained of God to punish the wicked and protect the good, it should be left free to perform its office in the whole body of Christendom without restriction and without respect to persons, whether it affects pope, bishops, priests, monks, nuns, or anyone else. If it were sufficient for the purpose of preventing secular authority from doing its work to say that among Christian offices it is inferior to that of preacher, confessor, or anyone of spiritual status, one would also have to prevent tailors, cobblers, stonemasons, carpenters, cooks, innkeepers, farmers, and the practitioners of all other secular trades from providing pope, bishops, priests, and monks with shoes, clothes, house, meat, and drink, as well as from paying them any tribute. But if these laypeople are allowed to do their proper work without restriction, what then are the Romanist scribes doing with their own laws, which exempt them from the jurisdiction of secular Christian authority? It is just so that they can be free to do evil and fulfill what St. Peter said: "False teachers will rise up among you who will deceive you, and with their false and fanciful talk, they will take advantage of you" (2 Peter 2:1–3).

For these reasons, Christian secular authority ought to exercise its office without hindrance, regardless of whether it is pope, bishop, or priest whom it affects. Whoever is guilty, let him suffer [punishment]. All that canon law has said to the contrary is the invention of Romanist presumption. For thus St. Paul says to all Christians, "Let every soul (I take that to mean the pope's soul also) be subject to governing authority, for it does not bear the sword in vain, but serves God by punishing the wicked and benefiting the good" (Romans 13:1, 4). St. Peter, too, says, "Be subject to all human ordinances for the sake of the Lord, who so wills it" (1 Peter 2:13, 15). He has also prophesied in 2 Peter 2:1, 3 that such men would arise and despise secular government. This is exactly what has happened through canon law.

So I think this first paper wall is overthrown. Inasmuch as secular rule has become a part of the Christian body, it is part of the spiritual estate, even though its work is physical. Therefore, its work should extend without hindrance to all the members of the whole body, to punish and use force whenever guilt deserves or necessity demands, without regard to whether the culprit is pope, bishop, or priest. Let the Romanists hurl threats and bans as they like. That is why guilty priests, when they are handed over to secular law, are first deprived of their priestly dignities. This would not be right unless the secular sword previously had had authority over these priests by divine right. Moreover, it is intolerable that in canon law so much importance is attached to the freedom, life, and property of the clergy, as though the laity were not also as spiritual and as good Christians as they, or did not also belong to the church. Why are your life and limb, your property and honor, so cheap and mine not, inasmuch as we are all Christians and have the same baptism, the same faith, the same Spirit, and all the rest? If a priest is murdered, the whole country is placed under interdict.[4] Why not when a peasant is murdered? How does this great difference come about between two men who are both Christians? It comes from the laws and fabrications of men.

It can, moreover, be no good spirit that has invented such exceptions and granted such license and impunity to sin. For if it is our duty to strive against the words and works of the devil and to drive him out in whatever way we can, as both Christ and his apostles command us, how have we come to the point that we have to do nothing and say nothing when the pope or his cohorts undertake devilish words and works? Ought we merely out of regard for these people allow the suppression of divine commandments and truth, which we have sworn in baptism to support with life and limb? Then we should have to answer for all the souls that would thereby be abandoned and led astray! It must, therefore, have been the chief devil himself who said what is written in the canon law, that if the pope were

4 Prohibition of performing all church rites.

so scandalously bad as to lead crowds of souls to the devil, still he could not be deposed. At Rome they build on this accursed and devilish foundation, and think that we should let all the world go to the devil rather than resist their knavery. If the fact that one man is set over others were sufficient reason why he should not be punished, then no Christian could punish another, since Christ commanded (Matthew 18:4; Luke 9:48) that all people should esteem themselves as the lowliest and the least. …

Attack on the second wall: The right to interpretation of the Bible

The Roman Church did not want the Bible to be in the hands of the people, but reserved it for the scholars and ministers of the Church. The highest authority for the interpretation of the Bible was the pope. Luther's objection to this was also based on his teaching of the universal priesthood. He cites many biblical examples to show that correct understanding of the Bible cannot be the exclusive prerogative of a supreme ecclesiastical authority. Faith is derived from the inner spiritual understanding of the Bible, which is why the Bible must be available to all.

The second wall is still more loosely built and less substantial. [The Romanists] want to be the only masters of Holy Scripture, although they never learn a thing from the Bible all their life long. They assume the sole authority for themselves, and, quite unashamed, they play about with words before our very eyes, trying to persuade us that the pope cannot err in matters of faith, regardless of whether he is righteous or wicked. Yet they cannot point to a single letter. This is why so many heretical and un-Christian, even unnatural, ordinances stand in the canon law. But there is no need to talk about these ordinances at present. Since these Romanists think the Holy Spirit never leaves them, no matter how ignorant and wicked they are, they become bold and decree only what they want. And if what they claim were true, why have Holy Scripture at all? Of what use is Scripture? Let us burn the Scripture and be satisfied with the unlearned gentlemen at Rome who possess the Holy Spirit! And yet the Holy Spirit can be possessed only by upright hearts. If I had not read the words with my own eyes, I would not have believed it possible for the devil to have made such stupid claims at Rome, and to have won supporters for them.

But so as not to fight them with mere words, we will quote the Scriptures. St. Paul says in 1 Corinthians 14:30, "If something better is revealed to anyone, though he is already sitting and listening to another in God's word, then the one who is speaking shall hold his peace and give place." What would be the point of this commandment if we were compelled to believe only the man who does the talking, or the man who is at the top? Even Christ said in John 6:45 that all Christians shall be taught by God. If it were to happen that the pope and his cohorts were wicked and not true Christians, were not taught by God and were without understanding, and at the same time some obscure person had a right understanding, why should the people not follow that one? Has the pope not erred many times? Who would help Christendom when the pope erred if we did not have others who had the Scriptures on their side and whom we could trust more than him?

Therefore, their claim that only the pope may interpret Scripture is an outrageous fancied fable. They cannot produce a single letter [of Scripture] to maintain that the interpretation of Scripture or the confirmation of its interpretation belongs to the pope alone. They themselves have usurped this power. And although they allege that this power was given to St. Peter when the keys were given him, it is clear enough that the keys were not given to Peter alone but to the whole community. Further, the keys were not ordained for doctrine or government, but only for the binding or loosing of sin. Whatever else or whatever more they arrogate to themselves on the basis of the keys is a mere fabrication. But Christ's words to Peter, "I have prayed for you that your faith fail not" (Luke 22:32), cannot be applied to the pope, since the majority of the popes have been without faith, as they must themselves confess. Besides, it is not only for Peter that Christ prayed, but also for all apostles and Christians, as he says in John 17:9, 20, "Father, I pray for those whom thou hast given me, and not for these only, but for all who believe on me through their word." Is that not clear enough?

Just think of it! The Romanists must admit that there are among us good Christians who have the true faith, spirit, understanding, word, and mind of Christ. Why, then, should we reject the word and understanding of good Christians and follow the pope, who has neither faith nor intelligence? To follow the pope would be to deny the whole faith as well as the Christian church. Again, if the article, "I believe in one holy Christian church," is correct, then the pope cannot be the only one who is right. Otherwise, we would have to pray, "I believe in the pope at Rome." This would reduce the Christian church to one man, and be nothing else than a devilish and hellish error.

Besides, if we are all priests, as was said above, and all have one faith, one gospel, one sacrament, why should we not also have the power to test and judge what is right or wrong in matters of faith? What becomes of Paul's words in 1 Corinthians 2:15, "A spiritual person judges all things and yet is judged by no one"? And 2 Corinthians 4:13, "We all have one spirit of faith"? Why, then, should not we perceive what is consistent with faith and what is not, just as well as an unbelieving pope does? We ought to become bold and free on the authority of all these texts, and many others. We ought not to allow the Spirit of freedom (Paul's appellation in 2 Corinthians 3:17) to be frightened off by the fabrications of the popes but ought rather to march boldly forward and test all that they do or leave undone by our faithful understanding of the Scriptures. We must compel the Romanists to follow not their own interpretation but the better one. Long ago Abraham had to listen to Sarah, although she was in more complete subjection to him than we are to anyone on earth (Genesis 21:12). And Balaam's donkey was wiser than the prophet himself (Numbers 22:21–35). If God spoke then through a donkey against a prophet, why should he not be able even now to speak through a righteous person against the pope? Similarly, St. Paul rebukes St. Peter as someone in error in Galatians 2:11–12. Therefore, it is the duty of every Christian to espouse the cause of the faith, to understand and defend it, and to denounce every error.

Attack on the third wall: Control of the councils

Since 325, when the first Ecumenical Council of the Church was held in Nicaea in today's Turkey, large general assemblies of bishops from the whole of Christendom have taken place in order to deal with the regulation of church issues. Luther considered that such a council would be able to reform the Church. But the pope had claimed for himself the competence to call and chair councils and to confirm – or refuse to confirm – their decisions. Once again, Luther argues with the general priesthood and the example of the Council of Nicaea, which was convened not by a pope but by the emperor Constantine, the first Roman emperor to profess Christianity.

The third wall falls of itself once the first two are down. For when the pope acts contrary to the Scriptures, it is our duty to stand by the Scriptures, to reprove him, and to constrain him, according to the word of Christ, Matthew 18:15–17, "If your brother sins against you, go and tell it to him, between you and him alone; if he does not listen to you, then take one or two others with you; if he does not listen to them, tell it to the church; if he does not listen to the church, consider him a heathen." Here every member is commanded to care for every other. How much more should we do this when the member that does evil is responsible for the government of the church, and by that one's evildoing is the cause of much harm and offense to the rest. But if I am to accuse such a person before the church, I must naturally call the church together.

[The Romanists] have no basis in Scripture for their claim that the pope alone has the right to call or confirm a council. It is just their own law, and it is only valid as long as it is not harmful to Christendom or contrary to the laws of God. But if the pope deserves punishment, this law ceases to be valid, for it is harmful to Christendom not to punish him by authority of a council.

Thus we read in Acts 15:6 that it was not St. Peter who called the Apostolic Council but the apostles and elders. If then that right had belonged to St. Peter alone, the council would not have been a Christian council, but a heretical *conciliabulum*. Even the Council of Nicaea, the most famous of all councils, was neither called nor confirmed by the bishop of Rome, but by the emperor Constantine. Many other emperors after him have done the same, and yet these councils were the most Christian of all. But if the pope alone has the right to convene councils, then these councils would all have been heretical. Further, when I examine the councils the pope did summon, I find that they did nothing of special importance.

Therefore, when necessity demands it, and the pope is an offense to Christendom, the first one who is able should, as true members of the whole body, do what can be done to bring about a truly free council. No one can do this so well as the secular authorities, especially since they are also fellow-Christians, fellow-priests, fellow-participants in spiritual authority, sharing power over all things. Whenever it is necessary or profitable, they ought to exercise the office and work that they have received from God over everyone. Would it not be unnatural if a fire broke out in a city and everybody were to stand by and let it burn on and on and consume everything that could burn because nobody had the authority of the mayor, or because, perhaps, the fire broke out in the mayor's house? In such a situation is it not the duty of every citizen to rouse and summon the rest? How much more should this be done in the spiritual city of Christ if a fire of offense breaks out, whether in the pope's government or anywhere else! The same argument holds if an enemy were to attack a city. The person who first rouses the others deserves honor and gratitude. Why, then, should that person not deserve honor who makes known the presence of the enemy from hell and rouses Christian people and calls them together?

All their boasting about an authority that dare not be opposed amounts to nothing at all. Nobody in Christendom has authority to do injury or to forbid the resisting of injury. There is no authority in the church except to foster improvement. Therefore, if the pope were to use his authority to prevent the calling of a free council, thereby preventing the improvement of the church, we should have regard neither for him nor for his authority. And if he were to hurl his bans and thunderbolts, we should despise his conduct as that of a madman, and we should instead ban him and drive him out as best we can, relying completely upon God. For his presumptuous authority is nothing, nor does he possess it. He is quickly defeated by a single text of Scripture, where Paul says to the Corinthians, "God has given us authority not to ruin Christendom, but to build it up" (2 Corinthians 10:8). Who will leap over the hurdle of this text? It is the power of the devil and of Antichrist, which resists the things that serve to build up Christendom. Such power is not to be obeyed, but rather resisted with life, property, and with all our might and main.

Even though a miracle were to be performed against secular authority on the pope's behalf, or if somebody were struck down by the plague - which they boast has sometimes happened - it should be considered as nothing but the work of the devil designed to destroy our faith in God. Christ foretold this in Matthew 24:24, "False Christs and false prophets shall come in my name, who shall perform signs and miracles in order to deceive even the elect." And Paul says in 2 Thessalonians 2:9 that Antichrist shall, through the power of Satan, be mighty in false miracles.

Let us, therefore, hold fast to this: Christian authority can do nothing against Christ. As St. Paul says, "We can do nothing against Christ, only for Christ" (2 Corinthians 13:8). But if an authority does anything against Christ, then it is that of the Antichrist and the devil, even if it were to rain and hail miracles and plagues. Miracles and plagues prove nothing, especially in these evil latter days. The whole of Scripture foretells such false miracles. This is why we must cling to the word of God with firm faith, and then the devil will soon drop his miracles!

With this I hope that all these wicked and lying terrors, with which the Romanists have long intimidated and dulled our consciences, have been overcome and that they, just like all of us, shall be made subject to the sword. For they have no right to interpret Scripture merely on their own authority and without learning. They have no authority to prevent a council, much less at their mere whim to put it under obligation, impose conditions on it, or deprive it of its freedom. When they do such things, they are truly in the fellowship of Antichrist and the devil. They have nothing at all of Christ except the name. …

Reform proposal 1: The Papacy

The first of Luther's reform proposals concerned the head of the Church, the papacy. In 1520, he still believed that it was possible to reform it. However, he already suspected that the papal throne in Rome was already occupied by the Antichrist, a figure prophesied in the New Testament for the end of time, who wanted to destroy the Church from within. In his immoderate rhetoric, Luther also toyed with the idea of taking violent action against the Pope and his entourage.

Let us now look at the matters that ought to be properly dealt with in councils, matters with which popes, cardinals, bishops, and all scholars ought properly to be occupied day and night if they loved Christ and his church. But if this is not the case, let ordinary people and the secular authorities take action, without regard to papal bans and fulminations, for [suffering under] an unjust ban is better than ten just and proper absolutions, and [trusting] one unjust, improper absolution is worse than ten just bans. Therefore, let us awake, dear Germans, and fear God more than mortals, lest we suffer the same fate of all the poor souls who are so lamentably lost through the shameless, devilish rule of the Romanists, and the devil grow stronger every day – as if it were possible that such a hellish regime could grow any worse, something that I can neither conceive nor believe.

First. It is horrible and shocking to see the head of Christendom, who boasts that he is the vicar of Christ and successor of St. Peter, going about in such a worldly and ostentatious style that neither king nor emperor can equal or approach him. He claims the title of "most holy" and "most spiritual," and yet he is worldlier than the world itself. He wears a triple crown, whereas the highest monarchs wear but one. If that is like the poverty of Christ and of St. Peter, then it is a new and strange kind of likeness! When anybody says anything against it, [the Romanists] bleat, "Heresy!" They refuse to hear how un-Christian and ungodly all this is. In my opinion, if the pope were to pray to God with tears, he would have to lay aside his triple crown, for the God we worship cannot put up with pride. In fact, the pope's office should be nothing else but to weep and pray for Christendom and to set an example of utter humility.

Be that as it may, this kind of splendor is offensive, and the pope is bound for the sake of his own salvation to set it aside. It was for this reason that St. Paul said, "Abstain from all practices which give offense" (1 Thessalonians 5:22), and in Romans 12:17, "We should do good, not only in the sight of God, but also in the sight of all people." An ordinary bishop's mitre ought to be good enough for the pope. It is in wisdom and holiness that he should be above his fellows. He ought to leave the crown of pride to Antichrist, as his predecessors did centuries ago. The Romanists say he is a lord of the earth. That is a lie! For Christ, whose vicar and vicegerent he claims to be, said to Pilate, "My kingdom is not of this world" (John 18:36). No vicar's rule can go beyond that of his lord. Moreover, he is not the vicar of Christ glorified but of Christ crucified. As Paul says, "I was determined to know nothing among you save Christ, and him only as the crucified" (1 Corinthians 2:2), and in Philippians 2:5–7, "This is how you should regard yourselves, as you see in Christ, who emptied himself and took upon himself the form of a servant." Or again in 1 Corinthians 1:23, "We preach Christ, the crucified." Now the Romanists make the pope a vicar of the glorified Christ in heaven, and some of them have allowed the devil to rule them so completely that they have maintained that the pope is above the angels in heaven and has them at his command. These are certainly the proper works of the real Antichrist. …

"Let us hang the thieves"

Since, then, such devilish rule is not only barefaced robbery, deceit, and the tyranny of the gates of hell but also ruinous to the body and soul of Christendom, it is our duty to exercise all diligence to protect Christendom from such misery and destruction. If we want to fight against the Turks, let us begin here where they are worst of all. If we are right in hanging thieves and beheading robbers, why should we let Roman

Avarice go free? He is the worst thief and robber that has ever been or could ever come into the world, and all in the holy name of Christ and St. Peter! Who can put up with it a moment longer and say nothing? Almost everything Avarice possesses has been procured by theft and robbery. It has never been otherwise, as all the history books prove. …

Reform proposal 13: Monastic life

When Luther developed his reform program in 1520, he was still a monk and still lived as a monk. Nevertheless, he also called for a reform of monastic life, which should be re–oriented to the beginnings and origins of monasticism. Monasteries should again serve education, and monks and nuns should no longer take life–long vows.

To my way of thinking, it would be a necessary measure, especially in our perilous times, to regulate convents and monasteries in the same way that they were regulated in the beginning, in the days of the apostles and for a long time afterward. In those days, convents and monasteries were all open for everyone to stay in them as long as they pleased. What else were the convents and monasteries but Christian schools where Scripture and the Christian life were taught, and where people were trained to rule and to preach? Thus we read that St. Agnes went to school, and we still see the same practice in some of the convents, like that at Quedlinburg and elsewhere. And in truth all monasteries and convents ought to be so free that God is served freely and not under compulsion. Later on, however, they became obsessed with vows and made of them an eternal prison. Consequently, these monastic vows are more highly regarded than the vows of baptism. We see, hear, read, and learn more and more about the fruit of all this every day. I can well suppose that this advice of mine will be regarded as the height of foolishness, but I am not concerned about that at the moment. I advise what seems good to me; let those who will reject it. I see for myself how the vows are kept, especially the vow of chastity. This vow has become universal in these monasteries, and yet it was never commanded by Christ. On the contrary, chastity is given to very few, as he himself says (Matthew 19:11–12), as well as St. Paul (1 Corinthians 7:7). It is my heartfelt wish that everybody be helped and that Christian souls not become entangled in self-contrived human traditions and laws. …

Reform proposal 25: The education system

At the time when Luther drew up his reform program, he was not only a monk but also a university professor. The reform of the educational system, whether universities or schools, was close to his heart. He wanted the Bible to be an integral and central component in education. Girls were to be given elementary education as well. At the universities, the heathen Greek philosopher Aristotle should no longer be given such prominence. Likewise, the study of the "Sentences" of the medieval theologian Peter Lombard, a collection of quotations from the church fathers, should no longer play such an intensive role for students and professors. Luther also took a critical look at the legal system of the time, which consisted of secular law on the one hand and ecclesiastical, so–called Canon Law on the other.

The universities, too, need a good, thorough reformation. I must say this, no matter whom it annoys. Everything the papacy has instituted and ordered serves only to increase sin and error. What else are the universities, unless they are utterly changed from what they have been hitherto, than what the book of Maccabees calls *gymnasia epheborum et graecae gloriae*? (2 Maccabees 4:9, 12). What are they but places where loose living is practiced, where little is taught of the Holy Scriptures and Christian faith, and where only the blind, heathen teacher Aristotle rules far more than Christ?

In this regard my advice would be that Aristotle's *Physics, Metaphysics, Concerning the Soul*, and *Ethics*, which hitherto have been thought to be his best books, should be completely discarded along with all the rest of his books that boast about nature, although nothing can be learned from them either about nature or the Spirit. Moreover, nobody has yet understood him, and many souls have been burdened with fruitless labor and study, at the cost of much precious time. I dare say that any potter has more knowledge of nature than is written in these books. It grieves me to the quick that this damned, arrogant, villainous heathen has deluded and made fools of so many of the best Christians with his misleading writings. God has sent him as a plague upon us on account of our sins. This wretched fellow in his best book, *Concerning the Soul*, even teaches that the soul dies with the body, although many have tried without success to save his reputation. As though we did not have the Holy Scriptures, in which we are fully instructed about all things, things about which Aristotle has not the faintest clue! And yet this dead heathen has conquered, obstructed, and almost succeeded in suppressing the books of the living God. When I think of this miserable business, I can only believe that the evil spirit has introduced the study [of Aristotle]. . . .

I would gladly agree to keeping Aristotle's books *Logic, Rhetoric*, and *Poetics*, or at least keeping and using them in an abridged form, as useful in training young people to speak and to preach properly. But the commentaries and notes must be abolished, and as Cicero's *Rhetoric* is read without commentaries and notes, so Aristotle's *Logic* should be read as it is without all these commentaries. But today nobody learns how to speak or how to preach from it. The whole thing has become nothing but a matter for wearying disputation. In addition to all this, there are, of course, the Latin, Greek, and Hebrew languages, as well as the mathematical disciplines and history. But all this I commend to the experts. In fact, reform would come readily if only we devoted ourselves seriously to it. Actually a great deal depends on it, for it is here in the universities that the Christian youth and our nobility, with whom the future of Christendom lies, will be educated and trained. Therefore, I believe that there is no work more worthy of pope or emperor than a thorough reform of the universities. And on the other hand, nothing could be more devilish or disastrous than unreformed universities.

I leave it to the physicians to reform their own faculties; I take the jurists and theologians for myself. I say first that it would be a good thing if canon law were completely blotted out, from the first letter to the last, especially the Decretals. More than enough is written in the Bible about how we should behave in all circumstances. The study of canon law only hinders the study of the Holy Scriptures. Moreover, the greater part smacks of nothing but greed and pride. Even if there were much in it that was good, it should still be destroyed, for the pope has the whole canon law imprisoned in the chamber of his heart, so that henceforth any study of it is just a waste of time and a farce. These days canon law is not what is written in the books of law, but whatever the pope and his flatterers want. Your cause may be thoroughly established in canon law, but the pope always has his "chamber of the heart" in the matter, and all law, and with it the whole world, has to be guided by that. Now it is often a villain, and even the devil himself who controls the chamber, and they proudly boast that it is the Holy Spirit who controls it! Thus they deal with Christ's poor people. They impose many laws upon them but obey none themselves. They compel others to obey these laws or buy their way out with money. ...

Secular law - God help us - has become a wilderness. Though it is much better, wiser, and more honest than the spiritual law, which has nothing good about it except its name, there is nevertheless far too much of it. Surely, wise rulers, along with Holy Scripture, would be more than enough law. As St. Paul says in 1 Corinthians 6:5–6, "Is there no one among you who can judge his neighbor's cause, that you must go to law before heathen courts?" It seems just to me that territorial laws and customs should take precedence over general imperial laws, and that the imperial laws be used only in case of necessity. Would God that every land were ruled by its own brief laws suitable to its gifts and peculiar character. This is how these lands were ruled before these imperial laws were designed, and as many lands are still ruled without them! Rambling and farfetched laws are only a burden to the people, and they hinder cases more than they help them. But I hope that others have already given more thought and attention to this matter than I am able to do.

My dear theologians have saved themselves worry and work. They just leave the Bible alone and lecture on the *Sentences*. I should have thought that the *Sentences* ought to be the first study for young students of theology, and the Bible left to the doctors. But today it is the other way round. The Bible comes first and is then put aside when the baccalaureate is received. The *Sentences* come last, and they occupy a doctor as long as he lives. There is such a solemn obligation attached to these *Sentences* that a person who is not a priest may well lecture on the Bible, but the sentences must be lectured on by someone who is a priest. As I see it, a married man may well be a Doctor of the Bible, but under no circumstances could he be a Doctor of the *Sentences*. How can we prosper when we behave so wrongly and give the Bible, the holy word of God, a back seat? To make things worse, the pope commands in the strongest language that his words are to be studied in the schools and used in the courts, but very little is thought of the gospel. Consequently, the gospel lies neglected in the schools and in the courts. It is pushed aside under the bench and gathers dust so that the scandalous laws of the pope alone may have full sway. If we bear the name and title of teachers of Holy Scripture, then by this criterion we ought to be compelled to teach the Holy Scripture and nothing else, although we all know that this high and mighty title is much too exalted for a person to take pride in it and allow being designated a Doctor of Holy Scripture. Yet that title might be permitted if the work justified the name. But nowadays, the *Sentences* alone dominate in such a way that we find among the theologians more pagan and human darkness than holy and certain doctrine of Scripture. What are we to do about it? I know of nothing else to do than to pray humbly to God to give us such real doctors of theology as we have in mind. Pope, emperor, and universities may make doctors of arts, of medicine, of laws, of the *Sentences*; but be assured that no one can make a doctor of Holy Scripture except the Holy Spirit from heaven. As Christ says in

John 6:45, "They must all be taught by God himself." Now the Holy Spirit does not care about red or brown birettas or other decorations. Nor does he ask whether a person is young or old, lay or cleric, monk or secular, unmarried or married. In fact, in ancient times he actually spoke through a donkey against the prophet who was riding it (Numbers 22:28). Would God that we were worthy to have such doctors given to us, regardless of whether they were lay or cleric, married or single! They now try to force the Holy Spirit into pope, bishops, and doctors, although there is not the slightest sign or indication whatever that he is in them.

The number of books on theology must be reduced and only the best ones published. It is not many books that make people learned or even much reading. It is, rather, a good book frequently read, no matter how small it is, that makes a person learned in the Scriptures and upright. Indeed, the writings of all the holy Fathers should be read only for a time so that through them we may be led into the Scriptures. As it is, however, we only read them these days to avoid going any further and getting into the Bible. We are like people who read the signposts and never travel the road they indicate. Our dear Fathers wanted to lead us to the Scriptures by their writings, but we use their works to get away from the Scriptures. Nevertheless, the Scripture alone is our vineyard in which we must all labor and toil.

Above all, the foremost reading for everybody, both in the universities and in the schools, should be Holy Scripture – and for the younger boys, the Gospels. And would God that every town had a girls' school as well, where the girls would be taught the gospel for an hour every day either in German or in Latin. But real schools! Monasteries and nunneries began long ago with that end in view, and it was a praiseworthy and Christian purpose, as we learn from the story of St. Agnes and of other saints. Those were the days of holy virgins and martyrs when all was well with Christendom. But today these monasteries and nunneries have come to nothing but praying and singing. Is it not only right that every Christian know the entire holy gospel by the age of nine or ten? Does not each person derive name and life from the gospel? A spinner or a seamstress teaches her daughter her craft in her early years. But today even the great, learned prelates and the very bishops do not know the gospel. …

Reform proposals for everyday life

At the end of his tract to the nobility, Luther deals with social grievances. Here, too, he proposes reforms. Luther was against every kind of luxury in everyday life. In the economic sphere, he rejected the lending of money at interest ("zynskauf"), which was just developing, and the new forms of credit transactions. He wanted to restrain the trade of the Fuggers in Augsburg, the largest firm of mercantile bankers in Germany.

Enough has now been said about the failings of the clergy, though you may and will find more if you look in the right place. Let us now take a look at some of those of the secular realm.

In the first place, there is a great need for a general law and decree in the German nation against boundlessly excessive and costly dress, because of which so many nobles and rich people are impoverished. God has certainly given us, as he has to other countries, enough wool, flax, linen, and everything else necessary for the seemly and honorable dress of every class. We do not need to waste fantastic sums for silk, velvet, golden ornaments, and foreign wares. I believe that even if the pope had not robbed us with his intolerable fleecing, we would still have more than enough of these home-grown robbers, the traders in silk and velvet. We see that now everybody wants to be like everybody else, and pride and envy are thereby aroused and increased among us, as we deserve. All this misery and much more besides would probably be avoided if only our ardor [for such things] would let us be thankfully content with the good things God has already given us.

It is also necessary to restrict the traffic in spices, which is another of the great ships in which money is carried out of the German lands. By the grace of God, more things to eat and drink grow here than in any other country, and they are just as tasty and good. Perhaps my proposals seem foolish, impractical, and give the impression that I want to ruin the greatest of all trades, that of commerce. But I am doing my best, and if there is no general improvement in these matters, then let him who will try his hand at improving them. I do not see that many good morals have ever come to a country through commerce, and in ancient times God made his people Israel dwell away from the sea because of this and did not let them engage in much commerce.

But the greatest misfortune of the German nation is certainly the *zynskauf*. If that did not exist, many people would have to leave unpurchased their silks, velvets, golden ornaments, spices, and display of every kind. This traffic has not existed much longer than a hundred years, and it has already brought almost all princes, endowed institutions, cities, nobles, and their heirs to poverty, misery, and ruin. If it goes on for another hundred years, Germany will not have a penny left, and the chances are we shall have to eat one another. The devil invented the practice, and by confirming it the pope has brought woe upon the whole world. Therefore, I beg and pray at this point that everyone open their eyes and see the ruin of their children and heirs. Ruin is not just at the door, it is already in the house. I pray and beseech emperor, princes, lords, and city councilors to condemn this trade as speedily as possible and prevent it from now on, regardless of whether the pope with all his unjust justice objects, or whether benefices or monasteries are based upon it. It is better for a city to have one benefice supported by honest legacies or revenue than to have a hundred benefices supported by *zynskauf*. Indeed, a benefice supported by a *zynskauf* is more grievous and oppressive than twenty supported by legacies. In fact, the *zynskauf* must be a sign and proof that the world has been sold to the devil because of its grievous sins and that at the same time we are losing both temporal and spiritual possessions. And yet we do not even notice it.

In this connection, we must put a bit in the mouth of the Fuggers and similar companies. How is it possible in the lifetime of one person to accumulate such great possessions, worthy of a king, legally and according to God's will? I don't know. But what I really cannot understand is how a person with one hundred gulden can make a profit of twenty in one year. Nor, for that matter, can I understand how a person with one gulden can make another – and make it not from tilling the soil or raising cattle, where the increase of wealth depends not on human wit but on God's blessing. I leave this to people who understand the ways of the world. As a theologian I have no further reproof to make on this subject except that it has an evil and offending appearance, about which St. Paul says, "Avoid every appearance or show of evil" (1 Thessalonians 5:22). I know full well that it would be a far godlier thing to increase agriculture and decrease commerce. I also know that those who work on the land and seek their livelihood from it according to the Scriptures do far better. All this was said to us and to everybody else in the story of Adam, "Cursed be the ground when you work it; it shall bear you thistles and thorns, and in the sweat of your face you shall eat your bread" (Genesis 3:17–19). There is still a lot of land lying fallow and neglected.

Next comes the abuse of eating and drinking, which gives us Germans a bad reputation in foreign lands, as though it were a special vice of ours. Preaching cannot stop it so deeply is it rooted and so firmly has it got the upper hand. The waste of money would be insignificant were it not for all the vices that accompany it – murder, adultery, stealing, blasphemy, and every other form of immorality. Government can do something to prevent it; otherwise, what Christ says will come to pass, that the last day shall come like a secret snare, when they shall be eating and drinking, marrying and wooing, building and planting, buying and selling. It is so much like what is now going on that I sincerely hope the Judgment Day is at hand, although very few people give it any thought.

Finally, is it not lamentable that we Christians tolerate open and common brothels in our midst, when all of us are baptized unto chastity? …

“On the Freedom of a Christian”

A second treatise by Luther from 1520 continues to be an inspiration even today. It deals with religious and theological issues affecting every single Christian. Following once again in the footsteps of Paul and Augustine, Luther makes a close connection between religion and the concept of freedom; this approach had a lasting influence on the history of Christian theology from that time on up to the present day. Religion has indeed in many cases been related to coercion and continues to do so. It is forced upon people, and it produces compulsion. For Luther, however, faith makes people free on the one hand, whilst on the other hand it may not be made the subject of constraints. Nonetheless, Luther sees freedom as based on the bond with God, leading to the obligation to serve one’s neighbor.

Martin Luther, Von der Freiheit eines Christenmenschen (1520): WA, Vol. 7, pp. 12–38.
Translation: Bertram Lee Woolf, Reformation Writings of Martin Luther, Vol. 1, New York: Philosophical Library 1953, pp. 356–379.

1. In order that we may have a true and proper understanding of what it is to be a Christian, or what is the freedom which Christ has won for us and given to us, and of which St. Paul often writes, I propose to begin with two propositions.

A Christian is free and independent in every respect, a bondservant to none.
A Christian is a dutiful servant in every respect, owing a duty to everyone.

These two axioms are clearly found in 1 Corinthians 9:19, where St. Paul says: "Though I am free from all men, I have made myself a servant to all." Again, Romans 13:8: "Owe no one anything, except to love one another. But love owes a duty, and is a bondservant of what she loves"; in the same way also in regard to Christ, Galatians 4:4: "God sent forth His Son, born of a woman, and made Him a bondservant of the law."

2. In order to understand these two antithetic assertions concerning freedom and bondage, we ought to remember that in every Christian there are two natures, a spiritual and a bodily. In as far as he possesses a soul, a Christian is a spiritual person, an inward, regenerate self; and in as far as he possesses flesh and blood, he is a sensual person, an outward, unregenerate self. Because of this difference, the Scriptures, in passages which directly contradict each other, speak of his freedom and bondage in the way I have just said.

The inner, spiritual person is free

Luther shows that the freedom of a Christian consists in the fact that external activities – works – are neither beneficial nor harmful for salvation. Freedom comes through Christ and is attained through faith. Even oppression and imprisonment cannot take this freedom away.

Luther also asks about the meaning of the divine commandments in Holy Scripture and says that they are meant to show humans that they are incapable of really doing good. In particular, someone who does many good things is often driven at heart by selfishness, and is therefore in reality a sinner. A person who has recognized this and accepts it in humility reaches for the divine grace offered to them in Christ and trusts in the promises contained in the Bible. Faith, according to Luther, unites the human soul with Christ like a bride with her bridegroom. As in a marriage, the partners hold all things in common; Christ absolves the soul from sin, allowing it to share in his righteousness. Christ also lets the believer share in his spiritual kingship and priesthood. The latter gives every Christian the right to come before God like a priest and to intercede with God on behalf of others.

In order to explain these complicated relationships, Luther, having distinguished between the outer and the inner person, deals first of all with the inner one.

3. When we consider the inner, spiritual man and see what belongs to him if he is to be a free and devout Christian, in fact and in name, it is evident that, whatever the name, no outer thing can make him either free or religious. For his religion and freedom, and, moreover, his sinfulness and servitude, are neither bodily nor outward. What avail is it to the soul if the body is free, active, and healthy; or eats, drinks, and lives as it likes? Again, what harm does it do to the soul if the body is imprisoned, ill and weakly; or is hungry, thirsty, and in pain, even if one does not bear it gladly? This sort of thing never touches the soul a little bit, nor makes it free or captive, religious or sinful.

4. Thus it does not help the soul if the body puts on sacred vestments as the priests and clergy do. It does not help even when the body is in church or in holy places, or when busy with sacred affairs; nor when the body is offering prayers, keeping fasts, or making pilgrimages, and doing other good works, which are performed only in and through the body. It must surely be something quite different which brings religion and freedom to the soul. For even a sinful man, or a hypocrite and pretender, may have all the afore-named things, do these

works, and follow these ways. Also, this is the way to make men nothing but sheer hypocrites. Further it does no harm to the soul if the body wears worldly clothes; tarries in worldly places, eats, drinks, does not go on pilgrimages, nor keep the appointed hours of prayer; and if it neglects all the works that hypocrites perform, as already said.

5. The only means, whether in heaven or on earth, whereby the soul can live, and be religious, free, and Christian, is the holy Gospel, the word of God preached by Christ. He Himself says in John 11:25, "I am the resurrection and the life. He that believeth in Me shall live eternally"; and John 14:6, "I am the way, the truth and the life"; and Matthew 4:4, "Man does not live by bread alone, but by every word that proceeds out of the mouth of God." Therefore, we can be certain that the soul can do without anything but the word of God; and apart from the word of God it has no means of help. When it has the word, however, it has no need of anything else. In short, it possesses food, joy, peace, light, ability, righteousness, truth, wisdom, freedom, and sufficient to overflowing of everything good. Thus we read in the Psalms, especially in Psalm 119, that the prophet cries only for the word of God. And in the Scriptures, the worst calamity, the worst sign of God's wrath, is when He withdraws His word from man. On the other hand, it is held the greatest grace when He sends forth His word, as it is written in Psalm 107:20: "He sent His word and helped them thereby." Christ came for no other object than to preach the word of God. Moreover all apostles, bishops, priests, and the whole clergy, were called and instituted only for the sake of the word; although, unfortunately, things happen differently nowadays.

6. You may ask, however: "What then is that word which gives such signal grace, and how shall I use it?" The answer is: It is nothing else than the message proclaimed by Jesus, as contained in the gospel; and this should be, and, in fact, is, so presented that you hear your God speak to you. It shows how all your life and labor are as nothing in God's sight, and how you and all that is in you, must eternally perish. If you truly believe this, and that you are indeed guilty, you necessarily despair of yourself; you believe that Hosea was right when he said: "O Israel, there is nought in you except your corruption, but in Me is your help" (Hosea 13:9). In order that you may come out of yourself and flee from yourself, i. e., escape your corruption, He sets you face to face with His beloved Son, Jesus Christ, and says to you by means of His living and comforting word: "You should surrender yourself to Him with firm faith, and trust Him gladly." Then, for your faith's sake, all your sins shall be forgiven and all your wickedness overcome. You yourself will be righteous, upright, serene, and devout. You will fulfill all commands, and be free from all things, as St. Paul says in Romans 1:17: "A justified Christian lives only by his faith"; and in Romans 10:4: "Christ is the end and the fulfillment of all commandments for them that believe in him." …

8. But how does it come about that faith alone can make one religious, and give such exceeding wealth apart from any works, seeing that so many laws, commandments, works, and other means are prescribed in the Scriptures? In this connection we must be sure to note and carefully remember that, as we shall see later, faith alone, apart from any act of ours, makes us religious, sets us free, and saves us. We should understand that the entire Holy Scriptures can be divided under two heads:

Commandment or God's Law, and Promise or Covenant. The commandments teach and prescribe many good works, but this does not mean that they are fulfilled by us. They give good instructions, but no assistance. They teach what man should do, but give no power to do it. Hence they are only fitted to show a man his own incapacity for goodness, and to make him learn to doubt himself. For this reason they are called the Old Testament, and all belong to the Old Testament. The commandment: "Thou shalt not have sinful appetites" (Exodus 20:17), shows that all of us are sinners, and there can be no man without sinful appetites, let him do what he may. Thereby a man learns not to depend on himself, but to seek help elsewhere in order that he may be without sinful appetites. Thus he may fulfill the commandment through another, although he could not do so of himself. In the same way, all other commandments are impossible to us.

9. Now when a man has learned from the commandments, and perceived his own incapacity, then he will be anxious to know how to keep the commandment, for unless he fulfills the commandment he will be damned. This will take away all his pride, and he will become as nothing in his own eyes; he will find nothing in himself to make him acceptable to God. Then comes the other word, the divine promise, the covenant which says: If you would fulfill all the commandments, and escape from your evil passions and sins, as the commandments urge and require, lo! believe on Christ. In Him I promise that you will find all the needful grace, righteousness, peace, and freedom. If you believe, you will possess; if you do not believe, you will not possess. What is impossible to you in attempting all the works of the commandments, which are necessarily many and yet of

no avail, will come to you quickly and easily through faith. I have summed everything up in faith alone, so that whoever has faith shall have all, and be saved; without faith, no one shall have anything. Thus God's covenants give what the commandments require, and bring about that for which the commandments are intended; all this is in order that everything, both commandment and fulfillment, might be God's own. He alone commands and alone fulfills. Therefore the covenants of God are the words of the New Testament, and their proper place is the New Testament.

10. Now these, and all God's words, are holy, true, right, peace-giving, free, and entirely good. The soul of the man who cleaves to them with a true faith will be so completely united with God that all the virtues of the word will become the qualities of his soul. Through faith and by God's word, the soul will become holy, righteous, true, peaceful, free, and entirely good, and he will become a true child of God. Thus it says in John 1:12: "He gave power to all them that believe in His name to become children of God." From this standpoint it is easy to see why faith can do so much, and why good works can never be equivalent to it. For works of merit are not such as to depend on the divine word as in the case of faith, nor can they live in the soul. Only the word and faith exercise sway in the soul. Just as iron becomes red like fire through its union with the fire, so does the soul become like the word through its union with the word. Thus we see that a Christian has sufficient in his faith. Works are not needed to make him become acceptable to God. And if such works are no longer a prerequisite, then assuredly all commandments and laws are like broken chains; and if his chains are broken, he is assuredly free. That

is Christian freedom, gained by faith alone. It is wrong to think this means that we can either be idle or do evil; rather it means that we have no need to perform works of merit in order to attain godliness and salvation. But we shall deal further with this matter later on. …

12. Faith not only gives the soul enough for her to become, like the divine word, gracious, free, and blessed. It also unites the soul with Christ, like a bride with the bridegroom, and, from this marriage, Christ and the soul become one body, as St. Paul says. Then the possessions of both are in common, whether fortune, misfortune, or anything else; so that what Christ has, also belongs to the believing soul, and what the soul has, will belong to Christ. If Christ has all good things, including blessedness, these will also belong to the soul. If the soul is full of trespasses and sins, these will belong to Christ. At this point a contest of happy exchanges takes place. Because Christ is God and man, and has never sinned, and because His sanctity is unconquerable, eternal, and almighty, He takes possession of the sins of the believing soul by virtue of her wedding ring, namely faith, and acts just as if He had committed those sins Himself. They are, of course, swallowed up and drowned in Him, for His unconquerable righteousness is stronger than any sin whatever. Thus the soul is cleansed from all her sins by virtue of her dowry, i. e., for the sake of her faith. She is made free and unfettered, and endowed with the eternal righteousness of Christ, her bridegroom. Is that not a happy household, when Christ, the rich, noble, and good bridegroom, takes the poor, despised, wicked little harlot in marriage, sets her free from all evil, and decks her with all good things? for her sins to damn her, for now they rest on Christ, and are swallowed up in

Him. In this way she has such a rich righteousness in her bridegroom that she can always withstand sins, although they indeed lie in wait for her. Paul speaks of this in 1 Corinthians 15:55–57: "Praise and thanks be to God, who has given us that victory in Christ Jesus, in which death is swallowed up together with sin." …

14. The next point to consider is the treasure we possess in Christ, and how valuable is the right kind of faith. Let us be clear that, before Old Testament times, as well as during them, God chose and reserved for Himself all the first-born, whether human or animal. Moreover, the eldest son was of special dignity, and had two great privileges as distinct from all the younger children: he was given authority, and he was a priest. The kingship and the priesthood were his. Thus, in practice, the eldest son was the master of all the other brothers; he was also a priest, or pope, of God. This is a figure symbolizing Jesus Christ, who is that self-same, human Son of God the Father by the Virgin Mary. He is therefore a king and a priest – but in the spiritual sense. His kingdom is not earthly, nor does it consist in earthly things, but in those of the spirit, such as truth, wisdom, peace, joy, salvation, and the like. Temporal goods are not excluded, however, for all things in heaven, earth, or hell are subject to Him, although He is unseen owing to the fact that He rules spiritually and invisibly.

Thus even His priesthood does not consist in rites and vestments such as we see among men. Rather it consists in the spirit, and is invisible, in order that He may stand continually before God's face, and offer Himself on behalf of those who are His, and do all that a devout priest should do. He prays for us, as St. Paul says in Romans 8:34; and also teaches us inwardly in our hearts. These two offices are right and proper for a priest; and therefore ordinary, human, and temporal priests pray and teach in the same manner.

15. Since Christ has the primogeniture with all appropriate honor and worth, He shares it with all Christians who are His, that, through faith, all may be kings and priests with Christ, as St. Peter says in 1 Peter 2:9: "You are a priestly kingdom and a royal priesthood." The result is that a Christian is lifted up by faith so high above all things that he becomes the spiritual lord of all, for nothing can hinder his salvation. Rather, everything is subject to him, and helps him to reach salvation. Thus St. Paul teaches in Romans 8:28: "Everything must help to secure the good of the elect", whether life, death, sin, piety, good or evil, or whatever it may be. So also, 1 Corinthians 3:21–22: "All things are yours, whether life or death, present or future", etc. It is not to be understood that we exercise material authority over all things, so that we possess or use them like ordinary men. Indeed as far as the body is concerned, we must die, for no one can avoid death. In the same way, we are necessarily subject to many other things, as we see exemplified also in Christ and His saints. For ours is a spiritual rulership, exercised even to the extent of repressing the body. Thus I can gain benefit in my soul quite apart from material things, and I can make even death and suffering of service to my salvation. That is surely a high and noble dignity, a proper and all-powerful lordship, a spiritual royalty. Nothing is so good or so evil but that it must serve me for good, if I have faith. Indeed, I need none of these things. My faith is sufficient for me. How precious then is the freedom and potency which Christians possess!

16. In addition, we are priests, and thus greater than mere kings, the reason being that priesthood makes us worthy to stand before God, and to pray for others. For to stand and pray before God's face is the prerogative of none except priests. Christ redeemed us that we might be able spiritually to act and pray on behalf of one another just as, in fact, a priest acts and prays on behalf of the people. But nothing avails to the benefit of a person who does not believe in Christ. He is nought but a slave; he is always worried; it is hard for him to pray, and his prayers do not come under God's eye. By contrast, who can fully conceive the honor and the elevation of a Christian? By virtue of his kingship he exercises authority over all things, and by virtue of his priesthood he exercises power with God, for God does what he asks and desires. Thus it is written in the book of Psalms: "God does the will of those that fear Him, and hears their prayers" (Psalm 145:19). This is an honor to which Christians attain through faith alone and not through any works. Thereby it becomes clear that a Christian always enjoys freedom, and is always master. He requires no good works to make him godly or to save him; faith brings everything in abundance to him. If he were so foolish as to think that by good works he would become godly, free, blessed, or a Christian, he would lose both faith and all else. He would be like the dog which, while carrying a piece of meat in its mouth, snapped at its reflection in the water, and thereby lost the meat and spoiled the reflection. …

The outer person is committed to service

In the second part of his tract on Christian freedom, Luther expounds his ethical teaching, showing that only the person who has become free in Christ through faith is able to do good to others selflessly. For this, he does not need commands in the sense of laws, but automatically does the right thing, filled by the love given to him by God, just as a good tree bears good fruit.

We now come to the second part, namely, to the outer man. Here we must deal with all those who take offense at the foregoing arguments, and are wont to say: "Oh! then if faith is the whole thing and sufficient in itself to make one religious, why are good works demanded? We shall be in good case without doing anything at all." No, my dear man, not so. That would perhaps be true if you were nothing but your inner self, and had become pure soul and pure spirit, a thing which will never happen before the last day. There will never be anything else on earth than a beginning and a growth; these will only be completed in the next world. That is why the apostle called it *primitias spiritus*, or the first-fruits of the spirit (Romans 8:23). From this fact we can understand what was said above: "*A Christian man is a dutiful menial, a bondservant to everyone*", which is as much as to say: "In as far as he is free, he requires to do nothing. In as far as he is a servant, he must do everything." How that happens, we shall now see.

20. Inwardly, and as regards his soul, a man is sufficiently justified by faith. He possesses all he ought to have, except that his very faith and sufficiency must always increase until his entry into the next life; nevertheless, he still remains on earth during his bodily life. Therefore he must rule his own body,

and he must mix with other people. That is where the need for good works enters. He must not be idle. Yes, the body must be disciplined and exercised with fasting, watching, laboring, and all due training, in order that it may be obedient to, and in harmony with, both the inner man and with faith; and not hinder nor oppose, as is its nature when it is not restrained. …

21. But none of these works must be done under the impression that a man becomes devout in God's sight thereby. …

23. Hence both expressions are true: "Good and devout works never make a man good and duteous; but a good and religious man does good and religious works." Nor do sinful works make a man sinful. Rather, it is a sinful man who does sinful works. Thus every argument proves that the person must first be good and godly; after that come all the works that are good. Good works proceed logically from a godly and good person. …

26. All this concerns meritorious works in general and those which a Christian may perform as far as his own self is concerned. But now we would speak of other actions, those which he does in relation to other men. For a man does not live alone, in his own body, but among other men, in the world. Therefore, he cannot remain without works in his contacts with others; he must speak to and co-operate with them, although none of these actions is necessary for his own godliness or salvation. …

27. … And although he is now quite free, yet a Christian ought voluntarily to make himself a servant and help his neighbor. He should associate and deal with him as God has done with

himself through Christ, everything being free, and nothing being sought except to please God: He should therefore think within himself: "Unworthy and guilty man that I am, and without any desert, yet my God, quite freely and out of pure mercy, has given me, in and through Christ, the full wealth of all religion and salvation, so that henceforth I need nothing except faith. So let it be. Yes, for the sake of such a Father, who has heaped upon me His superabundant good things, will I freely, gladly, and without reward, do what pleases Him. To my neighbor, I will be, as a Christian, what Christ has become to me, and do just what I see is needful, helpful, or acceptable to him, for I have enough of all things in Christ through my faith." Lo, that is how love and joy in God flow out of faith, and how love gives rise to a free, eager, and glad life of serving one's neighbor without reward. …

30. From all the foregoing, the conclusion follows that a Christian lives not in himself, but in Christ and his neighbor; in Christ by faith and in his neighbor by love. By faith he rises above himself unto God; from God he stoops below himself by love, and yet he remains always in God and in divine love, just as Christ says in John 1:51: "You will see the heavens open and the angels ascending and descending upon the Son of Man."

Yes, that is the true, spiritual, and Christian freedom. It liberates our hearts from all sins, laws, and commandments. It exceeds all other freedom as much as heaven the earth. God grant that we rightly understand and retain this freedom. Amen.

“On the Babylonian Captivity of the Church”

In addition to his address to the nobility and his tract on Christian freedom, Luther wrote a third fundamental treatise in 1520. Unlike the other two, it was intended for scholars and therefore formulated in Latin. In this text he accused the Roman Church of holding Christendom captive, as once the Babylonians held the people of Israel captive in the 6th century B.C., but in this case not externally, meaning physically, but internally and spiritually. This book “On the Babylonian Captivity of the Church” deals specifically with the doctrine of the sacraments. The medieval Church declared a total of seven ritual acts to be sacraments, meaning actions imparting divine grace to the faithful: baptism, confirmation, matrimony, extreme unction (today: anointing of the sick), holy orders, penance and the Lord’s Supper (Eucharist). Luther, however, insists that sacraments are only valid if they can be traced back to Jesus himself. And he only acknowledges acts connected, on the one hand, to a clear biblical promise (in the case of baptism, Jesus’ commission to baptize with the promise of salvation) and, on the other hand, to a clear symbolic ritual that is also to be found in the Bible (in the case of baptism, the three–fold immersion in water or pouring water on the head). Luther is in agreement with the church father Augustine that a sacrament consists of both word and sign, and he understands the sign as the word made visible. According to Luther, these conditions are only fulfilled in baptism and the Lord’s Supper, which he continues to regard as sacraments. In the first part of the treatise he also considered penance, combined with confession, to be a possible sacrament.

But Luther did not only change his mind with regard to the number of sacraments, but also called for changes in the concrete practice, which had in his opinion led to the “captivity” of the sacraments. He demands that at the Lord’s Supper the wine be offered to all. It had become customary since the 12th century to give the faithful only one “kind”, namely the bread, so that people used to refer simply to the "sacrament of the bread". Luther demands that the Lord's Supper be administered "in both kinds", to use the technical expression, meaning both as bread and wine.

Furthermore, Luther criticizes the doctrine, which also dated from the Middle Ages, that during the celebration of the Lord's Supper the words of the priest transform the substance of the bread into the body of Christ, and the wine into his blood, even though the elements remain outwardly (in their "accidental" property) bread and wine. This was called transubstantiation, a transformation of being. Whilst Luther also believed that Christ is bodily present at the Lord's Supper, he did not wish to use categories of Aristotelian philosophy to explain this, by which a distinction is made between the "substance" and the "accident" of an object and it is considered possible to transform something in substance while retaining its accidental properties. For Luther, bread is still bread, even if it is at the same time the real body of Christ, and wine is still wine, even if it is at the same time the real blood of Christ.

Lastly, Luther also rejects the teaching that the Lord's Supper is a good work accomplished by humans and pleasing to God, which imparts grace simply by being performed outwardly (the Latin term for this was: opus operatum). For Luther, the Lord's Supper is an act by which God grants faith and faith becomes aware of the grace of God. It is not a human act intended to please God. In Luther's view, the Mass – the worship service centered on the Lord's Supper – was a far cry from Christ's intention in instituting the Lord's Supper. Thinking that they were benefitting themselves, their relatives and even those who were deceased, people purchased large numbers of masses for money, and the celebration of such services had become a major source of income for the Church and its ministers.

Martin Luther, De captivitate Babylonica ecclesiae (1520):
WA, Vol. 6, pp. 489–573.
Translation: AL, Vol. 3, pp. 21–49.

On the Sacrament of the Bread

The first captivity: the cup for the priest alone

I shall tell you now what progress I have made as a result of my studies on the administration of this sacrament. … Now there are two passages that do bear very clearly upon this matter: the Gospel narratives of the Lord's Supper and Paul in 1 Corinthians 11:23–25. Let us examine these. Matthew 26:26–28, Mark 14:22–24, and Luke 22:19f. agree that Christ gave the whole sacrament to all his disciples. That Paul delivered both kinds is so certain that no one has ever had the temerity to say otherwise. Add to this that Matthew 26:27 reports that Christ did not say of the bread, "eat of it, all of you," but of the cup, "drink of it, all of you." Mark 14:23 likewise does not say, "they all ate of it," but "they all drank of it." Both attach the note of universality to the cup, not to the bread, as though the Spirit foresaw this schism, by which some would be forbidden to partake of the cup, which Christ desired should be common to all. How furiously, do you suppose, would they rave against us, if they had found the word "all" attached to the bread instead of to the cup? They would certainly leave us no loophole to escape. They would cry out and brand us as heretics and damn us as schismatics. But now, when the Scripture is on our side and against them, they will not allow themselves to be bound by any force of logic. Men of the most free will they are, even in the things that are God's; they change and change again, and throw everything into confusion.

I acknowledge that I am conquered by this argument, which to me is irrefutable. I have neither read nor heard nor found anything to say against it. For here the word and example of Christ stand unshaken when he says, not by way of permission, but of command: "Drink of it, all of you" (Matthew 26:27). For if all are to drink of it, and the words cannot be understood as addressed to the priests alone, then it is certainly an impious act to withhold the cup from the laymen when they desire it, even though an angel from heaven were to do it (Galatians 1:8). For when they say that the distribution of both kinds is left to the decision of the church, they make this assertion without reason and put it forth without authority. It can be ignored just as readily as it can be proved. It is of no avail against an opponent who confronts us with the word and work of Christ; he must be refuted with the word of Christ, but this we do not possess. If, however, either kind may be withheld from the laity, then with equal right and reason a part of baptism or penance might also be taken away from them by this same authority of the church. Therefore, just as baptism and absolution must be administered in their entirety, so the sacrament of the bread must be given in its entirety to all laymen, if they desire it …

But now I ask, where is the necessity, where is the religious duty, where is the practical use of denying both kinds, that is, the visible sign, to the laity, when everyone concedes to them the grace of the sacrament without the sign? If they concede the grace, which is the greater, why not the sign, which is the lesser? For in every sacrament the sign as such is incomparably less than the thing signified. What then, I ask, is to prevent them from conceding the lesser, when they concede the greater? Unless indeed, as it seems to me, it has come about by the permission of an angry God in order to give occasion for a schism in the church, to bring home to us how, having long ago lost the grace of the sacrament, we contend for the sign, which is the lesser, against that which is the most important and the chief thing; just as some men for the sake of ceremonies contend against love. This monstrous perversion seems to date from the time when we began to rage against Christian love for the sake of the riches of this world. Thus God would show us, by this terrible sign, how we esteem signs more than the things they signify. How preposterous it would be to admit that the faith of baptism is granted to the candidate for baptism, and yet to deny him the sign of this very faith, namely, the water! …

The first captivity of this sacrament, therefore, concerns its substance or completeness, which the tyranny of Rome has wrested from us. Not that those who use only one kind sin against Christ, for Christ did not command the use of either kind, but left it to the choice of each individual, when he said: "As often as you do this, do it in remembrance of me" (1 Corinthians 11:25). But they are the sinners, who forbid the giving of both kinds to those who wish to exercise this choice. The fault lies not with the laity, but with the priests. The sacrament does not belong to the priests, but to everyone. The priests are not lords but servants whose duty is to administer both kinds to those who desire them, as often as they desire them. If they wrest this right from the laity and deny it to them by force, they are tyrants; but the laity are without fault, whether they lack one kind or both kinds. In the meantime they must be preserved by their faith and by their desire for the complete sacrament. These same servants are likewise bound to administer baptism and absolution to everyone who seeks them, because he has a right to them; but if they do not administer them, the seeker has the full merit of his faith, while they will be accused before Christ as wicked servants. Thus the holy fathers of old in the desert did not receive the sacrament in any form for many years at a time. …

The second captivity: the doctrine of transubstantiation

The second captivity of this sacrament is less grievous as far as the conscience is concerned, yet the gravest of dangers threatens the person who would attack it, to say nothing of condemning it. …

My one concern at present is to remove all scruples of conscience, so that they need not fear being called heretics if they believe that real bread and real wine are present on the altar. …

But there are good grounds for my view, and this above all – no violence is to be done to the words of God, whether by human or angel. They are to be retained in their simplest meaning as far as possible. Unless the context manifestly compels it, they are not to be understood apart from their grammatical and proper sense, lest we give our adversaries occasion to make a mockery of all the Scriptures. Thus Origen was rightly repudiated long ago because, ignoring the grammatical sense, he turned the trees and everything else written concerning Paradise into allegories, from which one could have inferred that trees were not created by God. Even so here, when the Evangelists plainly write that Christ took bread (Matthew 26:26; Mark 14:22; Luke 22:19) and blessed it, and when the Book of Acts and the Apostle Paul in turn call it bread (Acts 2:46; 20:7; 1 Corinthians 10:16; 11:23, 26–28), we have to think of real bread and real wine, just as we do of a real cup (for even they do not say that the cup was transubstantiated). Since it is not necessary, therefore, to assume a transubstantiation effected by divine power, it must be regarded as a figment of the human mind, for it rests neither on the Scriptures nor on reason, as we shall see. …

The church kept the true faith for more than twelve hundred years, during which time the holy fathers never, at any time or place, mentioned this transubstantiation (an unnatural word and a dream), until the pseudo philosophy of Aristotle began to make its inroads into the church in these last three hundred years. …

And why could not Christ include his body in the substance of the bread just as well as in the accidents? In red-hot iron, for instance, the two substances, fire and iron, are so mingled that every part is both iron and fire. Why is it not even more possible that the body of Christ be contained in every part of the substance of the bread? …

What shall we say when Aristotle and these human doctrines are made to be the arbiters of such lofty and divine matters? Why do we not put aside such curiosity and cling simply to the words of Christ, willing to remain in ignorance of what takes place here and content that the real body of Christ is present by virtue of the words? Or is it necessary to comprehend the manner of the divine working in every detail? …

The third captivity: the doctrine of the Mass as a human work

The third captivity of this sacrament is by far the most wicked abuse of all, in consequence of which there is no opinion more generally held or more firmly believed in the church today than this, that the Mass is a good work and a sacrifice. And this abuse has brought an endless host of other abuses in its train, so that the faith of this sacrament has become utterly extinct and the holy sacrament has been turned into mere merchandise, a market, and a profit-making business. Hence participations, brotherhoods, intercessions, merits, anniversaries, memorial days, and similar goods are bought and sold, traded and bartered, in the church. On these the priests and monks depend for their entire livelihood. …

In the first place, in order that we might safely and happily attain to a true and free knowledge of this sacrament, we must be particularly careful to put aside whatever has been added to its original simple institution by human zeal and devotion: such things as vestments, ornaments, chants, prayers, organs, candles, and the whole pageantry of outward things. We must turn our eyes and hearts simply to the institution of Christ and this alone, and set nothing before us but the very word of Christ by which he instituted the sacrament, made it perfect, and committed it to us. For in that word, and in that word alone, reside the power, the nature, and the whole substance of the Mass. All the rest is the work of human beings, added to the word of Christ, and the Mass can be held and remain a Mass just as well without them. …

You see, therefore, that what we call the Mass is a promise of the forgiveness of sins made to us by God, and such a promise as has been confirmed by the death of the Son of God. …

From the above it will at once be seen what is the right and what is the wrong use of the Mass, and what is the worthy and what the unworthy preparation for it. If the Mass is a promise, as has been said, then access to it is to be gained, not with any works, or powers, or merits of one's own, but by faith alone. For where there is the word of the promising God, there must necessarily be the faith of the accepting person. It is plain, therefore, that the beginning of our salvation is a faith which clings to the word of the promising God, who, without any effort on our part, in free and unmerited mercy takes the initiative and offers us the word of his promise. …

From this you will see that nothing else is needed for a worthy holding of Mass than a faith that relies confidently on this promise, believes Christ to be true in these words of his, and does not doubt that these infinite blessings have been bestowed upon it. Hard on this faith there follows, of itself, a most sweet stirring of the heart, whereby the human spirit is enlarged and enriched (that is love, given by the Holy Spirit through faith in Christ), so that a person is drawn to Christ, that gracious and bounteous testator, and made a thoroughly new and different person. Who would not shed tears of gladness, indeed, almost faint for joy in Christ, if he believed with unshaken faith that this inestimable promise of Christ belonged to him? How could he help but love so great a benefactor, who of his own accord offers, promises, and grants such great riches and this eternal inheritance to one who is unworthy and deserving of something far different?

Therefore it is our one and only misfortune that we have many Masses in the world, and yet none, or very few of us, recognize, consider, and receive these promises and riches that are offered to us. …

Hence we see how great is God's wrath with us, in that God has permitted godless teachers to conceal the words of this testament from us, and thereby to extinguish this same faith, as far as they could. It is already easy to see what is the inevitable result of this extinguishing of the faith, namely, the most godless superstition of works. For where faith dies and the word of faith is silent, there works and the prescribing of works immediately crowd into their place. By them we have been carried away out of our own land, as into a Babylonian captivity, and despoiled of all our precious possessions. This has been the fate of the Mass; it has been converted by the teaching of godless people into a good work. They themselves call it an *opus operatum*, and by it they presume themselves to be all-powerful with God. Next they proceed to the very height of madness, and after inventing the lie that the Mass is effective simply by virtue of the act having been performed, they add another one to the effect that the Mass is none the less profitable to others even if it is harmful to some wicked priest who may be celebrating it. On such a foundation of sand they base their applications, participations, brotherhoods, anniversaries, and numberless other lucrative and profitable schemes of that kind.

Marriage and family

In his tract on the Babylonian captivity, Luther had dealt with the teaching on the sacraments and explained that matrimony was not to be counted among them. The medieval Church, like the Roman Catholic Church today, taught that marriage is a sacrament administered by the partners to each other and that this sacrament is indissoluble. Luther, on the other hand, described marriage as a "worldly thing" and was prepared to permit divorce and remarriage under certain conditions. He dealt with marriage in several of his writings. He explained that sexuality belongs to humanity as created by God, and that forgoing sexual activity is not an ideal to be aspired to, as was taught by the Church of his time. For this reason he rejects the celibacy of priests, who were obliged to remain unmarried, as is still the case for Roman Catholic clergy today; he argues that this is fundamentally contrary to human nature and clearly points out the harmful consequences of compulsory celibacy. Luther condemns the disdain for women, for marriage, housework and family that was widespread in his time.

Martin Luther, Vom ehelichen Leben (1522):
WA, Vol. 10/2, pp. 267–304.
Translation: AL, Vol. 5, pp. 40–77.

God has created humanity as male and female, intended to be partners

In the first part we shall consider which persons may enter into marriage with one another. In the first place, in order to proceed in order, let us first direct our attention to Genesis 1:27, "So God created humankind … male and female he created them." From this passage we may be assured that God divided humanity into two sections, namely, male and female, or a he and a she. This was so pleasing to him that he himself called it a good creation (Genesis 1:31). Therefore, each one of us must have the kind of body God has created for us. I cannot make myself a woman, nor can you make yourself a man; we do not have that power. But we are exactly as God created us: I a man and you a woman. Moreover, God wills to have this excellent handiwork honored as divine creation, and not despised. The man is not to despise or scoff at the woman or her body, nor the woman the man. Instead each one should honor the other's image and body as a divine and good creation that is well pleasing unto God.

In the second place, after God had made man and woman he blessed them and said to them, "Be fruitful and multiply" (Genesis 1:28). From this passage we may be assured that man and woman should and must come together in order to multiply. Now this [ordinance] is just as inflexible as the first, and no more to be despised and made fun of than the other, since God blesses marriage and does something over and above the act of creation. Hence, just as it is not within my power not to be a man, so it is not my prerogative to be without a woman. Again, just as it is not in your power not to be a woman, so it is not your prerogative to be without a man. For it is not a matter of free choice or decision but a natural and necessary thing, that whatever is a man must have a woman and whatever is a woman must have a man.

For this word that God speaks, "Be fruitful and multiply," is not a command. It is more than a command, namely, a divine ordinance [*werck*] that it is not our prerogative to hinder or ignore. Rather, it is just as necessary as the fact that I am a man, and more necessary than eating and drinking, emptying the bowels and bladder, sleeping and waking. It is a nature and disposition just as innate as the organs involved in it. Therefore, just as God does not command anyone to be a man or a woman but creates them the way they have to be, so he does not command them to multiply but creates them so that they have to multiply. And wherever individuals try to resist this, it remains irresistible nonetheless and goes its way through fornication, adultery, and secret sins[5], for this is a matter of nature and not of choice.

In the third place, God exempted three categories of individuals from this ordinance of creation, saying in Matthew 19:12 that "There are eunuchs who have been so from birth, and there are eunuchs who have been made eunuchs by others, and there are eunuchs who have made themselves eunuchs for the sake of the kingdom of heaven." Apart from these three groups, let no individual presume to be without a spouse. And whoever does not fall within one of these three categories should not consider anything except the estate of marriage. Otherwise it is simply impossible for you to remain righteous. For the Word of God that created you and said, "Be fruitful and multiply," abides and rules within you; you can by no means ignore it, or you will be bound to commit heinous sins without end. …

5 Masturbation.

Divorce and remarriage are allowed!

In the second part, we shall consider which persons may be divorced. I know of three grounds for divorce. The first, which has just been mentioned and was discussed above, is the situation in which the husband or wife is not equipped for marriage because of bodily or natural deficiencies of any sort. …

The second ground is adultery. …

The third case for divorce is that in which one of the parties deprives and avoids the other, refusing to fulfill the conjugal duty or to live with the other person. …

In addition to these three grounds for divorce, there is one more which would justify the sundering of husband and wife, but only in such a way that they must both refrain from remarrying or else become reconciled. This is the case where husband and wife cannot get along together for some reason other than the matter of the conjugal duty. …

What about a situation where one has an invalid spouse and has therefore become incapable of fulfilling the conjugal duty? May that person not take another [in marriage]? By no means. Let the individual serve the Lord in the person of the invalid and await God's good pleasure. Consider that in this invalid God has provided your household with a healing balm by which you are to gain heaven. Blessed and twice blessed are you when you recognize such a gift of grace and therefore serve your invalid spouse for God's sake.

Keeping house and bringing up children are divine works

What we would speak most of is the fact that the estate of marriage has universally fallen into such awful disrepute. There are many pagan books that treat of nothing but the depravity of womankind and the unhappiness of the estate of marriage, such that some have thought that even if Wisdom itself were a woman one should not marry. A Roman official was once supposed to encourage young men to take wives (because the country was in need of a large population on account of its incessant wars). Among other things he said to them, "My dear young men, if we could only live without women we would be spared a great deal of annoyance; but since we cannot do without them, take to yourselves wives," etc. He was criticized by some on the ground that his words were ill-considered and would only serve to discourage the young men. Others, on the contrary, said that because Metellus was a brave man he had spoken rightly, for an honorable man should speak the truth without fear or hypocrisy.

So they concluded that woman is a necessary evil, and that no household can be without such an evil. These are the words of blind heathen, who are ignorant of the fact that man and woman are God's creation. They blaspheme his work, as if man and woman just came into being spontaneously! I imagine that if women were to write books they would say exactly the same thing about men. What they have failed to set down in writing, however, they express with their grumbling and complaining whenever they get together.

Every day one encounters parents who forget their former misery because, like the mouse, they have now had their fill. They deter their children from marriage but entice them into priesthood and nunnery, citing the trials and troubles of married life. Thus do they bring their own children home to the Devil, as we daily observe; they provide them with ease for the body and hell for the soul. …

In order that we may not proceed as blindly, but rather conduct ourselves in a Christian manner, hold fast first of all to this, that man and woman are the work of God. Keep a tight rein on your heart and your lips; do not criticize his work, or call that evil which he himself has called good. He knows better than you yourself what is good and to your benefit, as he says in Genesis 2:18, "It is not good that the man should be alone; I will make him a helper as his partner." There you see that he calls the woman good, a helper. If you deem it otherwise, it is certainly your own fault, you neither understand nor believe God's word and work. See, with this statement of God one stops the mouths of all those who criticize and censure marriage. …

The world says of marriage, "Brief is the joy, lasting the bitterness." Let them say what they please; what God wills and creates is bound to be a laughingstock to them. The kind of joy and pleasure they have outside of wedlock they will be most acutely aware of, I suspect, in their consciences. To recognize the estate of marriage is something quite different from merely being married. He who is married but does not recognize the estate of marriage cannot continue in wedlock without bitterness, drudgery, and anguish; he will inevitably complain and blaspheme like the pagans and blind, irrational men. But he who recognizes the estate of marriage will find therein delight, love, and joy without end; as Solomon says, "He who finds a wife finds a good thing," etc. (Proverbs 18:22).

Now the ones who recognize the estate of marriage are those who firmly believe that God himself instituted it, brought husband and wife together, and ordained that they should beget children and care for them. For this they have God's word, Genesis 1:28, and they can be certain that he does not lie. They can therefore also be certain that the estate of marriage and everything that goes with it in the way of conduct, works, and suffering are pleasing to God. Now tell me, how can the heart have greater good, joy, and delight than in God, when one is certain that his estate, conduct, and work are pleasing to God? That is what it means to find a wife. Many *have* wives, but few *find* wives. Why? They are blind; they fail to see that their life and conduct with their wives is the work of God and pleasing in his sight. Could they but find that, then no wife would be so hateful, so ill-tempered, so ill-mannered, so poor, so sick that they would fail to find in her their heart's delight and would always be reproaching God for his work, creation, and will. And because they see that it is the good pleasure of their beloved Lord, they would be able to have peace in grief, joy in the midst of bitterness, happiness in the midst of tribulations, as the martyrs have in suffering. …

Now observe that when that clever harlot, our natural reason (which the pagans followed in trying to be most clever), takes a look at married life, she turns up her nose and says, "Alas, must I rock the baby, wash its diapers, make its bed, smell its stench, stay up nights with it, take care of it when it cries, heal its rashes and sores, and on top of that care for my wife, provide for her, labor at my trade, take care of this and take care of that, do this and do that, endure this and endure that, and whatever else of bitterness and drudgery married life involves? What, should I make such a prisoner of myself? O you poor, wretched fellow, have you taken a wife? Fie, fie upon such wretchedness and bitterness! It is better to remain free and lead a peaceful, carefree life; I will become a priest or a nun and compel my children to do likewise."

What then does Christian faith say to this? It opens its eyes, looks upon all these insignificant, distasteful, and despised duties in the Spirit, and is aware that they are all adorned with divine approval as with the costliest gold and jewels. It says, "O God, because I am certain that thou hast created me as a man and hast from my body begotten this child, I also know for a certainty that it meets with thy perfect pleasure. I confess to thee that I am not worthy to rock the little babe or wash its diapers, or to be entrusted with the care of the child and its mother. How is it that I, without any merit, have come to this distinction of being certain that I am serving thy creature and thy most precious will? O how gladly will I do so, though the duties should be even more insignificant and despised. Neither frost nor heat, neither drudgery nor labor, will distress or dissuade me, for I am certain that it is thus pleasing in thy sight."

A wife too should regard her duties in the same light, as she suckles the child, rocks and bathes it, and cares for it in other ways; and as she busies herself with other duties and renders help and obedience to her husband. These are truly golden and noble works. This is also how to comfort and encourage a woman in the pangs of childbirth, not by repeating St. Margaret legends and other silly old wives' tales but by speaking thus, "Dear Grete, remember that you are a woman, and that this work of God in you is pleasing to him. Trust joyfully in his will, and let him have his way with you. Work with all your might to bring forth the child. Should it mean your death, then depart happily, for you will die in a noble deed and in subservience to God. If you were not a woman you should now wish to be one for the sake of this very work alone, that you might thus gloriously suffer and even die in the performance of God's work and will. For here you have the word of God, who so created you and implanted within you this extremity." Tell me, is not this indeed (as Solomon says in Proverbs 18:22) "to obtain favor from the LORD," even in the midst of such extremity?

Now you tell me, when a father goes ahead and washes diapers or performs some other mean task for his child, and someone ridicules him as an effeminate fool - though that father is acting in the spirit just described and in Christian faith - my dear fellow you tell me, which of the two is most keenly ridiculing the other? God, with all his angels and creatures, is smiling - not because that father is washing diapers, but because he is doing so in Christian faith. Those who sneer at him and see only the task but not the faith are ridiculing God with all his creatures, as the biggest fool on earth. Indeed, they are only ridiculing themselves; with all their cleverness they are nothing but Devil's fools.

Whoever wishes to live in celibacy may do so

Here I will let the matter rest and leave to others the task of searching out further benefits and advantages of the estate of marriage. My purpose was only to enumerate those which a Christian can have for conducting one's married life in a Christian way, so that, as Solomon says, he may find his wife in the sight of God and obtain favor from the Lord (Proverbs 18:22). In saying this I do not wish to disparage virginity, or entice anyone away from virginity into marriage. Let each one act as one is able, and as one feels it has been given to one by God. I simply wanted to check those scandalmongers who place marriage so far beneath virginity that they dare to say: Even if the children should become holy (1 Corinthians 7:14), celibacy would still be better. One should not regard any estate as better in the sight of God than the estate of marriage. In a worldly sense celibacy is probably better, since it has fewer cares and anxieties. This is true, however, not for its own sake but in order that the celibate may better be able to preach and care for God's word, as St. Paul says in 1 Corinthians 7:32–34. It is God's word and the preaching that make celibacy – such as that of Christ and of Paul – better than the estate of marriage. In itself, however, the celibate life is far inferior. …

To sum the matter up: whoever finds oneself unsuited to the celibate life should see to it right away that one has something to do and to work at; then let that individual strike out in God's name and get married. A young man should marry at the age of twenty at the latest, a young woman at fifteen to eighteen; that's when they are still in good health and best suited for marriage. Let God worry about how they and their children are to be fed. God makes children; he will surely also feed them. Should he fail to exalt you and them here on earth, then take satisfaction in the fact that he has granted you a Christian marriage, and know that he will exalt you there; and be thankful to him for his gifts and favors. …

School and education

In his discourses on marriage, Luther advocated that family life and secular work should be appreciated more highly than life in monasteries and clerical professions. For him, education was necessary in order to be successful at work and in securing family livelihood. All boys and girls should learn reading, writing and arithmetic, in their own interests and for the benefit of society. But education should also be beneficial to religion. The general priesthood was only feasible if all people had a certain educational basis. In 1524, Luther addressed "the councilmen of all cities in Germany", requesting them to "establish and maintain Christian schools". The Reformation was also an educational movement. It promoted education for the masses and improved the education of the elite.

Martin Luther, An die Ratsherren aller Städte deutschen Landes, dass sie christliche Schulen aufrichten und halten sollen (1524): WA, Vol. 15, pp. 9–53.
Translation: AL, Vol. 5, pp. 253–256.

When I was a lad they had this maxim in school: *Non minus est negligere scholarem quam corrumpere virginem*; "It is just as bad to neglect a pupil as to despoil a virgin." The purpose of this maxim was to keep the schoolmasters on their toes, for in those days no greater sin was known than that of despoiling a virgin. But, dear Lord God, how light a sin it is to despoil virgins or wives (which, being a bodily and recognized sin, may be atoned for) in comparison with this sin of neglecting and despoiling precious souls, for the latter sin is not even recognized or acknowledged and is never atoned for. O woe unto the world forever and ever! Children are born every day and grow up in our midst, but alas!, there is no one to take charge of the youngsters and direct them. We just let matters take their own course. The monasteries and foundations should have seen to it; therefore, they are the very ones of whom Christ says, "Woe to the world because of stumbling blocks! If any of you put a stumbling block before one of the little ones who believes in me, it would be better for you if a great millstone were fastened around your neck and you were drowned in the depth of the sea" (Matthew 18:7, 6). They are nothing but devourers and destroyers of children.

Ah, you say, but all that is spoken to the parents; what business is it of councilmen and the authorities? Yes, that is true; but what if the parents fail to do their duty? Who then is to do it? Is it for this reason to be left undone, and the children neglected? How will the authorities and council then justify their position, that such matters are not their responsibility? There are various reasons why parents neglect this duty.

In the first place, there are some who lack the goodness and decency to do it, even if they had the ability. Instead, like the ostrich (Job 39:14–16), they deal cruelly with their young. They are content to have laid the eggs and brought children into the world; beyond this they will do nothing more. But these children are supposed to live among us and with us in the community. How then can reason, and especially Christian charity, allow that they grow up uneducated, to poison and pollute the other children until at last the whole city is ruined, as happened in Sodom and Gomorrah (Genesis 19:1–25), and Gibeah (Judges 19–20), and a number of other cities?

In the second place, unfortunately the great majority of parents are wholly unfit for this task. They do not know how children should be brought up and taught, for they themselves have learned nothing but how to care for their bellies. It takes extraordinary people to bring children up right and teach them well.

In the third place, even if parents had the ability and desire to do it themselves, they have neither the time nor the opportunity for it, in light of their other duties and the care of the household. Necessity compels us, therefore, to engage public schoolteachers for the children – unless each household were willing to engage its own private tutor. But that would be too heavy a burden for the average family, and many a promising child would again be neglected on account of poverty. Besides, many parents die, leaving orphans, and if we do not know from experience how they are cared for by their guardians it should be quite clear from the fact that God calls himself Father of orphans (Psalm 68:5), of those who are neglected by everyone else. Then too there are others who have no children of their own, and therefore take no interest in the training of children.

It therefore behooves the council and the authorities to devote the greatest care and attention to the young. Since the property, honor, and life of the whole city have been committed to their faithful keeping, they would be remiss in their duty before God and humanity if they did not seek its welfare and improvement day and night with all the means at their command. Now the welfare of a city does not consist solely in accumulating vast treasures, building mighty walls and magnificent buildings, and producing a goodly supply of guns and armor. Indeed, where such things are plentiful, and reckless fools get control of them, it is so much the worse and the city suffers even greater loss. A city's best and greatest welfare, safety, and strength consist rather in its having many able, learned, wise, honorable, and well-educated citizens. They can then readily gather, protect, and properly use treasure and all manner of property. ...

Since a city should and must have educated people, and since there is a universal dearth of them and complaint that they are nowhere to be found, we dare not wait until they grow up of themselves; neither can we carve them out of stone nor hew them out of wood. Nor will God perform miracles as long as people can solve their problems by means of the other gifts he has already granted them. Therefore, we must do our part and spare no labor or expense to produce and train such people ourselves. For whose fault is it that today our cities have so few capable people? Whose fault, if not that of authorities, who have left the young people to grow up like saplings in the forest, and have given no thought to their instruction and training? This is also why they have grown to maturity so misshapen that they cannot be used for building purposes, but are mere brushwood, fit only for kindling fires.

After all, secular government has to continue. Are we then to permit none but louts and boors to rule, when we can do better than that? That would certainly be a crude and senseless policy. We might as well make lords out of swine and wolves, and set them to rule over those who refuse to give any thought to how they are governed. Moreover, it is barbarous wickedness to think no further than this: We will rule now; what concern is it of ours how they will fare who come after us? Not over human beings, but over swine and dogs should such persons rule who play soldier to seek only their own profit or glory. Even if we took the utmost pains to develop a group of able, learned, and skilled people for positions in government, there would still be plenty of labor and anxious care involved in seeing that things went well. What then is to happen if we take no pains at all? …

Ministers and parishes

In 1520, in his address to the nobility, Luther had developed the doctrine of the universal priesthood. In 1523 he reiterated – "established by Scripture" – what he had already indicated at that time, namely, "that a Christian assembly or congregation has the right and power to judge all teaching and to call, appoint, and dismiss teachers". Luther developed the model of a "bottom–up" congregational structure, which was, however, never implemented as such in his time and in his church. Three years later he voiced his thoughts on a "third kind of worship service" alongside the Latin and German liturgies of the Word and the Eucharist; way ahead of his time, he outlined a model such as would later be practiced in Pietism and in free churches, or nowadays in grass–root congregations and house groups.

Martin Luther, Dass eine christliche Versammlung oder Gemeinde Recht und Macht habe, alle Lehre zu beurteilen und Lehrer zu berufen, ein- und abzusetzen, Grund und Ursache aus der Schrift (1523): WA, Vol. 11, pp. 401–416.
Translation: LW, Vol. 39, pp. 305–312.

First, it is necessary to know where and what the Christian congregation is, so that men do not engage in human affairs (as the non-Christians were accustomed to do) in the name of the Christian congregation. The sure mark by which the Christian congregation can be recognized is that the pure gospel is preached there. For just as the banner of an army is the sure sign by which one can know what kind of lord and army have taken to the field, so, too, the gospel is the sure sign by which one knows where Christ and his army are encamped. We have the sure promise of this from God in Isaiah 55:10–11, "My word" (says God) "that goes forth from my mouth shall not return empty to me; rather, as the rain falls from heaven to earth, making it fruitful, so shall my word also accomplish everything for which I sent it."

Thus we are certain that there must be Christians wherever the gospel is, no matter how few and how sinful and weak they may be. Likewise, where the gospel is absent and human teachings rule, there no Christians live but only pagans, no matter how numerous they are and how holy and upright their life may be.

Thus it undeniably follows that bishops, religious foundations, monasteries, and all who are associated with them have long since ceased to be Christians or Christian congregations, even though they have claimed they are more entitled to this name than anyone else. For whoever recognizes the gospel sees, hears, and understands that even today they insist on their human teachings, have driven the gospel far away from themselves, and are still driving it away. That is why one should consider pagan and worldly what these people do and pretend.

Second, in this matter of judging teachings and appointing or dismissing teachers or pastors, one should not care at all about human statutes, law, old precedent, usage, custom, etc., even if they were instituted by pope or emperor, prince or bishop, if one half or the whole world accepted them, or if they lasted one year or a thousand years. For the soul of man is something eternal, and more important than every temporal thing. That is why it must be ruled and seized only by the eternal word; for it is very disgraceful to rule consciences before God with human law and old custom. That is why this matter must be dealt with according to Scripture and God's word; for God's word and human teaching inevitably oppose each other when the latter tries to rule the soul. This we shall prove clearly with regard to our present discussion, in this manner:

Human words and teaching instituted and decreed that only bishops, scholars, and councils should be allowed to judge doctrine. Whatever they decided should be regarded as correct and as articles of faith by the whole world, as is sufficiently proven by their daily boasting about the pope's spiritual law. One hears almost nothing from them but such boasting that they have the power and right to judge what is Christian or what is heretical. The ordinary Christian is supposed to await their judgment and obey it. Do you see how shamelessly and foolishly this boasting, with which they intimidated the whole world and which is their highest stronghold and defense, rages against God's law and word?

Christ institutes the very opposite. He takes both the right and the power to judge teaching from the bishops, scholars, and councils and gives them to everyone and to all Christians equally when he says, John 10:4, "My sheep know my voice." Again, "My sheep do not follow strangers, but flee from them, for they do not know the voice of strangers" (John 10:5). Again, "No matter how many of them have come, they are thieves and murderers. But the sheep did not listen to them" (John 10:8).

Here you see clearly who has the right to judge doctrine: bishops, popes, scholars, and everyone else have the power to teach, but it is the sheep who are to judge whether they teach the voice [i. e., the words] of Christ or the voice of strangers. My dear, what can these water bubbles say against it, with their feet scraping, "Councils, councils! One must listen to the scholars, the bishops, the crowd; one must look at the old usage and custom"? Do you think the word of God should yield to your old usage, custom, and bishops? Never! That is why we let bishops and councils decide and institute whatever they please; when God's word is on our side we – and not they – shall judge what is right or wrong and they will have to yield to us and obey our word.

Here I think you can indeed see clearly enough how much trust should be placed in those who deal with souls by means of human words. Who cannot see that all bishops, religious foundations, monasteries, universities, and everything belonging to them rage against this clear word of Christ? They shamelessly take away the judgment of teaching from the sheep and annex it to themselves through their own law and blasphemy. That is why they should certainly be regarded as murderers and thieves, as wolves and apostate Christians, for they are openly convicted here not only of denying God's word but also of opposing and acting against it. Such action was quite appropriate for the Antichrist and his kingdom, according to the prophecy of St. Paul, 2 Thessalonians 2:3–4. ...

Thus we conclude that wherever there is a Christian congregation in possession of the gospel, it not only has the right and power but also the duty – on pain of losing the salvation of its souls and in accordance with the promise made to Christ in baptism – to avoid, to flee, to depose, and to withdraw from the authority that our bishops, abbots, monasteries, religious foundations, and the like are now exercising. For it is clearly evident that they teach and rule contrary to God and his word. This first point is established certainly and firmly enough, and one should depend upon it, that it is a divine right and a necessity for the salvation of souls to depose or to avoid such bishops, abbots, monasteries, and whatever is of their government.

Second, since a Christian congregation neither should nor could exist without God's word, it clearly follows from the previous [argument] that it nevertheless must have teachers and preachers who administer the word. And since in these last accursed times the bishops and the false spiritual government neither are nor wish to be teachers – moreover, they want neither to provide nor to tolerate any, and God should not be tempted to send new preachers from heaven – we must act according to Scripture and call and institute from among ourselves those who are found to be qualified and whom God has enlightened with reason and endowed with gifts to do so.

For no one can deny that every Christian possesses the word of God and is taught and anointed by God to be priest, as Christ says, John 6:45, "They shall all be taught by God," and Psalm 45:7, "God has anointed you with the oil of gladness on account of your fellows." These fellows are the Christians, Christ's brethren, who with him are consecrated priests, as Peter says too, 1 Peter 2:9, "You are a royal priesthood so that you may declare the virtue of him who called you into his marvelous light." …

If you say, "How can this be? If he is not called to do so he may indeed not preach, as you yourself have frequently taught," I answer that here you should put the Christian into two places. First, if he is in a place where there are no Christians he needs no other call than to be a Christian, called and anointed by God from within. Here it is his duty to preach and to teach the gospel to erring heathen or non-Christians, because of the duty of brotherly love, even though no man calls him to do so. This is what Stephen did, Acts 6–7, even though he had not been ordered into any office by the apostles. Yet he still preached and did great signs among the people. Again,

Philip, the deacon and Stephen's comrade, Acts 8:5, did the same thing even though the office of preaching was not commanded to him either. Again, Apollos did so too, Acts 18:25. In such a case a Christian looks with brotherly love at the need of the poor and perishing souls and does not wait until he is given a command or letter from a prince or bishop. For need breaks all laws and has none. Thus it is the duty of love to help if there is no one else who could or should help.

Second, if he is at a place where there are Christians who have the same power and right as he, he should not draw attention to himself. Instead, he should let himself be called and chosen to preach and to teach in the place of and by the command of the others. Indeed, a Christian has so much power that he may and even should make an appearance and teach among Christians - without a call from men - when he becomes aware that there is a lack of teachers, provided he does it in a decent and becoming manner. This was clearly described by St. Paul in 1 Corinthians 14:30, when he says, "If something is revealed to someone else sitting by, let the first be silent." Do you see what St. Paul does here? He tells the teacher to be silent and withdraw from the midst of the Christians; and he lets the listener appear, even without a call. All this is done because need knows no command.

If then St. Paul says here that anyone from the midst of the Christians may come forward if there is a need and calls him through such a word of God, and tells the other to withdraw and deposes him by the power of his word, how much more right does a whole congregation have to call someone into this office when there is a need, as there always is, especially now! For in the same passage St. Paul gives every Christian the power to teach among Christians if there is a need, saying, "You can all prophesy one by one, so that all may learn and all be admonished" (1 Corinthians 14:31). Again, "You should earnestly desire to prophesy, and do not forbid speaking in tongues; but all things should be done decently and in order" (1 Corinthians 14:39–40).

Let this passage be your sure foundation, because it gives such an overwhelming power to the Christian congregation to preach, to permit preaching, and to call. Especially if there is a need, it [this passage] calls everyone with a special call – without a call from men – so that we should have no doubt that the congregation which has the gospel may and should elect and call from among its members someone to teach the word in its place.

But if you say, "Did not St. Paul command Timothy and Titus to institute priests (1 Timothy 4:13; Titus 1:5), and do we not read, Acts 14:23, that Paul and Barnabas instituted priests among the congregations? (Therefore, the congregation cannot call anyone, nor can anyone draw attention to himself and preach among Christians; rather, one must have permission and authorization from bishops, abbots, or other prelates who represent the apostles)" I answer that if our bishops, abbots, etc., did represent the apostles, as they boast, one opinion would certainly be to let them do what Titus, Timothy, Paul, and Barnabas did when they instituted priests, etc. But since they represent the devil and are wolves who neither want to teach the gospel nor suffer it to be taught, they are as little concerned with instituting the office of preaching or pastoral care among Christians as the Turks or the Jews are. They should drive asses and lead dogs.

Moreover, if they were really decent bishops who wanted to have the gospel and wanted to institute decent preachers, they still could not and should not do so without the will, the election, and the call of the congregation – except in those cases where need made it necessary so that souls would not perish for lack of the divine word. For in such a need, as you have heard, not only may anyone procure a preacher, be it through pleas or the power of worldly authority, but he should also hurry to the scene himself and make an appearance and teach if he can – for need is need and has no limits – just as everyone should hurry to the scene of a fire in town and not wait until asked to come.

Otherwise, if there is no such need and if there are those who have the right, power, and grace to teach, no bishop should institute anyone without the election, will, and call of the congregation. Rather, he should confirm the one whom the congregation chose and called; if he does not do it, he [the elected man] is confirmed anyway by virtue of the congregation's call. Neither Titus nor Timothy nor Paul ever instituted a priest without the congregation's election and call. This is clearly proven by the sayings in Titus 1:7 and 1 Timothy 3:10, "A bishop or priest should be blameless," and, "Let the deacon be tested first." Now Titus could not have known which ones were blameless; such a report must come from the congregation, which must name the man. Again, we even read in Acts 6:1–6 regarding an even lesser office, that the apostles were not permitted to institute persons as deacons without the knowledge and consent of the congregation. Rather, the congregation elected and called the seven deacons, and the apostles confirmed them. If, then, the apostles were not permitted to institute, on their own authority, an office having to do only with the distribution of temporal food, how could they have dared to impose the highest office of preaching on anyone by their own power without the knowledge, will, and call of the congregation? …

Martin Luther, Deutsche Messe und Ordnung des Gottesdiensts (1526):
WA, Vol. 19, pp. 72–113.
Translation: AL, Vol. 3, p. 141.

An alternative form of worship

The third kind of service should be a truly Evangelical order and should not happen publicly on the town square for all sorts of people. But those who seriously want to be Christians and who profess the gospel with hand and mouth should sign in with their names and meet alone in a house to pray, to read, to baptize, to receive the sacrament, and to do other Christian works. According to this order, those who do not lead Christian lives could be known, reproved, corrected, excluded, or excommunicated, according to the rule of Christ, Matthew 18:15–17. Here one could also solicit gifts to be willingly given and distributed to the poor, according to St. Paul's example (2 Corinthians 9). Here would be no need of elaborate or excessive singing. Here one could practice a brief and beautiful order for baptism and the sacrament and center everything on the Word, prayer, and love. Here one could have a good, short catechism on the Creed, the Ten Commandments, and the Lord's Prayer. Basically, if one had the kind of people and persons who seriously wanted to be Christians, the regulations and practices would soon be ready.

But as yet I neither can nor desire to begin such a congregation or assembly or to make rules for it. For I have not yet the people or persons for it, nor do I see many who want it. …

"I will not recant!" The speech at Worms (1521)

The publication of Luther's theses on indulgences in 1517 had caused a scandal, and they led to the charge that he was a heretic. The trial on this account was concluded in Rome in 1520, when he was condemned by a papal "bull", an edict excluding him from the Roman Church. Subsequently, the authorities should have had him burned at the stake, but in April 1521, at the instigation of his sovereign, the Saxon Elector Frederick the Wise, he was summoned to the Imperial Diet in Worms and spoke before Emperor Charles V and representatives of the empire on 17 and 18 April. On 18 April, he held a long speech in Latin in which he refused to recant his writings. He ended with the simple words "God help me, Amen!" in German. The famous quotation "Here I stand; I can do no other" only appeared in later versions of the speech. But Luther's formidable stance at the Diet caused a sensation in any case. The text of his speech was published and also illustrated. Numerous pictures showed him standing alone, with the Bible in his hand, in front of the emperor – or even the pope, who was not actually present in Worms. But the pope was indeed Luther's true opponent, not the emperor. Seen in this light, it is precisely the pictures of Luther and the pope which struck to the core of the conflict.

Dictio d[octoris] Martini Lutheri coram caesare Carolo et principibus Wormaciae, in: Deutsche Reichstagsakten unter Kaiser Karl V., Vol. 2, 2nd ed., Göttingen 1962, pp. 551–555. Translation: LW, Vol. 32, pp. 101–131.

Most serene emperor, most illustrious princes, concerning those questions proposed to me yesterday on behalf of your serene majesty, whether I acknowledged as mine the books enumerated and published in my name and whether I wished to persevere in their defense or to retract them, I have given to the first question my full and complete answer, in which I still persist and shall persist forever. These books are mine and they have been published in my name by me, unless in the meantime, either through the craft or the mistaken wisdom of my emulators, something in them has been changed or wrongly cut out. For plainly I cannot acknowledge anything except what is mine alone and what has been written by me alone, to the exclusion of all interpretations of anyone at all.

In replying to the second question, I ask that your most serene majesty and your lordships may deign to note that my books are not all of the same kind.

For there are some in which I have discussed religious faith and morals simply and evangelically, so that even my enemies themselves are compelled to admit that these are useful, harmless, and clearly worthy to be read by Christians. Even the bull, although harsh and cruel, admits that some of my books are inoffensive, and yet allows these also to be condemned with a judgment which is utterly monstrous. Thus, if I should begin to disavow them, I ask you, what would I be doing? Would not I, alone of all men, be condemning the very truth upon which friends and enemies equally agree, striving alone against the harmonious confession of all?

Another group of my books attacks the papacy and the affairs of the papists as those who both by their doctrines and very wicked examples have laid waste the Christian world with evil that affects the spirit and the body. For no one can deny or conceal this fact, when the experience of all and the complaints of everyone witness that through the decrees of the pope and the doctrines of men the consciences of the faithful have been most miserably entangled, tortured, and torn to pieces. Also, property and possessions, especially in this illustrious nation of Germany, have been devoured by an unbelievable tyranny and are being devoured to this time without letup and by unworthy means. [Yet the papists] by their own decrees … warn that the papal laws and doctrines which are contrary to the gospel or the opinions of the fathers are to be regarded as erroneous and reprehensible. If, therefore, I should have retracted these writings, I should have done nothing other than to have added strength to this [papal] tyranny and I should have opened not only windows but doors to such great godlessness. It would rage farther and more freely than ever it has dared up to this time. Yes, from the proof of such a revocation on my part, their wholly lawless and unrestrained kingdom of wickedness would become still more intolerable for the already wretched people; and their rule would be further strengthened and established, especially if it should be reported that this evil deed had been done by me by virtue of the authority of your most serene majesty and of the whole Roman Empire. Good God! What a cover for wickedness and tyranny I should have then become.

I have written a third sort of book against some private and (as they say) distinguished individuals – those, namely, who strive to preserve the Roman tyranny and to destroy the godliness taught by me. Against these I confess I have been more violent than my religion or profession demands. But then, I do not set myself up as a saint; neither am I disputing about my life, but about the teaching of Christ. It is not proper for me to retract these works, because by this retraction it would again happen that tyranny and godlessness would, with my patronage, rule and rage among the people of God more violently than ever before.

However, because I am a man and not God, I am not able to shield my books with any other protection than that which my Lord Jesus Christ himself offered for his teaching. When questioned before Annas about his teaching and struck by a servant, he said: "If I have spoken wrongly, bear witness to the wrong" (John 18:19–23). If the Lord himself, who knew that he could not err, did not refuse to hear testimony against his teaching, even from the lowliest servant, how much more ought I, who am the lowest scum and able to do nothing except err, desire and expect that somebody should want to offer testimony against my teaching! Therefore, I ask by the mercy of God, may your most serene majesty, most illustrious lordships, or anyone at all who is able, either high or low, bear witness, expose my errors, overthrowing them by the writings of the prophets and the evangelists. Once I have been taught I shall be quite ready to renounce every error, and I shall be the first to cast my books into the fire. …

Since then your serene majesty and your lordships seek a simple answer, I will give it in this manner, neither horned nor toothed: Unless I am convinced by the testimony of the Scriptures or by clear reason (for I do not trust either in the pope or in councils alone, since it is well known that they have often erred and contradicted themselves), I am bound by the Scriptures I have quoted and my conscience is captive to the Word of God. I cannot and I will not retract anything, since it is neither safe nor right to go against conscience. May God help me, Amen.

Translating and interpreting the Bible

Luther's address to the Imperial Diet in Worms had shocked the emperor, but he did not break his promise, and thus allowed the monk from Wittenberg to depart. Nevertheless, Luther was now in great danger, because at the end of the assembly at Worms the emperor issued an edict declaring an imperial ban on Luther, consequent to the papal sentence of heresy from the previous year. Luther had now lost all his legal rights and was threatened by death at the stake. However, his sovereign Frederick the Wise had a plan of which Luther himself had no knowledge. He arranged for Luther to be "ambushed" in the Thuringian Forest close to Eisenach on his journey from Worms to Wittenberg and to be taken to Wartburg Castle for his own safety. It was there that Luther started to translate the New Testament from Greek into German. Later he was to translate the Hebrew Old Testament into German, so that the Luther Bible, to which his colleague Melanchthon contributed largely, was finished in the year 1534.

Luther was not the first person who translated the Bible into German, but he was the first one to translate it from the original languages into German and not from the Latin text, which was itself a translation. He considered his translation to be the first one to present the Bible in a kind of German which ordinary people could really understand.

Luther explained the principles of his biblical translation and interpretation in various short pamphlets and in the prefaces to his translations. Luther loved the Gospels, especially the Gospel of John, as well as some of Paul's letters, in particular the Letter to the Romans. They formed the basis for his interpretation of the entire Bible. Luther's preface to the Letter to the Romans is well known, in which he discusses the subject of faith and works. Luther was no friend of the Letter of James at all, and in 1522, in his preface to the New Testament, he described it as an "epistle of straw". He would have preferred to leave it out of his Bible, but he did not dare to do that. Instead, he positioned it further back, in contrast to the old Greek Bibles, where it is to be found between the

Epistles to the Hebrews and the Epistle of Peter. Luther placed James almost at the end, before the Epistle to Judas and Revelation, which Luther also did not appreciate.

For a Bible printed in 1530, Lucas Cranach did a woodcut with a double meaning. It shows the apostle Matthew (looking like Luther) writing his Gospel, but from another perspective Luther appears as an inspired translator in the guise of the Evangelist Matthew. Luther is sitting at a Renaissance writing desk. An angel, symbolizing Matthew, directs light onto him with the help of a mirror. A dove symbolizes the Holy Spirit. Luther is fully absorbed in his work. He shows no interest in the landscape, the castles and mountains, which can be seen through the window. Two chickens in the foreground could be an allusion to Matthew 23:37: God will gather the children of Jerusalem together as a hen gathers her chicks.

Martin Luther, Ein Sendbrief vom Dolmetschen (1530):
WA, Vol. 30/2, pp. 627–646.
Translation: AL, Vol. 6, pp. 24–30.

Fundamentals of Bible translations

First, if I, Doctor Luther, could have expected that all the papists taken together would be capable enough to translate a single chapter of the Scriptures correctly and well, I should certainly have mustered up enough humility to invite their aid and assistance in putting the New Testament into German. But because I knew – and still see with my own eyes – that none of them knows how to translate or to speak German, I spared them and myself that trouble. It is evident, indeed, that from my German translation they are learning to speak and write German, and so are stealing from me my language, of which they had little knowledge before. They do not thank me for it, however, but prefer to use it against me. However, I readily grant them this, for it tickles me that I have taught my ungrateful pupils, even my enemies, how to speak.

Second, you may say that I translated the New Testament conscientiously and to the best of my ability. I have compelled no one to read it, but have left that open, doing the work only as a service to those who could not do it better. No one is forbidden to do a better piece of work. If anyone does not want to read it, he can let it alone. I neither ask anybody to read it nor praise anyone who does so. It is my Testament and my translation, and it shall continue to be mine. If I have made some mistakes in it - though I am not conscious of any and would certainly be most unwilling to give a single letter a wrong translation intentionally - I will not allow the papists [to act] as judges. For their ears are still too long, and their hee-haws too weak, for them to criticize my translating. I know very well - and they know it even less than the miller's beast - how much skill, energy, sense, and brains are required in a good translator. For they have never tried it. …

We do not have to inquire of the literal Latin, how we are to speak German, as these jackasses do. Rather, we must inquire about this of the mother in the home, the children on the street, the common man in the marketplace. We must watch their mouth and be guided by their language, the way they speak, and do our translating accordingly. That way they will understand it and recognize that we are speaking German to them. …

For example, Christ says: *Ex abundantia cordis os loquitur* (Matthew 12:34; Luke 6:45). If I am to follow these jackasses, they will lay the original before me literally and translate thus: "Out of the abundance of the heart the mouth speaks." Tell me, is that speaking German? What German could understand something like that? What is "the abundance of the heart"? No German can say that; unless, perhaps, he was trying to say that someone was altogether too magnanimous or too courageous, though even that would not yet be correct. For "abundance of the heart" is not German, any more than "abundance of the house," "abundance of the stove," or "abundance of the bench" is German. But the mother in the home and the common man say this, "What fills the heart overflows the mouth." That is speaking good German, the kind that I have tried for – and, unfortunately, not always reached or hit upon. For the literal Latin is a great hindrance to speaking good German.

Martin Luther, Vorrede zum Brief des Paulus an die Römer (1522):
WA.DB, Vol. 7, pp. 2–27.
Translation: AL, Vol. 6, pp. 464–479.

The Epistle to the Romans: The chief part of the New Testament

This epistle is really the chief part of the New Testament, and is truly the purest gospel. It is worthy not only that every Christian should know it word for word, by heart, but also that he should occupy himself with it every day, as the daily bread of the soul. We can never read it or ponder over it too much; for the more we deal with it, the more precious it becomes and the better it tastes. Therefore I, too, will do my best, so far as God has given me power, to open the way into it through this preface, so that it may be the better understood by everyone. Heretofore it has been badly obscured by glosses and all kinds of idle talk, though in itself it is a bright light, almost sufficient to illuminate the entire Holy Scriptures.

To begin with, we must have knowledge of its language and know what St. Paul means by the words "law," "sin," "grace," "faith," "righteousness," "flesh," "spirit," and the like. Otherwise no reading of the book has any value. …

Faith is not the human notion and dream that some people call faith. When they see that no improvement of life and no good works follow - although they can hear and say much about faith - they fall into the error of saying, "Faith is not enough; one must do works in order to be righteous and be saved." This is due to the fact that when they hear the gospel, they get busy and by their own powers create an idea in their heart which says, "I believe"; they take this then to be a true faith. But, as it is a human figment and idea that never reaches the depths of the heart, nothing comes of it either, and no improvement follows.

Faith, however, is a divine work in us which changes us and makes us to be born anew of God, John 1:12–13. It kills the old Adam and makes us altogether different, in heart and spirit and mind and powers; and it brings with it the Holy Spirit. O, it is a living, busy, active, mighty thing, this faith. It is impossible for it not to be doing good works incessantly. It does not ask whether good works are to be done, but before the question is asked, it has already done them, and is constantly doing them. Whoever does not do such works, however, is an unbeliever. A person gropes and looks around for faith and good works, but knows neither what faith is nor what good works are. Yet that one talks and talks, with many words, about faith and good works.

Faith is a living, daring confidence in God's grace, so sure and certain that the believer would stake one's life on it a thousand times. This knowledge of and confidence in God's grace makes people glad and bold and happy in dealing with God and with all creatures. And this is the work which the Holy Spirit performs in faith. Because of it, without compulsion, a person is ready and glad to do good to everyone, to serve everyone, to suffer everything, out of love and praise to God who has shown this grace. Thus, it is impossible to separate works from faith, quite as impossible as to separate heat and light from fire. Beware, therefore, of your own false notions and of the idle talkers who imagine themselves wise enough to make decisions about faith and good works, and yet are the greatest fools. Pray God that he may work faith in you. Otherwise you will surely remain forever without faith, regardless of what you may think or do. …

In this epistle we thus find most abundantly the things that a Christian ought to know, namely, what is law, gospel, sin, punishment, grace, faith, righteousness, Christ, God, good works, love, hope, and the cross; and also how we are to conduct ourselves toward everyone, be he righteous or sinner, strong or weak, friend or foe – and even toward our own selves. Moreover, this is all ably supported with Scripture and proved by St. Paul's own example and that of the prophets, so that one could not wish for anything more. Therefore it appears that he wanted in this one epistle to sum up briefly the whole Christian and evangelical doctrine, and to prepare an introduction to the entire Old Testament. For, without doubt, whoever has this epistle well in his heart has with him the light and power of the Old Testament. Therefore let all Christians be familiar with it and exercise themselves in it continually. To this end may God give his grace. Amen. …

Martin Luther, Vorrede zum Jakobus- und Judasbrief (1522):
WA.DB, Vol. 7, pp. 384–387.
Translation: LW, Vol. 35, pp. 395–398.

The Epistle of James is not the work of an apostle!

Though this epistle of St. James was rejected by the ancients, I praise it and consider it a good book, because it sets up no doctrines of men but vigorously promulgates the law of God. However, to state my own opinion about it, though without prejudice to anyone, I do not regard it as the writing of an apostle; and my reasons follow.

In the first place it is flatly against St. Paul and all the rest of Scripture in ascribing justification to works (James 2:24). It says that Abraham was justified by his works when he offered his son Isaac (James 2:21); though in Romans 4:2–22, St. Paul teaches to the contrary that Abraham was justified apart from works, by his faith alone, before he had offered his son, and proves it by Moses in Genesis 15:6. Now although this epistle might be helped and an interpretation devised for this justification by works, it cannot be defended in its application to works (James 2:23) of Moses' statement in Genesis 15:6. For Moses is speaking here only of Abraham's faith, and not of his works, as St. Paul demonstrates in Romans 4. This fault, therefore, proves that this epistle is not the work of any apostle.

In the second place its purpose is to teach Christians, but in all this long teaching it does not once mention the Passion, the resurrection, or the Spirit of Christ. He names Christ several times; however he teaches nothing about him, but only speaks of general faith in God. Now it is the office of a true apostle to preach of the Passion and resurrection and office of Christ, and to lay the foundation for faith in him, as Christ himself says in John 15:27, "You shall bear witness to me." All the genuine sacred books agree in this, that all of them preach and inculcate [*treiben*] Christ. And that is the true test by which to judge all books, when we see whether or not they inculcate Christ. For all the Scriptures show us Christ, Romans 3:21; and St. Paul will know nothing but Christ, 1 Corinthians 2:2. Whatever does not teach Christ is not yet apostolic, even though St. Peter or St. Paul does the teaching. Again, whatever preaches Christ would be apostolic, even if Judas, Annas, Pilate, and Herod were doing it.

But this James does nothing more than drive to the law and to its works. Besides, he throws things together so chaotically that it seems to me he must have been some good, pious man, who took a few sayings from the disciples of the apostles and thus tossed them off on paper. Or it may perhaps have been written by someone on the basis of his preaching. He calls the law a "law of liberty" (James 1:25), though Paul calls it a law of slavery, of wrath, of death, and of sin.

Moreover he cites the sayings of St. Peter (in James 5:20): "Love covers a multitude of sins" (1 Peter 4:8), and again (in 4:10), "Humble yourselves under the hand of God" (1 Peter 5:6); also the saying of St. Paul in Galatians 5:17, "The Spirit lusteth against envy." And yet, in point of time, St. James was put to death by Herod (Acts 12:2) in Jerusalem, before St. Peter. So it seems that [this author] came long after St. Peter and St. Paul.

In a word, he wanted to guard against those who relied on faith without works, but was unequal to the task. He tries to accomplish by harping on the law what the apostles accomplish by stimulating people to love. Therefore I cannot include him among the chief books, though I would not thereby prevent anyone from including or extolling him as he pleases, for there are otherwise many good sayings in him. “One man’s word is no man’s word”, says a worldly proverb. In that case, how should this one man prove to be right in contradiction to Paul and all other scripture? …

Consideration for the weak!

Luther lived incognito in Wartburg castle. In order not to be recognized, the monk disguised himself as a nobleman. Martin Luther let his hair and beard grow and became "Junker Jörg". He turned his back on monasticism inwardly as well and wrote a book criticizing the monks' vows, which prompted many monks and nuns to leave their monasteries.

During the time when Luther was living at Wartburg Castle, in the summer, autumn and winter of 1521, his companions advanced the cause of the Reformation in Wittenberg. Melanchthon and especially Karlstadt, another of Luther's fellow professors, initiated practical changes such as the reform of the worship service. This led to fierce controversy, and Luther followed the developments with concern.

In the spring of 1522, he hastened back to Wittenberg. On Invocavit Sunday, March 1522, he held a famous sermon in which he put a stop to the practical changes and urged his listeners to be patient with those who were weak, that is, with those people who still held on to the old faith and traditions in their hearts.

Martin Luther, Acht Sermone, gepredigt zu Wittenberg
in der Fastenzeit (1522): WA, Vol. 10/3, pp.1–64, 430–439.
Translation: AL, Vol. 4, pp. 14–19.

The summons of death comes to us all, and no one can die for another. All must fight their own battle with death by themselves, alone. We can shout into one another's ears but everyone must individually be prepared for the time of death, for I will not be with you then nor you with me. Therefore each person must personally know and be armed with the chief things that concern a Christian. And these are what you, my beloved, heard from me many times in the past.

In the first place, we must know that we are the children of wrath and all our works, intentions, and thoughts are nothing at all. Here we need a clear, strong text to bear out this point. Such is the saying of St. Paul in Ephesians 2:3. Note this well; and though there are many such in the Bible, I do not wish to overwhelm you with many texts.

Second, God has sent us the only-begotten Son that we may believe in him so that whoever trusts in him shall be free from sin and a child of God, as John declares in his first chapter, "To all who believed in his name, he gave power to become children of God" (John 1:12). Here we should all be well versed in the Bible and ready to confront the devil with many passages.

With respect to these two points I do not feel that there has been anything wrong or lacking. They have been rightly preached to you, and I should be sorry if it were otherwise. Indeed, I am well aware and dare say that you are more learned than I, and that there are not only one, two, three, or four, but perhaps ten or more who have this awareness.

Third, we must also have love and through love we must do to one another as God has done to us through faith. For without love faith is nothing, as St. Paul says (1 Corinthians 13:1): "If I had the tongues of angels and could speak of the highest things in faith, and have not love, I am nothing." And here, dear friends, have you not grievously failed? I see no signs of love among you and I observe very well that you have not been grateful to God for his rich gifts and treasures. Here let us beware lest Wittenberg become Capernaum (cf. Matthew 11:23).

I notice that you have a great deal to say of the doctrine of faith and love which is preached to you, and this is no wonder; an ass can almost intone the lessons, and why should you not be able to repeat the doctrines and formulas? Dear friends, the kingdom of God - and we are that kingdom - does not consist in talk or words but in activity, in deeds, in works and exercises (1 Corinthians 4:20; 1 John 3:18). God does not want hearers and repeaters of words but followers and doers, and this occurs in faith through love (James 1:22; Galatians 5:2). For a faith without love is not enough - rather it is not faith at all, but a counterfeit of faith, just as a face seen in a mirror is not a real face, but merely the reflection of a face (1 Corinthians 13:12).

Fourth, we also need patience. For whoever has faith trusts in God and shows love to their neighbor, practicing it day by day, will undoubtedly suffer persecution. For the devil never sleeps, but constantly gives believers plenty of trouble. But patience works and produces hope (Romans 5:4), which freely yields itself to God and realizes itself in God. Thus faith, by much affliction and persecution, ever increases, and is strengthened day by day. A heart thus blessed with virtues can never rest or restrain itself, but rather pours itself out again for the benefit and service of the brethren, just as God has done to it.

And here, dear friends, believers must not insist upon their own rights, but must see what may be useful and helpful to their brothers and sisters, as Paul says, *Omnia mihi licent, sed non omnia expediunt*, "'All things are lawful for me,' but not all things are helpful" (1 Corinthians 6:12). For we are not all equally strong in faith and some of you have even stronger faith than I. Therefore we must not look upon ourselves, or our strength, or our prestige, but upon our neighbor, for God has said through Moses: I have borne and reared you, as a mother does her child (Deuteronomy 1:31). What does a mother do to her child?

First she gives it milk, then gruel, then eggs and soft food, whereas if she turned about and gave it solid food, the child would never thrive (cf. 1 Corinthians 3:2; Hebrews 5:12–13). So we should also deal with our brothers and sisters, have patience with them for a time, have patience with their weakness and help them bear it (Galatians 6:2); we should also give them milk-food, too (1 Peter 2:2; cf. Romans 14:1–3), as was done with us, until they, too, grow strong. In this way, we do not travel heavenward alone but bring those brothers and sisters who are not yet our friends with us. If all mothers were to abandon their children, where would we have been? Dear friend, if you have suckled long enough, do not at once cut off the breast, but let your neighbor be suckled as you were. If I had been here, I would not have gone so far as you have. The cause is good but there has been too much haste. For there are still brothers and sisters on the other side who belong to us and must still be won.

Let me illustrate. The sun has two properties, light and heat. No king has power enough to bend or guide the light of the sun; it remains fixed in its place. But the heat may be turned and guided, even as it always still comes from the sun. Thus faith must always remain pure and immovable in our hearts, never wavering; but love bends and turns so that our neighbor may grasp and follow it. There are some who can run, others must walk, still others can hardly creep (cf. 1 Corinthians 8:7–13). Therefore we must not look upon our own abilities, but upon our neighbor's powers, so that those who are weak in faith and attempt to follow the strong may not be snatched up by the devil. Therefore, dear friends, follow me; I have never been a destroyer. I was also the first whom God set to this task. I cannot run away but will remain as long as God allows. I was also the first one to whom God revealed that his word should be preached to you. I am also sure that you have the clear word of God.

Let us, therefore, act with fear and humility, casting ourselves at one another's feet, reaching out our hands to one another, and helping each other. I will do my part, which is no more than my duty, to love you even as I love my own soul. For here we battle not against popes, bishops, or anyone else, but against the devil, and do you imagine he is asleep (cf. Ephesians 6:12; 1 Peter 5:8)? He sleeps not, but sees the true light rising, and to keep it from shining into his eyes he would like to make a flank attack - and he will succeed, if we are not on our guard. I know him well, and I hope, too, that with the help of God, I am his master. But if we yield him but an inch, we must soon look to it how we may be rid of him. Therefore all those have erred who have helped and consented to abolish the Mass; not that it was not a good thing, but that it was not done in an orderly way. You say it was right according to the Scriptures. I agree, but what becomes of order? For it was done in wantonness, with no regard for proper order and with offense to your neighbor. If, beforehand, you had called upon God in earnest prayer and had obtained the aid of the authorities, one could be certain that it had come from God. ...

I was not so far away that you could not reach me with a letter, whereas not the slightest communication was sent to me. If you were going to begin something and make me responsible for it, that would have been too much for me. I will not do it [i.e., assume the responsibility]. Here one can see that you do not have the Spirit, even though you do have a deep knowledge of the Scriptures. ...

I, too, would like to begin many things, in which but few would follow me, but what is the use? For I know that when the conflicts come those who have begun such things would not be able to persevere and would be the first to retreat. How would it be, if I brought the crowds to the point of attack and then if I – who had been the first to exhort others – would then flee death rather than steadfastly face it? How the poor people would be deceived!

Let us, therefore, feed others also with the milk which we received, until they too become strong in faith. For there are many who are otherwise in accord with us and who would also gladly accept this thing, but they do not yet fully understand it – these we drive away. Therefore, let us show love to our neighbors; if we do not do this, our work will not endure. We must have patience with them for a long time yet and not cast out those who are still weak in faith; how much to do or not to do depends on what love requires and what does no harm to our faith. If we do not earnestly pray to God and act rightly in this matter, it looks to me as if all the complaints that we have heaped upon the papists will fall upon us. Therefore I could no longer remain away, but was compelled to come and say these things to you.

Elementary Christian doctrine: The Catechism

For Luther, reformation meant first and foremost spiritual instruction and liberation of conscience. This was the goal of his Bible translation, his sermons and his books. Practical changes were of secondary importance for him. The two catechisms he wrote in the late 1520s, the Small Catechism and the Large Catechism, also served this purpose. Catechisms, which had existed in Christianity since time immemorial, summarized the Christian doctrines and expanded them on the basis of the Ten Commandments, the Creed and the Lord's Prayer. Luther and many of his reformer colleagues created new, Protestant catechisms. They were used in churches, schools and families for instruction in matters of faith and served as homiletic and didactic aids for pastors and schoolteachers. Luther's Small Catechism was intended for this purpose. His Large Catechism, on the other hand, was more like a textbook of theology and was intended above all to equip the preachers themselves. Luther's handbooks of faith became a great success and are still used today. In Lutheran churches they have the status of confessional documents. Luther's Small Catechism is still to be found in the hymnbook of every Protestant church in Germany.

Luther's explanation of the First Commandment in the Great Catechism is famous on the grounds of its definition of a god: "Anything on which your heart relies and depends, is really your God." When money and wealth become a god, or rather an idol, Luther describes them as "mammon" with reference to Luke 16:9. In his teaching on baptism, Luther dealt with infant baptism, among other topics, because quite a number of adherents to the Reformation doubted its validity; Luther discredited them as "sectarians". As proof of the validity and efficacy of infant baptism, he refers to recognized theologians of the Middle Ages such as Bernhard of Clairvaux and Jean Gerson, but also to Johann Hus, who was condemned as a heretic. All three of them are good examples for the work of the Holy Spirit, says Luther, despite or rather because they had been baptized as children. In addition, Luther shows that penance, which was still considered a sacrament by the Roman Catholic Church, is actually nothing more than a return to baptism. He appreciated this practice, including the confession of sin connected with it.

Martin Luther, Der große Katechismus:
WA, Vol. 30/1, pp. 123–238.
Translation: AL, Vol. 2, pp. 300–304. and pp. 388–402.

The First Commandment

"You are to have no other gods."
That is, you are to regard me alone as your God. What does this mean, and how is it to be understood? What does "to have a god" mean, or what is God? Answer: God is that in which we are to look for all good and in which we are to find refuge in all need. Therefore, to have a god is nothing else than to trust and believe in that one with your whole heart. As I have often said, it is the trust and faith of the heart alone that make both God and an idol. If your faith and trust are right, then your God is the true one. Conversely, where your trust is false and wrong, there you do not have the true God. For these two belong together, faith and God. Anything on which your heart relies and depends, I say, that is really your God.

The intention of this commandment, therefore, is to require true faith and confidence of the heart, which fly straight to the one true God and cling to God alone. What this means is: "See to it that you let me alone be your God, and never search for another." In other words: "Whatever good thing you lack, look to me for it and seek it from me, and whenever you suffer misfortune and distress, crawl to me and cling to me. I, I myself, will give you what you need and help you out of every danger. Only do not let your heart cling to or rest in anyone else."

So that it may be understood and remembered, I must explain this a little more plainly by citing some everyday examples of the opposite. There are some who think that they have God and everything they need when they have money and property; they trust in them and boast in them so stubbornly and securely that they care for no one else. They, too, have a god - mammon by name, that is, money and property - on which they set their whole heart. This is the most common idol on earth. Those who have money and property feel secure, happy, and fearless, as if they were sitting in the midst of paradise. On the other hand, those who have nothing doubt and despair as if they knew of no god at all. We will find very few who are cheerful, who do not fret and complain, if they do not have mammon. This desire for wealth clings and sticks to our nature all the way to the grave. So, too, those who boast of great learning, wisdom, power, prestige, friendship, and honor and who trust in them have a god also, but not the one, true God. Notice again, how presumptuous, secure, and proud people are when they have such possessions, and how despondent they are when they lack them or when they are taken away. Therefore, I repeat, the correct interpretation of this commandment is that to have a god is to have something in which the heart trusts completely.

Again, look at what we used to do in our blindness under the papacy. Anyone who had a toothache fasted and called on St. Apollonia; those who worried about their house burning down appealed to St. Laurence as their patron; if they were afraid of the plague, they made a vow to St. Sebastian or Roch.

There were countless other such abominations, and everyone selected their own saints and worshiped them and invoked their help in time of need. In this category also belong those who go so far as to make a pact with the devil so that it may give them plenty of money, help them in love affairs, protect their cattle, recover lost property, etc., as magicians and sorcerers do. All of them place their heart and trust elsewhere than in the true God, from whom they neither expect nor seek any good thing. ...

Thus you can easily understand what and how much this commandment requires, namely, that one's whole heart and confidence be placed in God alone, and in no one else. To have a God, as you can well imagine, does not mean to grasp God with your fingers, or to put God into a purse, or to shut God up in a box. Rather, you lay hold of God when your heart grasps and clings to God. Clinging with your heart is nothing else than entrusting yourself completely to God who wishes to turn us away from everything else apart from God and to draw us to God as the one, eternal good. It is as if God said: "What you formerly sought from the saints, or what you hoped to receive from mammon or from anything else, turn to me for all of this; look on me as the one who will help you and lavish all good things upon you richly." ... This much, however, should be said to the common people, so that they may mark well and remember the sense of this commandment: We are to trust in God alone, to look to God alone, and to expect God to give us only good things; for it is God who gives us body, life, food, drink, nourishment, health, protection, peace, and all necessary temporal and eternal blessings. In addition, God protects us from misfortune and rescues and delivers us when any evil befalls us. It is God alone (as I have repeated often enough) from whom we receive everything good and by whom we are delivered from all misfortune. This, I think, is why we Germans from ancient times have called God by a name more elegant and worthy than found in any other language, a name derived from the word "good," because God is an eternal fountain who overflows with pure goodness and from whom pours forth all that is truly good. ...

Although much that is good comes to us from human beings, nevertheless, anything received according to God's command and ordinance in fact comes from God. Our parents and all authorities – as well as everyone who is a neighbor – have received the command to do us all kinds of good. So we receive our blessings not from them, but from God through them. Creatures are only the hands, channels, and means through which God bestows all blessings. For example, God gives to the mother breasts and milk for her infant or gives grain and all sorts of fruits from the earth for sustenance – things that no creature could produce by itself. No one, therefore, should presume to take or give anything unless God has commanded it. This forces us to recognize God's gifts and give God thanks, as this commandment requires. Therefore, we should not spurn even this way of receiving such things through God's creatures, nor are we through arrogance to seek other methods and ways than those God has commanded. For that would not be receiving them from God, but seeking them from ourselves. ...

Let us, then, learn well the First Commandment, that we may see how God will tolerate no presumption nor any trust in any other object, and how he requires nothing higher of us than confidence from the heart for everything good. Thus we may proceed rightly and straightforwardly, using all the blessings which God gives, just like a shoemaker who uses his needle, awl, and thread for work and then lays them aside. Or like a traveler who uses an inn with food and bed only for temporal necessity. Each person should follow God's order in their own station, not allowing any of these goods to hold dominion over them or become an idol. Enough said about the First Commandment. We have expounded it in many words, because it is of the utmost importance. For, as we have said before, when the heart is united with God and this commandment is kept, all the rest follows of its own accord.

Concerning Baptism

We must still say something about our two sacraments instituted by Christ. For every Christian ought to have at least some brief, elementary instruction about them, because without them no one can be a Christian, although unfortunately nothing was taught about them in the past. First, we shall take up baptism, through which we are initially received into the Christian community. In order that it may be readily understood, we shall treat it in a systematic way and limit ourselves to that which is necessary for us to know. How it is to be maintained and defended against heretics and sectarians we shall leave to the scholars. In the first place, we must above all be familiar with the words on which baptism is founded and to which everything is related that is to be said on the subject, namely, where the Lord Christ says in the last chapter of Matthew 28:19: "Go into all the world, teach all the nonbelievers, and baptize them in the name of the Father and of the Son and of the Holy Spirit." Likewise, in the last chapter of Mark 16:16: "The one who believes and is baptized will be saved; but the one who does not believe will be condemned."

Observe, first, that these words contain God's commandment and institution, so that no one may doubt that baptism is of divine origin, not something devised or invented by human beings. As truly as I can say that the Ten Commandments, the Creed, and the Lord's Prayer were not spun out of anyone's imagination but are revealed and given by God, so I can boast that baptism is no human plaything but is instituted by God alone. Moreover, it is solemnly and strictly commanded that we must be baptized or we shall not be saved, so that we are not to regard it as an indifferent matter, like putting on a new red coat. It is of the greatest importance that we regard baptism as excellent, glorious, and exalted. It is the chief cause of our contentions and battles, because the world is now full of sects who scream that baptism is an external thing and that external things are of no use. But no matter how external it may be, here stand God's word and command that have instituted, established, and confirmed baptism. What God institutes and commands cannot be useless. Rather, it is a most precious thing, even though to all appearances it may not be worth a straw. If people used to consider it a great thing when the pope dispensed indulgences with his letters and bulls and confirmed altars and churches solely by virtue of his letters and seals, then we ought to regard baptism as much greater and more precious because God has commanded it. What is more, it is performed in God's name. So the words read, "Go, baptize," not "in your name" but "in God's name."

To be baptized in God's name is to be baptized not by human beings but by God and God's own doing. Although it is performed by human hands, it is nevertheless truly God's own act. …

Thus, we must regard baptism and put it to use in such a way that we may draw strength and comfort from it when our sins or conscience oppress us, and say: "But I am baptized! And if I have been baptized, I have the promise that I shall be saved and have eternal life, both in soul and body." This is the reason why these two things are done in baptism; the body has water poured over it because all it can receive is the water, and in addition the word is spoken so that the soul may receive it. Because the water and the word together constitute one baptism, both body and soul shall be saved and live forever: the soul through the word in which it believes, the body because it is united with the soul and apprehends baptism in the only way it can. No greater jewel, therefore, can adorn our body and soul than baptism, for through it we become completely holy and blessed, which no other kind of life and no work on earth can acquire. Let this suffice concerning the nature, benefits, and use of baptism as serves the present purpose.

At this point, we come to a question that the devil uses to confuse the world through its sects, namely, about infant baptism. Do children believe, and is it right to baptize them? To this we reply briefly: Let the simple dismiss this question and leave it to the learned. But if you wish to answer, then reply in this way: That the baptism of infants is pleasing to Christ is sufficiently proved from God's own work. God has sanctified many who have been thus baptized and has given them the Holy Spirit. Even today there still are many whose teaching and lives attest that they have the Holy Spirit. Similarly by God's grace we have been given the power to interpret the Scriptures and to know Christ, which is impossible without the Holy Spirit. But if God did not accept the baptism of infants, God would not have given any of them the Holy Spirit – or any part of her. In short, all this time down to the present day there would have been no person on earth who could have been a

Christian. Because God has confirmed baptism through the bestowal of the Holy Spirit, as we have perceived in some of the Fathers, such as St. Bernard, Gerson, John Hus, and others, and because the holy Christian church will not disappear until the end of the world, so they must confess that it is pleasing to God. For God cannot contradict God's own self, support lies and wickedness, or give God's grace or Spirit for such ends. This is just about the best and strongest proof for the simple and unlearned. For no one can take from us or overthrow this article, "I believe in one holy Christian church, the communion of saints," etc.

Further, we say, we do not put the main emphasis on whether the person baptized believes or not, for in the latter case baptism does not become invalid. Everything depends on the word and commandment of God. ...

Finally, we must also know what baptism signifies and why God ordained precisely this sign and external ceremony for the sacrament by which we are first received into the Christian community. This act or ceremony consists of being dipped into the water, which covers us completely, and being drawn out again. These two parts, being dipped under the water and emerging from it, point to the power and effect of baptism, which is nothing else than the slaying of the old creature and the resurrection of the new creature, both of which must continue in us our whole lives long. Thus a Christian life is nothing else than a daily baptism, begun once and continuing ever after. For we must keep at it without ceasing, always purging whatever pertains to the old creature, so that whatever belongs to the new creature may come forth. What is the old creature? It is what is born in us from Adam and Eve, irascible, spiteful, envious, unchaste, greedy, lazy, proud - yes - and unbelieving;

it is beset with all vices and by nature has nothing good in it. Now, when we enter Christ's kingdom, this corruption must daily decrease so that the longer we live the gentler and more patient and meek we become, and the more we break away from greed, hatred, envy, and pride. …

Here you see that baptism, both by its power and by its signification, comprehends also the third sacrament, formerly called penance, which is really nothing else than baptism. What is repentance but an earnest attack on the old creature and an entering into a new life? If you live in repentance, therefore, you are walking in baptism, which not only announces this new life but also produces, begins, and exercises it. In baptism we are given the grace, Spirit, and strength to suppress the old creature so that the new may come forth and grow strong. Therefore baptism remains forever. Even though someone falls from it and sins, we always have access to it so that we may again subdue the old creature. But we need not have the water poured over us again. Even if we were immersed in water a hundred times, it would nevertheless not be more than one baptism, and the effect and significance would continue and remain. Repentance, therefore, is nothing else than a return and approach to baptism, to resume and practice what has earlier been begun but abandoned. …

Thus we see what a great and excellent thing baptism is, which snatches us from the jaws of the devil and makes us God's own, overcomes and takes away sin and daily strengthens the new person, and always endures and remains until we pass out of this misery into eternal glory. Therefore let all Christians regard their baptism as the daily garment that they are to wear all the time. Every day they should be found in faith and with its fruits, suppressing the old creature and growing up in the new. If we want to be Christians, we must practice the work that makes us Christians and let those who fall away return to it. As Christ, the mercy seat, does not withdraw from us or forbid us to return to him even though we sin, so all his treasures and gifts remain. As we have once obtained forgiveness of sins in baptism, so forgiveness remains day by day as long as we live, that is, as long as we carry the old creature around our necks.

Luther's prayer guide

The Reformation broke with many types of expression of Christian piety. Prayers were no longer offered to the saints, pilgrimages no longer took place, indulgences could no longer be purchased. In Luther's opinion, the essence of the Christian faith lay rather in listening to the lively proclamation of the gospel and in prayer. Luther wrote a great deal on the subject of prayer and also testified in many ways to his own prayer life. One of his works which is particularly impressive and still inspiring for personal prayer today was dedicated by him in 1535 to "a good friend" under the title "A Simple Way to Pray".

In his own piety, Luther was not concerned with doing pious works, but with seeking true self-knowledge and being certain of God's mercy. This comes out very clearly when you read this guide to prayer. Luther never saw himself as a saint, but always – as is very much apparent in this little handbook – as a sinner. Nevertheless, he was regarded and portrayed as a saint even during his lifetime.

Martin Luther, Eine einfältige Weise zu beten (1535):
WA, Vol. 38, pp. 351–375.
Translation: AL, Vol. 4, pp. 256–278.

First, when I feel that I have become cold and listless in prayer because of other tasks or thoughts (for the flesh and the devil always impede and obstruct prayer), I take my little psalter, hurry to my room, or, if it be the day and hour for it, to the church where a congregation is assembled and, as time permits, I say the Ten Commandments, the Creed, and, if I have time, some words of Christ or of Paul, or some psalms, out loud to myself just as a child might do.

It is a good thing to let prayer be the first business of the morning and the last at night. Diligently guard against those false, deluding ideas, which tell you, "Wait a little while. I will pray in an hour; first I must attend to this or that." Such thoughts get you away from prayer into other affairs that so hold your attention and involve you that nothing comes of prayer for that day.

This is especially so in emergencies when you have some tasks that seem as good or better than prayer. There is a saying ascribed to St. Jerome[6]: "Everything a believer does is prayer," and a proverb, "He who works faithfully prays twice." This can be said because a believer fears and honors God in his work and remembers the commandment not to wrong anyone, or to try to steal, overcharge, or embezzle. Such thoughts and such faith undoubtedly transform his work into prayer and a sacrifice of praise. Then again, the contrary must also be true that the work of an unbeliever is outright cursing and so he who works faithlessly curses twice. By the thoughts of his heart as well as his work he scorns God. He thinks about violating the commandment and about how to take advantage of his neighbor, to steal and to embezzle. For, what else can such thoughts be but vain curses against God and man, which makes one's work and effort a double curse by which a man also curses himself. In the end such people are beggars and bunglers.

Christ openly speaks of continual prayer in Luke 11, "Pray without ceasing." One must unceasingly guard against sin and wrongdoing, something one cannot do unless one fears God and keeps his commandment in mind, as Psalm 1:2 says,

---

6 Church father, lived c. 347 to c. 420.

"Blessed is he who meditates upon God's law day and night, etc." Yet we must be careful not to break the habit of true prayer and imagine other works to be necessary which, after all, are nothing of the kind. Thus at the end we become lazy and lax, cold and listless toward prayer. The devil who besets us is not lax nor lazy, and our flesh is all too ready and eager to sin and is averse to the spirit of prayer.

Now, when your heart has been warmed by such recitation to yourself [of the Ten Commandments, the words of Christ, etc.] and is intent upon the matter, kneel or stand with your hands folded and your eyes are directed toward heaven and speak out loud or think as briefly as you can:

"O Heavenly Father, dear God, I am a poor unworthy sinner. I do not deserve to raise my eyes or hands toward you or to pray. But because you have commanded us all to pray and have promised to hear us and because you have taught us through your dear Son, Jesus Christ, both how and what to pray, I come to you in obedience to your word, trusting in your gracious promise. I pray in the name of my Lord Jesus Christ together with all your saints and Christians on earth as he has taught me: 'Our Father in heaven … .'"

The Lord's Prayer

The First Petition

Pray through the whole prayer, word for word, then repeat one part or as much as you wish, perhaps the first petition: "Hallowed be your name," and say: "Yes, Lord God, dear Father, hallowed be your name, both in us and throughout the whole world. Destroy and root out the abominations, idolatry, and heresy of the Turk, the pope, and all false teachers and factious spirits who falsely bear your name and thus shamefully abuse it and horribly blaspheme it. They insistently boast that they teach your word and the laws of the church, though they really use the devil's lies and trickery in your name to wretchedly seduce so many poor souls throughout the world, even killing and shedding much innocent blood, and in such persecution they believe that they render you a divine service. Dear Lord God, convert and restrain [them]. Convert those who are still to be converted that they with us and we with them may hallow and praise your name, both with true and pure doctrine and with a good and holy life. Restrain those who are unwilling to be converted so that they are forced to cease from misusing, defiling, and dishonoring your holy name and from misleading the poor people. Amen."

The Second Petition

"Your kingdom come." Say: "O dear Lord, God and Father, you see how worldly wisdom and reason not only profane your name and ascribe the honor due to you to lies and to the devil, but how they also take the power, might, wealth, and glory which you have given them on earth for ruling the world and thereby serving you, and use it in their own ambition to oppose your kingdom. They are many and mighty, thick, fat, and full; they plague and hinder the tiny flock of your kingdom who are weak, despised, and few. They will not tolerate your flock on earth and think that by plaguing them they render a great and godly service to you. Dear Lord, God and Father, convert [them] and defend [us]. Convert those who are still to become children and members of your kingdom so that they with us and we with them may serve you in your kingdom in right faith and true love and that from your kingdom, which has begun, we may enter into your eternal kingdom. Defend us against those who will not turn away their might and power from the destruction of your kingdom so that when they are cast down from their thrones and humbled, they will have to cease from their efforts. Amen."

The Third Petition

"Your will be done on earth as it is in heaven." Say: "O dear Lord, God and Father, you know that the world, if it cannot destroy your name or exterminate your kingdom, is busy day and night with wicked tricks, carrying out many intrigues and strange attacks, whispering together in secret counsel, giving mutual encouragement and support, threatening and spouting off, going about with every evil intention to destroy your name, word, kingdom, and children. Therefore, dear Lord, God and Father, convert [them] and defend [us]. Convert those who have yet to acknowledge your good will that they with us and we with them may obey your will and for your sake readily, patiently, and joyously bear every evil, cross, and adversity, and thereby acknowledge, test, and experience your kind, gracious, and perfect will. But defend us against those who in their rage, fury, hate, threats, and evil desires do not cease to do us harm. Make their wicked schemes, tricks, and devices come to nothing so that these may be turned against them, as we sing in Psalm 7:16. Amen." …

The Sixth Petition

"And lead us not into temptation." Say: "O dear Lord, Father and God, keep us bold and alert, passionate and eager in your word and service, so that we do not become complacent, lazy, and sluggish as though we had already achieved everything. In that way the fierce devil cannot beguile us, surprise us, and deprive us of your precious word or stir up strife and factions among us and lead us into other sin and disgrace, both spiritually and physically. Rather grant us wisdom and strength through your spirit that we may valiantly resist him and gain the victory. Amen."

The Seventh Petition

"But deliver us from evil." Say: "O dear Lord, God and Father, this wretched life is so full of misery, misfortune, and uncertainty, so full of faithlessness and malice (as St. Paul says, "The days are evil" (Ephesians 5:16) that we might easily grow weary of life and long for death. But you, dear Father, know our frailty; therefore help us to pass in safety through so much wickedness and villainy; and, when our time comes, in your mercy grant us a gracious final hour and a blessed departure from this vale of sorrows so that in the face of death we do not become fearful or despondent but in firm faith commit our souls into your hands. Amen."

Finally, mark this, that you must always speak the "Amen" firmly. Never doubt that God in his mercy will surely hear you and say "yes" to your prayers. Never think that you are kneeling or standing alone, rather think that the whole of Christendom, all devout Christians, are standing there beside you and you are standing among them in a common, united petition which God cannot disdain. Do not leave your prayer without having said or thought, "Very well, God has heard my prayer; this I know as a certainty and a truth." That is what Amen means.

You should also know that I do not want you to recite all these words in your prayer. That would make it nothing but mere chatter and idle prattle, read word for word out of a book as were the rosaries by the laity and the prayers of the clerics and monks. Rather do I want your heart to be stirred and guided concerning the thoughts that ought to be comprehended in the Lord's Prayer. These thoughts may be expressed, if your heart is rightly warmed and inclined toward prayer, in many different ways and with more words or fewer. I do not bind myself to such words or syllables, but say my prayers in one fashion today, in another tomorrow, depending upon my mood and feeling. I stay however, as nearly as I can, with the same general thoughts and ideas. It may happen occasionally that I may wander among so many ideas in one petition that I forgo the other six. If such an abundance of good thoughts comes to us we ought to disregard the other petitions, make room for such thoughts, listen in silence, and under no circumstances obstruct them. The Holy Spirit himself preaches here, and one word of his sermon is far better than a thousand of our prayers. Many times I have learned more from one prayer than I might have learned from much reading and speculation. It is of great importance that the heart be made ready and eager for prayer. As the Preacher says, "Prepare your heart for prayer, and do not tempt God" (Ecclesiasticus 18:23). What else is it but tempting God when your mouth babbles and the heart is distracted? ... This in short is the way I use the Lord's Prayer when I pray it. To this day I suckle at the Lord's Prayer like a child, and as an old man eat and drink from it and never get my fill. It is the very best prayer, even better than the psalter, which is so very dear to me. It is surely evident that a real master composed and taught it. What a great shame that the prayer of such a master is prattled and chattered so irreverently all over the world! How many pray the Lord's Prayer several thousand times in the course of a year, and if they were to keep on doing so for a thousand years they would not have tasted nor prayed one letter or one stroke of a letter of it! In a word, the Lord's Prayer is the greatest martyr on earth (along with the name and word of God). Everybody tortures and abuses it; few take comfort and joy in its proper use.

The Ten Commandments as a model for prayer

If I have time and opportunity to go through the Lord's Prayer, I do the same with the Ten Commandments. I take one part after another and free myself as much as possible from distractions in order to pray. I divide each commandment into four parts, thereby fashioning a garland of four entwined strands. That is, I think of each commandment as, first, instruction, which is really what it is intended to be, and consider what the Lord God so earnestly demands of me. Second, I turn it into a thanksgiving; third, a confession; and fourth, a prayer. I do so in thoughts or words such as these:

The First Commandment

"I am the Lord your God, etc. You are to have no other gods besides me, etc." Here I first consider that God expects and teaches me to trust him sincerely in all things. It is his most earnest intention to be my God, so I must think of him in this way at the risk of losing eternal salvation. My heart must not build upon anything else or trust in any other thing, be it wealth, prestige, wisdom, might, holiness, or any other creature.

Second, I give thanks for God's infinite compassion by which he has come to me, a lost mortal, in such a fatherly way and, without my asking, seeking, or deserving him, has offered to be my God, to care for me, and to be my comfort, protection, help, and strength in every time of need. We poor blind mortals have sought so many gods and would have to seek them still if he did not enable us to hear him openly tell us in our own language that he wants to be our God. How could we ever – in all eternity – thank God enough!

Third, I confess and acknowledge my great sin and ingratitude for having so shamefully despised such a sublime teaching and precious gift throughout my whole life, and for having horridly provoked his wrath by countless acts of idolatry. I repent of these and ask for his grace.

Fourth, I pray and say: "O my God and Lord, help me by your grace to learn and understand your commandments more fully every day and to live by them in sincere confidence. Preserve my heart so that I shall never again become forgetful and ungrateful, that I may never seek after other gods or other consolation on earth or in any creature, but cling truly and solely to you, my only God. Amen, dear Lord God and Father. Amen."

The Second Commandment

Afterward, if time and inclination permit, the Second Commandment likewise in four strands, in this way:

"You are not to take the name of the Lord your God in vain," etc. First, I learn that I should regard God's name as honorable, holy, and beautiful. I should not swear, curse, lie, be boastful, nor seek honor and repute for myself, but instead I should humbly invoke his name, pray, adore, praise, and extol it. I should let it be all my honor and glory that he is my God and that I am his lowly creature and unworthy servant.

Second, I give thanks to him for these precious gifts, that he has revealed and imparted his name to me, that I can glory in his name and be called God's servant and creature, etc., that his name is my refuge like a mighty fortress to which the righteous man can flee and find protection, as Solomon says (Proverbs 18:10).

Third, I confess and acknowledge that I have grievously and shamefully sinned against this commandment all my life. I have not only failed to invoke, extol, and honor his holy name, but have also been ungrateful for such gifts and have, by swearing, lying, and betraying, misused them in the pursuit of shame and sin. This I regret and ask grace and forgiveness, etc.

Fourth, I ask for help and strength henceforth to learn [to obey] this commandment and to be preserved from such evil ingratitude, abuse, and sin against his holy name, and that I may be found grateful in revering and honoring his name.

I repeat here what I previously said in reference to the Lord's Prayer: if in the midst of such thoughts the Holy Spirit begins to preach in your heart with rich, enlightening thoughts, honor him by letting go of these prepared thoughts; be still and listen to him who can do better than you can. Remember what he says and note it well and you will behold wondrous things in the law of God, as David says (Psalm 119:18).

"You are to sanctify the day of rest." I learn from this, first of all, that the day of rest has not been instituted for the sake of being idle or indulging in worldly pleasures, but in order that we may observe it respectfully. However, it is not sanctified by our works and actions – since our works are not holy – but by the word of God, which alone is wholly pure and sacred and which sanctifies everything that comes in contact with it, be it time, place, person, labor, rest, etc. For through the word our works are also sanctified. As St. Paul says in 1 Timothy 4:5, "Every creature is sanctified by the word and prayer." I realize therefore that on the day of rest I must, above all, hear and contemplate God's word. Thereafter I should give thanks in my own words, praise God for all his benefits, and pray for myself and for the whole world. He who so conducts himself on the day of rest sanctifies it. He who fails to do so is worse than the person who works on the day of rest.

Second, I thank God in this commandment for the great and beautiful goodness and grace which he has given us through his word and preaching. And he has instructed us to make use of it, especially on the day of rest, for meditation by the human heart can never exhaust such a treasure. His word is the only light in the darkness of this life, a word of life, consolation, and supreme blessedness. Where this precious and saving word is absent, nothing remains but empty and terrifying darkness, error and factions, death and every calamity, and the devil's own tyranny, as we can see with our own eyes every day.

Third, I confess and acknowledge great sin and wicked ingratitude on my part because all my life I have made disgraceful use of the day of rest and have thereby despised his precious and dear word so miserably. I have been too lazy, listless, and tired of the word to listen to it, let alone to have desired it sincerely or to have been grateful for it. I have let my dear God proclaim his word to me in vain, have abandoned the noble treasure, and have trampled it underfoot. He has tolerated this in his great and divine mercy and has not ceased in his fatherly, divine love and faithfulness to keep on preaching to me and calling me to the salvation of my soul. For this I repent and ask for grace and forgiveness.

Fourth, I pray for myself and for the whole world that the gracious Father may preserve us in his holy word and not withdraw it from us because of our sin, ingratitude, and laziness. May he preserve us from factious spirits and false teachers, and may he send faithful and honest laborers into his harvest, that is, devout pastors and preachers. May he grant us grace humbly to hear, accept, and honor their words as his own words and to offer our sincere thanks and praise.

The Fourth Commandment

"You are to honor your father and your mother." First, I learn here to acknowledge God, my Creator; how wondrously he has created me, body and soul; and how he has given me life through my parents and has instilled in them the desire to care for me, the fruit of their bodies, with all their power. He has brought me into this world, has sustained and cared for me, nurtured and educated me with great diligence, carefulness, and concern, through danger, trouble, and work. Up to this very hour he has protected me, his creature, and helped me in countless dangers and troubles. It is as though he were creating me anew every moment. But the devil does not willingly concede us one single moment of life.

Second, I thank the rich and gracious Creator on behalf of myself and all the world that he has established and assured in this commandment the increase and preservation of the human race, that is, of households and of states. Without these two institutions or governments the world could not tand a single year, because without government there can be no peace, and where there is no peace there can be no family; without family, children cannot be begotten or raised, and fatherhood and motherhood would cease to be. It is the purpose of this commandment to guard and preserve both family and state, to admonish children and subjects to be obedient. This must happen and, if it does not, he will let no violation go unpunished – otherwise children would have torn the household apart long ago by their disobedience, and subjects would have laid waste to the state through rebellion, because they outnumber parents and rulers. This is therefore an indescribable blessing.

Third, I confess and acknowledge my wicked disobedience and sin; in defiance of God's commandment I have not honored or obeyed my parents; I have often provoked and offended them, have been impatient with their parental discipline, have grumbled about and scorned their loving admonition and have preferred to go along with loose company and evil companions. God afflicts such disobedient children and withholds from them a long life; many of them succumb and perish in disgrace before they reach adulthood. Whoever does not obey father and mother must obey the executioner or otherwise come, through God's wrath, to an evil end, etc. Of all this I repent and ask for grace and forgiveness.

Fourth, I pray for myself and for all the world that God would bestow his grace and pour his blessing richly upon the family and the state, so that from this time on we may be devout, honor our parents, obey our superiors, and resist the devil when he entices us to be disobedient and rebellious. Grant that we may help improve home and nation by our actions and thus preserve the peace, all to the praise and glory of God for our own benefit and for the prosperity of all. Grant that we may acknowledge these his gifts and be thankful for them. At this point we should add a prayer for our parents and superiors, that God may grant them understanding and wisdom to govern and rule us in peace and happiness. May he preserve them from tyranny, from riot and fury, and turn them from such things so that they honor God's word and do not persecute or do injustice to anyone. Such excellent gifts must be sought by prayer, as St. Paul teaches; otherwise the devil will reign in the palace and everything will fall into chaos and confusion. …

The Fifth Commandment

"You are not to kill." Here I learn, first of all, that God desires me to love my neighbor, so that I do him no bodily harm, either by word or action, neither injure nor take revenge upon him in anger, vexation, envy, hatred, or for any evil reason. I should realize that I am obliged to assist and counsel him in every bodily need. In this commandment God commands me to protect my neighbor's body and in turn commands my neighbor to protect my own. As Sirach says, "He has committed to each of us his neighbor."

Second, I give thanks for such ineffable love, care, and faithfulness toward me by which he has placed such a strong protection and wall around my body. All are obliged to look after what is mine and protect me, and I, in turn, must behave likewise toward all others. He upholds this command and, where it is not observed, he has established the sword as punishment for those who do not live up to it. Were it not for this excellent commandment and ordinance, the devil would instigate such a massacre among men that no one could live in safety for a single hour – as happens when God becomes angry and inflicts punishment upon a disobedient and ungrateful world.

Third, I confess and lament my own wickedness and that of the world, not only that we are so terribly ungrateful for such fatherly love and care toward us – but what is especially scandalous, that we do not acknowledge this commandment and teaching, are unwilling to learn it, and neglect it as though it did not concern us or we had no part in it. We amble along complacently, feeling no remorse that, in defiance of this commandment, we despise our neighbors, desert them, persecute, injure, or even kill them in our thoughts. We indulge in anger, rage, and villainy as though we were doing a fine and noble thing. Really, it is high time that we started to deplore and bewail how much we have acted like rogues and like blind, wild, and unfeeling people who tread on, kick, scratch, tear, bite, and devour one another like furious beasts and pay no heed to this serious command of God, etc.

Fourth, I pray the dear Father to lead us to an understanding of this his sacred commandment and to help us keep it and live in accordance with it. May God preserve us from the murderer who is the master of every form of murder and violence. May God grant us his rich grace that we and all others may treat each other in kindly, gentle, and generous ways, forgiving one another from the heart, bearing each other's faults and shortcomings in a Christian and brotherly manner, and thus living together in true peace and unity, as the commandment teaches and requires us to do. ...

The Ninth and Tenth Commandments

"You are not to covet your neighbor's house." Similarly, "his wife," etc. This teaches us first that we shall not dispossess our neighbor of his goods under pretense of legal claims, or reduce, divert, or extort what is his, but help him to keep what is his, just as we wish to be done for ourselves. It is also a protection against the subtleties and chicaneries of shrewd manipulators who will receive their punishment in the end.

Second, we should render thanks to him. Third, we should repentantly and sorrowfully confess our sins. ...

These are the Ten Commandments in their fourfold aspect, namely, as a little book of instruction, a book of thanksgiving, a penitential book, and a prayer book. They are intended to help the heart come to itself and to be warmed up to pray. Take care, however, not to undertake all of this or so much that one becomes weary in spirit. Likewise, a good prayer should not be lengthy or drawn out, but frequent and ardent. It is enough to consider one section or half a section which kindles a fire in the heart. This the Spirit will grant us and continually instruct us in when, by God's word, our hearts have been cleared and freed of outside thoughts and concerns.

The bondage of the human will and the hidden God

Apart from those of his books that were to lead to a renewed, vibrant, Protestant piety, Luther also wrote demanding works of theology intended for scholars and academics. Of these, the most important, not only in Luther's own opinion, was his treatise of 1525 on the question of whether or not humans have a free will. Luther had first raised this question in 1516, and then in 1518 he took it up in theses which he presented for discussion at the University of Heidelberg. Even as early as that, he had postulated – a bone of contention not only for his contemporaries but also today – that humans are not free to make their own choice for God or against him, for or against belief, for or against salvation. But Luther's position provoked outspoken opposition. In 1524, the respected humanist Erasmus of Rotterdam, who was living in Basel at the time, penned a "diatribe", a polemical essay refuting Luther and maintaining that human beings do indeed have free will, even if only to a limited extent.

Luther responded with his book "On the Bondage of the Will" (De servo arbitrio), in which he not only repeated and expanded his Heidelberg position, but also stated his position on numerous other difficult questions of theology. Luther used harsh words to express his disagreement with Erasmus, who always expressed himself in a polite and modest way. He dismissed the arguments of this great and internationally respected scholar in blunt and polemical language, so that Erasmus forthwith wanted to have nothing more to do with Luther and the Reformation, but consistently remained faithful to the old church instead.

Luther was supremely self–confident in contradicting great scholars and powerful churchmen, gladly disparaging the great theologians of the Middle Ages as "sophists". He justified this by the fact that he was a doctor of theology and had thus gained insights that fundamentally challenged conventional theology and philosophy. He had received his doctorate in Wittenberg in 1512.

Martin Luther, De servo arbitrio (1525): WA, Vol. 18, pp. 600–787.
Translation: AL, Vol. 2, pp. 158–257.

Now first we will begin quite properly with the definition you give of free choice, where you say: "By free choice in this place we mean a power of the human will by which a man can apply himself to the things which lead to eternal salvation, or turn away from them." It is very prudent of you to give only a bare definition and not to explain (as others usually do) any part of it – perhaps because you were afraid you might be shipwrecked on more than one point.

I am thus compelled to look at your definition in detail. The thing defined, if it is examined closely, is certainly itself wider than the definition, which is of a kind that the Sophists would call "vicious," a term they apply whenever a definition does not exhaust the thing defined. For we have shown above that free choice properly belongs to no one but God alone. You might perhaps rightly attribute some measure of choice to man, but to attribute free choice to him in relation to divine things is too much; for the term "free choice," in the judgment of everyone's ears, means (strictly speaking) that which can do and does, in relation to God, whatever it pleases, uninhibited by any law or any sovereign authority. For you would not call a slave free, who acts under the sovereign authority of his master; and still less rightly can we call a man or angel free, when they live under the absolute sovereignty of God (not to mention sin and death) in such a way that they cannot subsist for a moment by their own strength. …

Let us come to those parts of the definition on which the whole matter hinges. Some of them are plain enough, but others shun the light as though guiltily aware that they have everything to fear; yet nothing ought to be more plainly and unhesitatingly expressed than a definition, since to define obscurely is the same as giving no definition at all. . . . I take it, then, that what is meant by "a power of the human will" is a capacity or faculty or ability or aptitude for willing, unwilling, selecting, neglecting, approving, rejecting, and whatever other actions of the will there are. Now, what it means for that same power to "apply itself" and to "turn away" I do not see, unless it is precisely this willing and unwilling, selecting, neglecting, approving, rejecting, or in other words, precisely the action of the will. So that we must imagine this power to be something between the will itself and its action, as the means by which the will itself produces the action of willing and unwilling, and by which the action of willing and unwilling is itself produced. Anything else it is impossible either to imagine or conceive here. If I am mistaken, let the author be blamed who has given the definition, not I who am trying to understand it; for as the lawyers rightly say, if a man speaks obscurely when he could speak more clearly, his words are to be interpreted against himself. . . . There is need of plain, blunt speaking for the sake of teaching and understanding. Now, the things which lead to eternal salvation I take to be the words and works of God, which are presented to the human will so that it may apply itself to them or turn away from them. By the words of God, moreover, I mean both the law and the gospel, the law requiring works and the gospel faith. For there is nothing else that leads either to the grace of God or to eternal salvation except the word and work of God, since grace or the Spirit is life itself, to which we are led by God's word and work.

This life or eternal salvation, however, is something that passes human comprehension, as Paul quotes from Isaiah 64:4

in 1 Corinthians 2:9: “What no eye has seen, nor ear heard, nor the heart of man conceived, what God has prepared for those who love him.” It is also included among the chief articles of our faith, where we say [in the creed]: “And the life everlasting.” And what free choice is worth in relation to this article, Paul shows in 1 Corinthians 2:10, where he says: “God has revealed it to us through his Spirit.” This means that unless the Spirit had revealed it, no man’s heart would have any knowledge or notion of it, much less be able to apply itself to it or seek after it. Take a look at experience. What have the most distinguished minds among the heathen thought about the future life and the resurrection? Is it not the case that the more distinguished they have been, the more absurd the idea of a future life and resurrection has seemed to them to be? Were they not talented philosophers and Greeks who when Paul taught these things at Athens called him a babbler and a preacher of foreign divinities (Acts 17:18)? Porcius Festus called Paul mad (Acts 26:24) on account of his preaching of eternal life. … For privately there is simply no one, unless he is thoroughly imbued with the Holy Spirit, who knows, believes, or desires eternal salvation, even though they never stop talking and writing about it. …

On the authority of Erasmus, then, free choice is a power of the will that is able of itself to will and unwill the word and work of God, by which it is led to those things which exceed both its grasp and its perception. But if it can will and unwill, it can also love and hate, and if it can love and hate, it can also in some small degree do the works of the law and believe the gospel. For if you can will or unwill anything, you must to some extent be able to perform something by that will, even if someone else prevents your completing it. Now, in that case, since the works of God which lead to salvation include death, the cross, and all the evils of the world, the human will must be able to will both death and its own perdition. Indeed, it can will everything when it can will the word and work of God; for how can there be anything anywhere that is below, above, within, or without the word and work of God, except God himself? But what is left here to grace and the Holy Spirit? This plainly means attributing divinity to free choice, since to will the law and the gospel, to unwill sin and to will death, belongs to divine power alone, as Paul says in more than one place (1 Corinthians 2:14; 2 Corinthians 3:5). …

Your definition is therefore to be condemned even by the standards of the Sophists, who if only they were not so enraged by blind envy of me, would be rampaging instead against your book. As it is, since it is Luther you are attacking, everything you say is holy and catholic, even if you contradict both yourself and them, so great is the endurance of saintly men.

I do not say this because I approve the view of the Sophists regarding free choice, but because I consider it more tolerable than that of Erasmus, since they come nearer the truth. For although they do not say, as I do, that free choice is nothing, yet when they … say that it can do nothing without grace, they take sides against Erasmus; indeed, they seem to take sides against themselves too, and to be racked with dissension merely about a word, as if they were fonder of controversy than of truth, as might be expected of Sophists. For suppose one of the least objectionable Sophists were brought to me, with whom I could discuss these things privately in intimate conversation and ask for his free and candid judgment in some such way as this: If anyone told you that a thing was free which could operate by its own power only in one direction (the bad one), while in the other (the good one) it could of course operate, though not by its own power, but only by the help of another – would you be able to keep a straight face, my friend? By that sort of method I can easily make out that a stone or a log of wood has free choice because it can move both upward and downward, though by its own power only downward, and upward only by the help of another. …

You regard as hard, though probable enough, the opinion of those who deny that man can will the good without special grace. They deny that he can begin, progress, or reach his goal, etc.; and this you approve because it leaves man to desire and endeavor, but does not leave him with anything to ascribe to his own powers. Harder, you think, is the opinion of those who contend that free choice is of no avail save to sin, that grace alone accomplishes good in us, etc. But hardest is the view of those who say that free choice is a mere empty name, that it is God who works both good and evil in us, and that all things which happen come about by sheer necessity. It is against these last two positions that you profess to be writing.

Do you really know what you are saying, my dear Erasmus? You express here three opinions as if they belonged to three different schools, not realizing that they are the same thing variously stated, in different words at different times, by us who remain the same persons and exponents of one school only.

But let us draw your attention to this and point out the carelessness or stupidity of your judgment. I ask you, how does the definition of free choice given by you earlier square with this first and probable enough opinion? For you said there that free choice is a power of the human will by which a man can apply himself to the good; but here you say, and approve of its being said, that man without grace cannot will good. The definition asserts what the illustration of it denies, and there is found in your free choice both a Yes and a No, so that you at once both approve and condemn us, and condemn and approve also yourself, in one and the same dogma and article. Or do you think it is not good to apply oneself to the things which pertain to eternal salvation?

That is what your definition attributes to free choice; and yet there is no need of grace if there were so much good in free choice that it could apply itself to the good. Hence the free choice you define is a different thing from the free choice you defend; so now Erasmus, in contrast to the rest of us, has two free choices, and those entirely at variance with each other.

But let us put aside that free choice which the definition has invented, and look at the contrary one which the "opinion" itself implies. You grant that man cannot will good without special grace – for we are not now discussing what the grace of God can do, but what man can do without grace. You grant, then, that free choice cannot will good. This means nothing else but that it cannot apply itself to the things which pertain to eternal salvation, as your definition cheerfully stated it could. Indeed, you say a little before, that the human will since the Fall is so depraved that having lost its liberty, it is obliged to serve sin and cannot bring itself back to any better issue. … What an exquisitely free choice, which has lost its liberty and is called by Erasmus himself a slave of sin! When Luther said this, nothing more absurd had ever been heard, nothing more mischievous than this paradox could be published, so that even diatribes must be written against him!

The first opinion, then, when compared with itself, is such as to deny that man can will anything good, and yet to maintain that a desire is left to him which nevertheless is not his own.

Now, let us compare it with the other two. The second is that harder one which holds that free choice avails for nothing but sinning. …

The third and hardest opinion is that of Wycliffe[7] and Luther, that free choice is an empty name and all that we do comes about by sheer necessity. It is with these two views that Diatribe quarrels. Here I admit that perhaps I am not good enough at Latin or German to have been able to put the fact of the matter plainly into words; but God is my witness that I meant to say nothing else, and to have nothing else understood, by the words of the last two opinions than what is stated in the first opinion. … For when it has been conceded and agreed that free choice, having lost its liberty, is perforce in bondage to sin and cannot will anything good, I can make no other sense of these words than that free choice is an empty phrase, of which the reality has been lost. Lost liberty, according to my grammar, is no liberty at all, and to give the name of liberty to something that has no liberty, is to employ an empty phrase. If I am wrong here, let anyone put me right who can; if these things are obscure and ambiguous, let anyone who is able shed light on them and settle what they mean. I for my part cannot call lost health, health; and if I ascribed it to a sick person, I do not think I should have ascribed anything but an empty name.

But let us have done with verbal monstrosities. For who can bear this abuse of language by which we both say that man has free choice and at the same time assert that having lost his liberty he is perforce in bondage to sin and can will nothing good?

---

[7] 14th-century English theologian condemned as a heretic.

These things are contrary to common sense and completely destroy the common use of language. … For when a man has lost his liberty and is forced to serve sin and cannot will good, what can be more truly inferred about him than that he sins, or wills evil, necessarily? …

Scripture, however, represents man as one who is not only bound, wretched, captive, sick, and dead (Ephesians 2:1), but in addition to his other miseries is afflicted, through the agency of Satan his prince, with this misery of blindness, so that he believes himself to be free, happy, unfettered, able, well, and alive. For Satan knows that if men were aware of their misery, he would not be able to retain a single one of them in his kingdom, because God could not but at once pity and succour them in their acknowledged and crying wretchedness, seeing he is so highly extolled throughout Scripture as being near to the contrite in heart (Psalms 34:18), as Christ too declares himself according to Isaiah 61:1, to have been sent to preach the gospel to the poor and to bind up the brokenhearted (Luke 4:18). Accordingly, it is Satan's work to prevent men from recognizing their plight and to keep them presuming that they can do everything they are told. But the work of Moses or a lawgiver is the opposite of this, namely, to make man's plight plain to him by means of the law and thus to break and confound him by self-knowledge, so as to prepare him for grace and send him to Christ that he may be saved. They are therefore not absurd but emphatically serious and necessary things that are done by the law. …

Biblical promises do not prove free will

In his diatribe, Erasmus quotes Ezekiel 33:11 and other passages where God says, "I desire not the death of a sinner, but rather that the sinner may turn and live", claiming that they prove a certain freedom of will. Luther counters this by arguing that in this way Erasmus turns a word of promise into a legal precept. In Luther's interpretation of the Bible, the distinction between law and promise is fundamental. He accuses Erasmus of not recognizing and observing this distinction. For Luther, words of the law are actually intended to convict sinners of their sins and to make them fear. Words of promise have the purpose of comforting the afflicted sinner. According to Luther, neither of these words proves the freedom of the will, but they rather contradict it.

It is an evangelical word and the sweetest comfort in every way for miserable sinners, where Ezekiel (Ezekiel 33:11) says: "I desire not the death of a sinner, but rather that he may turn and live," like Psalm 30:5: "For his anger is but for a moment, and his favor is for a lifetime." Then there is Psalm 69:16: "How sweet is thy mercy, O Lord" and "For I am merciful" (Jeremiah 3:12), and also Christ's saying in Matthew 11:28: "Come unto me, all you who labor, and I will give you rest," and that in Exodus 20:6: "I show mercy to many thousands, to those who love me."

What, indeed, does almost more than half of Holy Scripture contain but sheer promises of grace, in which mercy, life, peace, and salvation are offered by God to men? And what else do words of promise have to say but this: "I desire not the death of a sinner"? Is it not the same thing to say, "I am merciful," as to say, "I am not angry, I do not want to punish, I do not want you to die, I want to pardon, I want to spare"? And if these divine promises were not there to raise up consciences afflicted with the sense of sin and terrified with the fear of death and judgment, what place would there be for pardon or hope? What sinner would not despair? But just as free choice is not proved by other words of mercy or promise or comfort, so neither is it proved by this one: "I desire not the death of a sinner," etc.

But our Diatribe, again making no distinction between words of law and of promise, takes this verse of Ezekiel as an expression of the law, and expounds it thus: "I desire not the death of a sinner," that is, "I do not want him to sin mortally or become a sinner liable to death, but rather that he may turn from his sin, if he has committed any, and so may live." For if she did not expound it so, it would not serve her purpose at all. But this means completely throwing overboard the loveliest thing in Ezekiel, "I desire not death." If that is how in our blindness we wish to read and understand the Scriptures, what wonder is it if they are obscure and ambiguous? For he does not say, "I desire not the sin of a man," but, "I desire not the death of a sinner," plainly showing that he is speaking of the penalty of sin, which the sinner experiences for his sin, namely, the fear of death. And he lifts up and comforts the sinner from his affliction and despair, so as not to quench the smoking flax and break the bruised reed (Isaiah 42:3), but to give hope of pardon and salvation, so that he may rather be converted (by turning to salvation from the penalty of death) and live, that is, be at peace and happy with an untroubled conscience. For this also must be observed, that just as the voice of the law is not raised except over those who do not feel or acknowledge their sin, as Paul says in Romans 3:20: "Through the law comes knowledge of sin," so the word of grace does not come except to those who feel their sin and are troubled and tempted to despair. Thus in all expressions of the law you see that sin is revealed, inasmuch as we are shown what we ought to do, just as you see in all the words of promise, on the other hand, that the evil is indicated under which sinners, or those who are to be lifted up, are laboring. Here, for instance, "I desire not the death of a sinner" explicitly names death and the sinner, that is, the evil that is felt as well as the person who feels it. But in the words "Love God with all your heart," (Matthew 22:37) we are shown the good we ought to do, not the evil we feel, in order that we may recognize how unable we are to do that good.

Hence nothing could have been more inappropriately quoted in support of free choice than this passage of Ezekiel, which actually stands in the strongest opposition to free choice. For here we are shown what free choice is like, and what it can do about sin when sin is recognized, or about its own conversion to God; that is to say, nothing but fall into a worse state and add despair and impenitence to its sins, if God did not quickly come to its aid and call it back and raise it up by a word of promise. For God's solicitude in promising grace to recall and restore the sinner is a sufficiently strong and reliable argument that free choice by itself cannot but go from bad to worse and (as Scripture says) fall down into hell (Proverbs 5:5), unless you credit God with such levity as to pour out words of promise in profusion for the mere pleasure of talking, and not because they are in any way necessary for our salvation. So you can see that not only all the words of the law stand against free choice, but also all the words of promise utterly refute it; which means that Scripture in its entirety stands opposed to it. This word, therefore, "I desire not the death of a sinner," has as you see no other object than the preaching and offering of divine mercy throughout the world, a mercy that only the afflicted and those tormented by the fear of death receive with joy and gratitude, because in them the law has already fulfilled its office and brought the knowledge of sin. Those, however, who have not yet experienced the office of the law, and neither recognize sin nor feel death, have no use for the mercy promised by that word.

Ignore the hidden God, regard the revealed God

Now Luther, like Erasmus in his diatribe, is confronted with the question of God. If a human has no free will, does that mean that it is not the sinner who is responsible for the death caused by sins, but ultimately God himself? Then how can God lament the death of the sinner, although he himself brings it about? Does it not follow from God's lamentation over the death of sinners that they themselves, not God, are responsible for their death? That means that sinners have a free will, but do not use it to save themselves from death. While this provides Erasmus with further arguments to support his claim for the freedom of the will, Luther differentiates between God and God – between the God who is openly revealed in the Word and desires the salvation of all human beings, and the God who is high above us, hidden from us, ordaining all things in a way that is beyond our comprehension. Luther puts it succinctly: "Things above us are no business of ours." His motto is: pay attention to God revealed in the preaching of the Word, look to his mercy and do not seek to understand his inscrutable plan.

But why some are touched by the law and others are not, so that the former accept and the latter despise the offered grace, is another question and one not dealt with by Ezekiel in this passage. For he is here speaking of the preached and offered mercy of God, not of that hidden and awful will of God whereby he ordains by his own counsel which and what sort of persons he wills to be recipients and partakers of his preached and offered mercy. This will is not to be inquired into, but reverently adored, as by far the most awe-inspiring secret of the Divine Majesty, reserved for himself alone and forbidden to us …

When now Diatribe pertly asks, “Does the good Lord deplore the death of his people, which he himself works in them?” – for this really does seem absurd – we reply, as we have already said, that we have to argue in one way about God or the will of God as preached, revealed, offered, and worshiped, and in another way about God as he is not preached, not revealed, not offered, not worshiped. To the extent, therefore, that God hides himself and wills to be unknown to us, it is no business of ours. For here the saying truly applies, “Things above us are no business of ours.” And lest anyone should think this is a distinction of my own, I am following Paul, who writes to the Thessalonians concerning Antichrist that he will exalt himself above every God that is preached and worshiped (2 Thessalonians 2:4). This plainly shows that someone can be exalted above God as he is preached and worshiped, that is, above the word and rite through which God is known to us and has dealings with us; but above God as he is not worshiped and not preached, but as he is in his own nature and majesty, nothing can be exalted, but all things are under his mighty hand. God must therefore be left to himself in his own majesty, for in this regard we have nothing to do with him, nor has he willed that we should have anything to do with him. But we have something to do with him insofar as he is clothed and set forth in his Word, through which he offers himself to us and which is the beauty and glory with which the psalmist celebrates him as being clothed (Psalm 21:5). In this regard we say, the good God does not deplore the death of his people which he works in them, but he deplores the death which he finds in his people and desires to remove from them. For it is this that God as he is preached is concerned with, namely, that sin and death should be taken away and we should be saved. For "he sent his word and healed them" (Psalm 107:20). But God hidden in his majesty neither deplores nor takes away death, but works life, death, and all in all (1 Corinthians 12:6). For there he has not bound himself by his word, but has kept himself free over all things.

Diatribe, however, deceives herself in her ignorance by not making any distinction between God preached and God hidden, that is, between the Word of God and God himself. God does many things that he does not disclose to us in his word; he also wills many things which he does not disclose himself as willing in his word. Thus he does not will the death of a sinner, according to his word; but he wills it according to that inscrutable will of his. It is our business, however, to pay attention to the word and leave that inscrutable will alone, for we must be guided by the word and not by that inscrutable will. After all, who can direct himself by a will completely inscrutable and unknowable? It is enough to know simply that there is a certain inscrutable will in God, and as to what, why, and how far it wills, that is something we have no right whatever to inquire into, hanker after, care about, or meddle with, but only to fear and adore. It is therefore right to say, "If God does not desire our death, the fact that we perish must be imputed to our own will." It is right, I mean, if you speak of God as preached; for he wills all men to be saved (1 Timothy 2:4), seeing he comes with the word of salvation to all, and the fault is in the will that does not admit him, as he says in Matthew 23:37: "How often would I have gathered your children, and you would not!" But why that majesty of his does not remove or change this defect of our will in all men, since it is not in man's power to do so, or why he imputes this defect to man, when man cannot help having it, we have no right to inquire; and though you may do a lot of inquiring, you will never find out. It is as Paul says in Romans 9:20: "Who are you, to answer back to God?" …

The presence of Christ in bread and wine

A second controversy which broke out in the mid–1520s had even more far–reaching consequences than Luther's dispute with Erasmus over the question of the freedom of the human will. Luther and the Zurich Reformer Ulrich Zwingli disagreed in their understanding of the Lord's Supper. While Luther, together with the medieval and Roman Church, maintained that bread was the body of Christ in this sacrament, and only rejected the doctrine of transubstantiation, i. e. the rational explanation of the mystery, Zwingli understood bread to be a symbol of the body of Christ. In the words of institution "This is my body", Jesus had meant "This signifies …", "This is a symbol of my body". Luther vigorously contradicted Zwingli, deeming him to be a "Schwärmer" ("fanatic") and a spiritualist, who did not properly accept the written word of the Bible. In 1526 and several other times, he wrote pamphlets "Against the Fanatics". Zwingli's followers struck back and polemicized against Luther and his supporters, accusing them, like the medieval Arabic–Islamic philosopher Averroes, of wanting to eat God.

Martin Luther, Sermon von dem Sakrament des Leibes und Blutes Christi, wider die Schwarmgeister (1526): WA 19, pp. 482–523. Translation: LW, Vol. 36, pp. 329–361.

In this sacrament there are two things that should be known and proclaimed. First, what one should believe. In Latin this is called the *objectum fidei*, that is, the work or thing in which one believes, or to which one is to adhere. Second, the faith itself, or the use which one should properly make of that in which he believes. The first lies outside the heart and is presented to our eyes externally, namely, the sacrament itself, concerning which we believe that Christ's body and blood are truly present in the bread and wine. The second is internal, within the heart, and cannot be externalized. It consists in the attitude which the heart should have toward the external sacrament. Up to now I have not preached very much about the first part, but have treated only the second, which is also the best part. But because the first part is now being assailed by many, and the preachers, even those who are considered the best, are splitting up into factions over the matter, so that in foreign lands a large number are already pouncing upon it and maintaining that Christ's body and blood are not present in the bread and wine, the times demand that I say something on this subject also.

At the outset I will say this, however: if anyone is thought to be engulfed in such an error, I would earnestly advise him to abstain from the sacrament until he emerges from his error and becomes strong in the faith. For we have before us the clear text and the plain words of Christ: "Take, eat; this is my body, which is given for you. Drink of it, all of you, this is my blood, which is poured out for you. Do this in remembrance of me" (Matthew 26:26–28; Mark 14:22–24; Luke 22:19–20). These are the words on which we take our stand. They are so simply and clearly stated that even they, our adversaries, must confess that it is difficult to interpret them otherwise. Yet they pass these clear words by and follow their own thoughts, making darkness for themselves in the midst of the bright light.

If anyone wishes to pursue a true course and not come to grief, let him beware of the clever idea, inspired by the devil in this matter everywhere, that he may suck the egg dry and leave us the shell, that is, remove the body and blood of Christ from the bread and wine, so that it remains no more than mere bread, such as the baker bakes. In accordance with this clever idea our opponents mock us at their pleasure, charging that we are eaters of flesh and drinkers of blood and that we worship a baked God. In former times that desperate renegade, Averroes … similarly mocked and slandered the faithful, maintaining that there is no people on earth more despicable than the Christians, because they devour their own God, which no other people had ever done. Was this not an exquisitely clever saying? Such are the tricks which the devil is playing against us nowadays everywhere.

Now God is the sort of person who likes to do what is foolish and useless in the eyes of the world, as Paul says in 1 Corinthians 1:23: "We preach Christ crucified, a stumbling block to the Jews and folly to the Gentiles." And again: "For since, in the wisdom of God, the world did not know God through wisdom, it pleased God through the folly of what we preach to save those who believe in him" (1 Corinthians 1:21). Well then, if anyone does not believe this, let him believe accordingly that it is mere bread, or a batch of bread. Anyone who has failed to grasp the faith may thenceforth believe whatever he likes, it makes no difference. Just as when someone is on the point of drowning, whether he drowns in a brook or in the middle of a stream, he is drowned just the same. So I say of these fanatics: if they let go of the word, let them believe whatever they like and squabble as long as they like. It has already happened that six or seven sects have arisen over the sacrament, but all of them under the delusion that Christ's flesh and blood are not present.

This comes about, I maintain, because in the first place they have not adhered to the words, and then because they have followed their own thoughts and have seen that if Christ were present in the bread and wine and were distributed so widely everywhere and if each person were to eat this Christ, that would be an awkward situation. This has been their first thought. Hence they have a colored glass before their eyes, and therefore the words must mean what they think. This is what all factious spirits do: they first concoct an opinion. If it pleases them, they then attempt to force the Scriptures to agree with it. But whoever derives the right faith from the words will believe like this: Whether Christ enters into the bread or the cup or into whatever he will, God grant that as long as I have the words, I will not seek or speculate any further; what he says, I will keep. Thus the believer envelops himself in the Word, will not let himself be turned aside from it, and is also thereby sustained.

"On Secular Authority"

One of Luther's topics which leads to controversy is his teaching on authority. In his time, Luther faced the challenge of establishing the necessity of authorities and the Christian's duty to obey them. The reason was that some of his Protestant contemporaries drew the conclusion from his theology that whoever is truly pious has no further need of authorities. On the contrary, Luther stressed that one should be obedient to authority. And in later times, when the social and political conditions had fundamentally changed, it was particularly those churches which adhered to Luther's opinions that advocated strict obedience to authority. It has therefore repeatedly been suggested that Luther's doctrine concerning authority was partly to blame for the fact that the Protestant churches largely failed during the National Socialist era.

However, in studying Luther's texts, one can discover that he was also extremely critical of the authorities. His severe judgment of the worldly rulers was only exceeded by his criticism of the pope. Luther considers authorities to be necessary to restrain the evil in the world. But Luther believes that the authorities should not interfere in religious affairs, especially in matters of conscience. They are not even responsible for driving out false doctrine and heretics. Thus, in 1523, Luther adopted a somewhat different position to that of his address to the nobility three years beforehand. The reason that Luther wrote a new treatise "On Secular Authority" was that in various Catholic areas, including Bavaria and Brandenburg, the authorities had ordered Luther's Bible translation to be confiscated. Luther limits the scope of the authorities and also outlines the way rulers should exercise government if they truly see themselves as Christians.

Every authority is entitled to employ power for law enforcement – the sword, as Luther puts it. But how does that fit in with Jesus' Sermon on the Mount? Luther rejects the traditional doctrine of the Church, which said that the Sermon on the Mount was not a commandment for all Christians, but was only valid as divine advice or a recommendation for Christians living an especially perfect life, such as clergy and monks. They were indeed not supposed to take up arms. Luther refuted this interpretation of the Sermon on the Mount by the "sophists", Luther's scornful name for traditional theologians. He developed his doctrine of the two kingdoms instead. A Christian lives on the one hand in the kingdom of Christ, on the other hand in the kingdom of the earthly world. The Sermon on the Mount is valid in the kingdom of Christ, but not in the kingdom of the world, not in society, politics or international relations. This means that a Christian renounces violence and revenge for himself and among Christians, but at the same time he is ready to use violence to protect his neighbor and to ward off evil. This so-called "two kingdoms doctrine" of Luther remains the subject of extremely controversial discussion even today.

Martin Luther: Von weltlicher Obrigkeit, wie weit man ihr
Gehorsam schuldig sei (1523): WA 11, pp. 229–281.
Translation: AL, Vol. 5, pp. 88–122.

Some time ago I addressed a little book to the German nobility, setting forth their Christian office and function. But how they responded to it is only too evident. I must therefore change my tactics and this time prescribe to them what they should omit and not do. I expect, however, that they will conform to this new effort exactly as they did to the first, and that they will remain princes and never become Christians. For God the Almighty has made our rulers mad; they actually think they can do – and order their subjects to do – whatever they please. And the subjects make the mistake of believing that they in turn are bound to obey their rulers in everything. It has gone so far that the rulers have begun ordering the people to get rid of certain books, and to believe and conform to what the rulers prescribe. They are thereby presumptuously setting themselves in God's place, lording it over men's consciences and faith, and testing the patience of the Holy Spirit with their foolish notions. Nevertheless, they let it be known that they are not to be contradicted, and are still to be called gracious lords.

They issue public proclamations, and say that this is the emperor's command and that they want to be obedient Christian princes, just as if they really meant it and no one noticed the scoundrel behind the mask. If the emperor were to take a castle or a city from them or command some other injustice, we should then see how quickly they would find themselves obliged to resist the emperor and disobey him. But when it comes to fleecing the poor or exercising their arbitrary will on the word of God, it becomes a matter of "obedience to the imperial command." Such people were formerly called scoundrels; now they have to be called obedient Christian princes. Still, they will not permit anyone to appear before them for a hearing or to defend himself, no matter how humbly he may petition. If the emperor or anyone else were to treat them this way, they would regard it as quite intolerable. Such are the princes who today rule the Empire in the German lands. This is also why things must be going so well in all the lands, as we see.

Because the raging of such fools tends toward the suppression of the Christian faith, the denying of the divine word, and the blaspheming of the Divine Majesty, I can and will no longer just look at my ungracious lords and angry nobles; I must resist them, at least with words. And since I have not been in terror of their idol, the pope, who threatens to deprive me of soul and of heaven, I must show that I am not in terror of his lackeys and windbags, who threaten to deprive me of body and of earth.

God grant that they may have to rage until the gray cloaks perish, and help us that we may not die of their threats. Amen.

Authorities are necessary

First, we must properly justify the secular law and sword, so no one will doubt that it is in the world by God's will and ordinance. The passages that justify it are the following: Romans 13:1–2: "Let every soul be subject to authority and government, for there is no authority except from God; the authority that everywhere exists has been ordained by God. Whoever resists that authority resists God's ordinance, and he who resists God's ordinance will incur condemnation." Again, in 1 Peter 2:13–14, "Be subject to every kind of human ordinance, whether it be to the king as supreme, or to governors, as those who have been sent by him to punish the wicked and to praise the good."

This same law of the secular sword has existed from the beginning of the world. For when Cain slew his brother Abel, he was in such great terror of being killed in turn that God placed a special prohibition on it and suspended the sword for his sake, so that no one was to slay him (Genesis 4:14–15). He would not have had this fear if he had not seen and heard from Adam that murderers are to be slain. Moreover, after the Flood, God reestablished and confirmed this in unmistakable terms when he said in Genesis 9:6, "Whoever sheds human blood, by human hands shall that person's blood be shed." This cannot be understood as a plague or punishment of God upon murderers, for many murderers remain alive because of penance or pardon and eventually die by means other than the sword. Rather, it is said of the law of the sword, that a murderer is guilty of death and in justice is to be slain by the sword. Now if justice should be hindered or the sword have become negligent, so that the murderer dies a natural death, Scripture is not on that account false when it says, "Whoever sheds human blood, by human hands shall that person's blood be shed." The credit or blame belongs to mortals if this law instituted by God is not carried out; just as other commandments of God, too, are broken.

Afterward it is also confirmed by the law of Moses, Exodus 21:14, "For it anyone wantonly kills another, you shall take the killer from my altar to be executed." And again, in the same chapter (Exodus 21:23–25), "A life for a life, an eye for an eye, a tooth for a tooth, a foot for a foot, a hand for a hand, a wound for a wound, a stripe for a stripe." In addition, Christ also confirms it when he says to Peter in the garden, "Whoever takes the sword will perish by the sword" (Matthew 26:52), which is to be interpreted exactly like the Genesis 9:6 passage, "Whoever sheds human blood," etc. Christ is undoubtedly referring in these words to that very passage, which he thereby wishes to cite and to confirm. John the Baptist also teaches the same thing. When the soldiers asked him what they should do, he answered, "Do neither violence nor injustice to any one, and be content with your wages" (Luke 3:14). If the sword were not a godly estate, he should have directed them to get out of it, since he was supposed to make the people perfect and instruct them in a proper Christian way. Hence, it is certain and clear enough that it is God's will that the secular sword and law be used for the punishment of the wicked and the protection of the good.

Second. It speaks powerfully to the contrary that Christ says in Matthew 5:38–41, "You have heard that it was said to your ancestors: An eye for an eye, a tooth for a tooth. But I say to you, Do not resist evil; but if anyone strikes you on the right cheek, turn the other cheek also. And if anyone would sue you and take your coat, surrender your cloak as well. And if anyone forces you to go one mile, go a second mile as well," etc. Likewise Paul in Romans 12:19, "Beloved, defend not yourselves, but leave it to the wrath of God; for it is written, 'Vengeance is mine; I will repay, says the Lord.'" And in Matthew 5:44, "Love your enemies, do good to them that hate you." And again, in 1 Peter 3:9, "Do not return evil for evil, or reviling for reviling," etc. These and similar passages certainly make it appear as though in the New Testament Christians have no secular sword.

For this reason too the sophists say that Christ has thereby abolished the law of Moses. Of such commandments they make "counsels" for the perfect. They divide Christian teaching and Christendom into two. One part they call the perfect, and assign to it such counsels. The other they call the imperfect, and assign to it the commandments. This they do out of sheer wantonness and caprice, without any basis in Scripture. They fail to see that in the same passage Christ lays such stress on his teaching that he is unwilling to have the least word of it set aside, and condemns to hell those who do not love their enemies. Therefore, we must interpret these passages differently, so that Christ's words may apply to everyone alike, whether perfect or imperfect. For perfection and imperfection do not consist in works, and do not establish any distinct external order among Christians. They exist rather in the heart, in faith and love, so that those who believe and love the most are the perfect ones, whether they be outwardly male or female, prince or peasant, monk or layperson. For love and faith produce no sects or outward differences.

Third. Here we must divide the children of Adam and the whole human race into two parts, the first belonging to the kingdom of God, the second to the kingdom of the world. Those who belong to the kingdom of God are all the true believers who are in Christ and under Christ, for Christ is King and Lord in the kingdom of God, as Psalm 2:6 and all of Scripture says. For this reason he came, that he might begin God's kingdom and establish it in the world. Therefore, he says before Pilate, "My kingdom is not of the world, but everyone who is of the truth hears my voice" (John 18:36–37). In the gospel he continually refers to the kingdom of God, and says, "Mend your ways, the kingdom of God is at hand" (Matthew 3:2; 4:17; 10:7); again, "Seek first the kingdom of God and his righteousness" (Matthew 6:33). He also calls the gospel a gospel of the kingdom of God, because it teaches, governs, and upholds God's kingdom.

Now observe, these people need no secular law or sword. If all the world were composed of real Christians, that is, true believers, there would be neither need nor use for prince, king, lord, sword, or law. What purpose would they serve? For Christians have in their hearts the Holy Spirit, who both teaches and causes them to do injustice to no one, to love everyone, and to suffer injustice and even death willingly and cheerfully at the hands of anyone. Where there is nothing but the unadulterated doing of right and bearing of wrong, there is no need for quarrels, disputes, courts, judicial penalties, law, or sword. For this reason it is impossible that the secular sword and law should find any work to do among Christians, since they do of their own accord much more than all laws and precepts can demand, just as Paul says in 1 Timothy 1:9, no law is given to the righteous but rather to the unrighteous. …

Fourth. All who are not Christians belong to the kingdom of the world and are under the law. For since there are few true believers, and still fewer who live a Christian life and who neither resist evil nor themselves do any evil, God has provided for them a different government beyond the Christian estate and kingdom of God. He has subjected them to the sword so that, even though they would like to, they are unable to practice their wickedness, and if they do practice it they cannot do so without fear or with success and impunity. It is just as when a dangerous wild beast is bound with chains and ropes so that it cannot bite and tear as it would normally do, even though it would like to; whereas a tame and gentle animal needs no restraint, but is harmless despite the lack of chains and ropes. ...

If anyone attempted to rule the world by the gospel and to abolish all secular law and sword on the ground that all are baptized and Christian, and that, according to the gospel, there shall be among them no law or sword – or need for either – pray tell me, friend, what would he be doing? He would be loosing the ropes and chains of the savage wild beasts and letting them bite and mangle everyone, meanwhile insisting that they were harmless, tame, and gentle creatures; but I would have the proof in my wounds. Just so would the wicked under the name of Christian abuse evangelical freedom, carry on their rascality, and insist that they were Christians, subject neither to law nor sword, as some are already raving and ranting.

To such a one we must say: Certainly it is true that Christians, so far as they themselves are concerned, are subject neither to law nor sword, and have need of neither. But take heed and first fill the world with real Christians before you attempt to rule it in a Christian and evangelical manner. This you will never accomplish; for the world and the multitude are and will remain un-Christian, even if they are all baptized and Christian in name. Christians are few and far between (as the saying goes). Therefore, it is out of the question that there should be a common Christian government over the whole world, or indeed over a single country or any considerable body of people, for the wicked always outnumber the good. Hence, a man who would venture to govern an entire country or the world with the gospel would be like a shepherd who should put together in one fold wolves, lions, eagles, and sheep, and let them mingle freely with one another, saying, "Help yourselves, and be good and peaceful toward one another. The fold is open, there is plenty of food. You need have no fear of dogs and clubs." The sheep would doubtless keep the peace and allow themselves to be fed and governed peacefully, but they would not live long, nor would one beast survive another.

For this reason one must carefully distinguish between these two governments. Both must be permitted to remain; the one to produce righteousness, the other to bring about external peace and prevent evil deeds. Neither one is sufficient in the world without the other. No one can become righteous in the sight of God by means of secular government, without Christ's spiritual government. Christ's government does not extend over all people; rather, Christians are always a minority in the midst of non-Christians. Where secular government or law alone governs, there sheer hypocrisy is inevitable, even though the commandments be God's very own. For without the Holy Spirit in the heart no one becomes truly righteous, no matter how fine their works may be. On the other hand, where spiritual government alone governs land and people, there wickedness is given free rein and the door is open for all manner of knavery, for the world as a whole cannot receive or comprehend it.

Now you see the intent of the words of Christ that we quoted above from Matthew 5:39, that Christians should not go to law or use the secular sword among themselves. Actually, he says this only to his dear Christians, those who alone accept it and act accordingly, who do not make "counsels" out of it as the sophists do, but in their heart are so disposed and conditioned by the Spirit that they do evil to no one and willingly endure evil at the hands of others. If all the world were Christians, then these words would apply to all, and all would act accordingly. Since, however, they are un-Christian these words do not apply to them and they do not act accordingly, but are under another government in which those who are not Christian are kept under external constraint and compelled to keep the peace and do what is good. . . .

Fifth. But you say: since then Christians do not need the secular sword or law, why does Paul say to all Christians in Romans 13:1, "Let all souls be subject to the governing authorities," and St. Peter, "Be subject to every human ordinance" (1 Peter 2:13), etc., as quoted above? Answer: I have just said that Christians, among themselves and by and for themselves, need no law or sword, since it is neither necessary nor useful for them. But because true Christians live and labor on earth not for themselves alone but for their neighbors, they do by the very nature of their spirit even what they themselves have no need of but is needful and useful to their neighbors. Since, however, the sword is most beneficial and necessary for the whole world in order to preserve peace, punish sin, and restrain the wicked, Christians submit most willingly to the rule of the sword, pay their taxes, honor those in authority, serve, help, and do all they can to assist government, that it may continue to function and be held in honor and fear. Although they have no need of these things for themselves – to them they are not essential – they nevertheless concern themselves about what is of service and benefit to others, as Paul teaches in Ephesians 5:21–6:9.

Just as they perform all other works of love that they themselves do not need – they do not visit the sick in order that they themselves may be made well, or feed others because they themselves need food – so they serve government not because they need it but for the sake of others, that they may be protected and that the wicked may not become worse. They lose nothing by this; such service in no way harms them, yet it is of great benefit to the world. If they did not so serve they would not be acting as Christians but rather contrary to love; they would also be setting a bad example to others, who in like manner would not submit to authority, even though they were not Christians. In this way the gospel would be brought into disrepute, as though it taught insurrection and produced self-centered people unwilling to benefit or serve others, when in fact it makes Christians servants of all. Thus in Matthew 17:27 Christ paid the half-shekel tax that he might not offend them, although he had no need to do so. …

Sixth. You ask whether a Christian too may bear the secular sword and punish the wicked, since Christ's words, "Do not resist evil," are so clear and definite that the sophists have had to make of them a "counsel." Answer: You have now heard two propositions. One is that the sword can have no place among Christians; therefore, you cannot bear it among Christians or hold it over them, for they do not need it. The question, therefore, must be referred to the other crowd, who are not Christians, whether you may bear it there in a Christian manner. Here the other proposition applies, that you are under obligation to serve and assist the sword by whatever means you can, with body, goods, honor, and soul. For it is a service that you do not need but is very beneficial and essential for the whole world and for your neighbor. Therefore, if you see that there is a lack of hangmen, bailiffs, judges, lords, or princes, and you find that you are qualified, you should offer your services and seek the position, so that essential government may not be despised and become enfeebled or perish. The world cannot and dare not dispense with it.

The reason for this is that in such a case you would be entering entirely into the service of others with works that would be of advantage neither to yourself nor to your property or honor, but only to your neighbor and to others. You would be doing it not with the purpose of avenging yourself or returning evil for evil, but for the good of your neighbor and for the maintenance of the safety and peace of others. For yourself and your goods you would conduct yourself according to the gospel and suffer injustice as a good Christian. For yourself you would abide by the gospel and govern yourself according to Christ's word, gladly turning the other cheek and letting the cloak go with the coat when the matter concerned you and your cause. In this way the two propositions are brought into harmony with one another: at one and the same time you satisfy God's kingdom inwardly and the kingdom of the world outwardly. You suffer evil and injustice, and yet at the same time you punish evil and injustice; you do not resist evil, and yet at the same time, you do resist it. In the one case, you consider yourself and what is yours; in the other, you consider your neighbor and what is his. In what concerns you and yours, you govern yourself by the gospel and suffer injustice toward yourself as a true Christian; in what concerns the person or property of others, you govern yourself according to love and tolerate no injustice toward your neighbor. The gospel does not forbid this; to the contrary, in another place it actually commands it. …

You ask: Why did Christ and the apostles not bear the sword? Answer: You tell me, why did Christ not take a wife, or become a cobbler or a tailor? If an office or vocation were to be regarded as disreputable on the ground that Christ did not pursue it himself, what would become of all the offices and vocations other than the ministry, the one occupation he did follow? Christ pursued his own office and vocation, but he did not thereby reject any other. It was not incumbent upon him to bear the sword, for he was to exercise only that function by which his kingdom is governed and that actually serves his kingdom. Now, it is not essential to his kingdom that he be a married man, a cobbler, tailor, farmer, prince, hangman, or bailiff; neither is the secular sword or law essential to it, but only God's Word and Spirit. It is by these that his people are ruled inwardly. This is the office that he also exercised then and still exercises now, always bestowing God's Word and Spirit. And in this office the apostles and all spiritual rulers had to follow him. For they are so busily occupied with the spiritual sword, the Word of God, that to do their job properly they must perforce ignore the secular sword and leave it to others who do not have to preach, even though it is not contrary to their calling to use it, as I have said. For each one must attend to the duties of his own calling.

Therefore, although Christ did not bear or prescribe the sword, it is sufficient that he did not forbid or abolish it but rather confirmed it; just as it is sufficient that he did not abolish the estate of marriage but confirmed it, though without himself taking a wife or setting forth a teaching concerning it.

For he had to manifest himself wholly in connection with that estate and calling which alone expressly served his kingdom, lest from his example there should be deduced the justification or necessity of teaching and believing that the kingdom of God could not exist without matrimony and the sword and similar externals (since Christ's example is necessarily binding), when in fact it exists solely by God's Word and Spirit. This was and had to be Christ's peculiar function as the supreme king in this kingdom. Since not all Christians, however, have this same office (although they could have it), it is fitting that they should have some other external office by which God may also be served.

From all this it follows what the true meaning of Christ's words is in Matthew 5:39, "Do not resist evil," etc. Namely that Christians should be so disposed that they will suffer every evil and injustice without avenging themselves, and will not seek legal redress in the courts but have no need whatever for secular authority and law for their own sake. On behalf of others, however, they may and should seek vengeance, justice, protection, and help, and do as much as they can to achieve it. Likewise, government should, on its own initiative or through the instigation of others, help and protect them too, without any complaint, application, or instigation on their own part. If it fails to do this, they should permit themselves to be despoiled and slandered; they should not resist evil, as Christ's words say. …

The power of the authorities is limited

We come now to the main part of this treatise. Having learned that there must be secular government on earth, and how it is to be exercised in a Christian and salutary manner, we must now learn how long its arm is and how far its hand reaches, so that it does not reach too far and encroach upon God's kingdom and government. It is absolutely essential for us to know this, for where secular authority is given too wide a scope, intolerable and terrible injury follows; on the other hand, it is also not without injury where it is restricted too narrowly. In the one case, it punishes too much; in the latter case, too little. To err in this direction, however, and punish too little is more tolerable, for it is always better to let a scoundrel live than to put a godly person to death. The world has plenty of scoundrels anyway and must continue to have them, but godly people are scarce.

It is to be noted first that the two classes of Adam's children – the one in God's kingdom under Christ and the other in the kingdom of the world under secular government, as was said above – have two kinds of law. For every kingdom must have its own laws and statutes; without law no kingdom or government can survive, as everyday experience amply shows. Secular government has laws that extend no further than to life and property and external matters on earth, for God cannot and will not permit anyone but himself to rule over the soul. Therefore, where secular authority presumes to prescribe laws for the soul, it encroaches upon God's authority and only misleads souls and destroys them. We want to make this so clear that everyone will grasp it, and that our fine Junkers, the princes and bishops, will see what fools they are when they seek to coerce the people with their laws and commandments into believing this or that. …

It is therefore the height of folly when they command that one shall believe the Church, the Fathers, and the Councils, though there be no word of God for it. It is not the church but the Devil's apostles who command such things, for the church commands nothing unless it knows for certain that it is God's word. As St. Peter puts it, "Whoever speaks, let him speak as the word of God" (1 Peter 4:11). It will be a long time, however, before they can ever prove that the decrees of the councils are God's word. Still more foolish is it when they assert that kings, princes, and the crowd of ordinary people must believe thus and so. My dear man, we are not baptized into kings, or princes, or even into the crowd, but into Christ and God himself. Neither are we called kings, princes, or common people, but Christians. No one shall or can command the soul unless he is able to show it the way to heaven; but this no human being can do, only God alone. Therefore, in matters that concern the salvation of souls nothing but God's word shall be taught and accepted. …

If your prince or secular ruler commands you to side with the pope, to believe thus and so, or to get rid of certain books, you should say, "It is not fitting that Lucifer should sit at the side of God. Gracious sir, I owe you obedience in body and property; command me within the limits of your authority on earth, and I will obey. But if you command me to believe or to get rid of certain books, I will not obey; for then you are a tyrant and overreach yourself, commanding where you have neither the right nor the authority," etc. Should he seize your property on account of this and punish such disobedience, then blessed are you; thank God that you are worthy to suffer for the sake of the divine word. Let him rage, fool that he is; he will meet his judge. For I tell you, if you fail to withstand him, if you give in to him and let him take away your faith and your books, you have truly denied God. …

You should know that since the beginning of the world a wise prince is a rare bird indeed, and an upright prince even rarer. They are generally the biggest fools or the worst scoundrels on earth; therefore, one must constantly expect the worst from them and look for little good, especially in divine matters that concern the salvation of souls. They are God's jailers and hangmen; his divine wrath uses them to punish the wicked and to maintain outward peace. Our God is a great lord. Therefore he must also have such noble, highborn, and rich hangmen and bailiffs, and he desires that everyone accord them riches, honor, and fear in great abundance. It pleases his divine will that we call his hangmen gracious lords, fall at their feet, and be subject to them in all humility, so long as they do not ply their trade too far and try to become shepherds instead of hangmen. If a prince should happen to be wise, upright, or a Christian, that is one of the great miracles, the most precious token of divine grace upon his land. For the usual course of events accords with the passage from Isaiah 3:4, "I will make children their princes, and open-mouthed fools shall rule over them"; and in Hosea 13:11, "I will give you a king in my anger, and take him away in my wrath." The world is too wicked, and does not deserve to have many wise and upright princes. Frogs must have their storks.

Again you say, "Secular authority is not forcing anyone to believe but merely seeing to it externally that no one deceives the people by false doctrine; how could heretics otherwise be restrained?" Answer: This the bishops should do, for this office has been entrusted to them and not to the princes. Heresy can never be restrained by force. One will have to tackle the problem in some other way, for heresy must be opposed and dealt with otherwise than with the sword. God's word must do the fighting here. If it does not succeed, then secular authority will certainly not succeed either, even if it were to drench the world in blood. Heresy is a spiritual matter, which cannot be hacked to pieces with iron, consumed by fire, or drowned in water. God's word alone avails here, as Paul says in 2 Corinthians 10:4–5, "Our weapons are not carnal, but mighty in God to destroy every argument and proud obstacle that exalts itself against the knowledge of God, and to take every thought captive in the service of Christ." …

Principles for the rule of a Christian Administration

Now that we know how far secular authority extends, the time has come to inquire how a prince should make use of it. This is for the sake of those princes – of whom there are very few indeed – who would like to be Christian princes and lords as well, and who desire to enter into the life to come. Christ himself describes the nature of secular princes in Luke 22:25, where he says, "The princes of this world exercise lordship, and those that are in authority proceed with force." For if they are lords by birth or by election they think it only right that they should be served and should rule by force. He who would be a Christian prince must certainly lay aside any intent to exercise lordship or to proceed with force. For cursed and condemned is every sort of life lived and sought for the benefit and good of one's self; cursed are all works not done in love. They are done in love, however, when they are directed not toward one's own pleasure, benefit, honor, comfort, and welfare but wholeheartedly toward the benefit, honor, and welfare of others. …

First. He must take thought for his subjects, and devote himself wholeheartedly to them. This he does when he directs his every thought to making himself useful and beneficial to them; when instead of thinking, "the land and people belong to me, I will do what best pleases me," he thinks rather, "I belong to the land and the people, I shall do what is useful and good for them. My concern will be not how to lord it over them and dominate them, but how to protect and maintain them in peace and plenty." He should picture Christ to himself, and say, "Behold, Christ, the highest prince, came to serve me; he did not seek to gain power, goods, and honor from me, but considered only my need, and directed all things to the end that I should gain power, goods, and honor from him and through him. I will do likewise, seeking from my subjects not my own advantage but theirs. I will use my office to serve and protect them, listen to them and defend them, and govern to the sole end that they, not I, may benefit and profit from my rule." Thus should a prince in his heart empty himself of his power and authority, and take unto himself the needs of his subjects, dealing with them as though they were his own needs. For this is what Christ did for us (Philippians 2:7); and these are the proper works of Christian love.

Now you will say, "Who would then want to be a prince? That would make the princely estate the worst on earth, full of trouble, labor, and unpleasantness. What would become of princely amusements - dancing, hunting, racing, gaming, and similar worldly pleasures?" I answer: We are not here teaching how a secular prince is to live, but how a secular prince is to be a Christian, so that he may also reach heaven. Who is not aware that a prince is a rare beast in heaven? I do not speak with any hope that secular princes will give heed, but on the chance that there might be one who would also like to be a Christian, and to know how he should act. Of this I am certain, that God's word will not bow down or submit to princes; princes must rather submit themselves to God's word. It is sufficient for me simply to point out that it is not impossible for a prince to be a Christian, although it is a rare thing and beset with difficulties. If they would so manage things that their dancing, hunting, and racing were done without injury to their subjects, and if they would otherwise conduct their office in love toward them, God would not be so harsh as to begrudge them their dancing and hunting and racing. But they would soon find out for themselves that if they gave their subjects the care and attention required by their office, many a fine dance, hunt, race, and game would have to be missed. …

Are wars allowed? Is it permissible for a Christian to be a soldier?

Closely connected with the question of authority is the question: Are Christian rulers allowed to wage wars, and is it right for Christians to be soldiers? It was Luther's principle to follow the New Testament strictly in matters of theology and ethics, so that one would suppose that he would say no to both questions, for Jesus had given the clear commandment: "Love your enemies …" (Matthew 5:44). Luther indeed dealt with this issue in 1526, and declared that warfare is a "work of love", as long as it ultimately serves peace. However, in Luther's view, it was not permissible for subjects to wage war against the authorities, and he even prohibits the deposition of a tyrant by violent means. On the other hand, if a ruler has gone mad, he may be removed from office and imprisoned. It is also possible to refuse to do military service, in particular to participate in manifestly unjust wars.

Martin Luther, Ob Kriegsleute auch in seligem Stande sein können (1526): WA, Vol. 19, pp. 616–662.
Translation: AL, Vol. 5, pp. 192–227.

It is not my intention to explain here at length how the occupation and work of a soldier are right and godly in themselves because I have written a great deal about this in my book *Temporal [Secular] Authority: To What Extent It Should Be Obeyed*. Indeed, I might boast here that not since the time of the apostles have the temporal sword and temporal government been so clearly described or so highly praised as by me. Even my enemies must acknowledge this. But the true reward that I have earned for this is that my doctrine has been critiqued and condemned as seditious and as encouraging resistance to rulers. God be praised for that! For because the sword has been instituted by God to punish the evil, protect the good, and preserve peace (Romans 13:1–4; 1 Peter 2:13–14), it is powerfully and sufficiently proven that war and killing, along with all the things that accompany war and martial law, have been instituted by God. What else is war but the punishment of wrong and evil? Why does anyone go to war other than a desire for peace and obedience?

Now slaying and robbing do not seem to be an act of love. A simple man therefore thinks that this is not a Christian deed and that Christians should not do this. In truth, however, even this is a work of love. A good doctor, faced with a grave disease, must sometimes amputate or destroy a hand, foot, ear, or eye, to save the body. Looking only at the amputated organ he appears to be a cruel and merciless man. But looking at it from the perspective of the body, which the doctor wants to save, he is in truth a fine and upright man who is doing a good Christian deed as far as the work itself is concerned.

In the same way, when I think of the work of a soldier who punishes the wicked, kills the evildoer, and creates so much misery, it seems to be an un-Christian work, completely contrary to Christian love. But when I think of how it protects the good – wife and child, house and farm, property and honor – and keeps and preserves the peace, then I see how precious and godly this work is; and I observe that it also amputates a leg or a hand, so that the whole body does not perish. For if the sword were not on guard to preserve the peace, everything in the world would be ruined by upheaval. Therefore, such a war is nothing other than a very brief turmoil that prevents an everlasting and immeasurable upheaval – a small misfortune that prevents a great misfortune. …

To sum up, in thinking about a soldier's office we must not focus on the killing, burning, striking, hitting, seizing, etc. This is what children see with their limited and restricted vision when they regard a doctor as only a sawbones who amputates the hand or the leg, but do not see that he does this in order to save the whole body. So, too, we must look upon the office of the soldier or the sword with the eyes of an adult and see why this office slays and acts so cruelly. Then it will prove itself to be an office that is, in itself, godly – as needful and useful to the world as eating and drinking or any other work. There are, however, some who abuse this office, and strike and kill people needlessly simply because of their own impulsive desires. But that is the fault of the persons, not of the office, for where is there an office or a work or anything else so good that self-willed, wicked people do not abuse it? They are like crazed physicians who would needlessly amputate a healthy hand just because they wanted to. Indeed, they are a part of that general disorder that must be prevented by just wars and the sword and be forced into peace. It always happens, and always has happened, that those who begin war unnecessarily are defeated. For ultimately, they cannot escape God's judgment and sword. In the end God's justice finds them and strikes …

So then, we have this to say about people who live under military law or who are involved in fighting a war. First, war may be made by three kinds of people. When an equal makes war against his equal – that is, neither of the two persons is the vassal or subject of the other even though one may not be as great or glorious or mighty as the other. Second, an overlord may fight against his subject. Or a subject may fight against his overlord.

Now let us take the third case first. Here is what the law says, "No one shall fight or make war against his overlord; for a man owes his overlord obedience, honor, and fear" (Romans 13:1–7). If you chop over your head, the chips fall in your eyes. And Solomon says, "If you throw a stone into the air, it will land on your own head" (Proverbs 26:27). That is the law in a nutshell. God has instituted it and humans have accepted it – for it is impossible both to obey and to resist, to be subject to your lords and to disdain them. …

It is only right that if a prince, king, or lord becomes insane, he should be deposed and put under restraint, for he is no longer to be considered a human since his reason is gone. "That is true," you say, "a raving tyrant is also clearly insane; or is to be considered even worse than an insane man, for he does much more harm." Here an answer is problematic, for such arguments seem very impressive and seem to be in accord with justice and equity. Nevertheless, it is my opinion that madmen and tyrants are not the same, for a madman can neither do nor tolerate anything reasonable. There is no hope for him because the light of reason has gone out. A tyrant, however, may do things that are far worse, but he still has a conscience and he still knows that he is doing wrong. There is also hope that he may improve, allowing someone to talk to him and instruct him, and that he might follow this advice. We can never hope that an insane man will do this for he is like a clod or a stone.

Furthermore, it would have bad consequences or set a bad example. If it is considered permissible to murder or depose tyrants, the practice soon spreads and it would become commonplace to arbitrarily call men tyrants who are not tyrants, and even to kill them if the mob takes a notion to do so. Roman history shows us clearly how this can happen. They killed many of their emperors simply because they did not like him or he did not do what they wanted, that is, let them be lords and make him their fool. This happened to Galba, Pertinax, Gordian, Alexander, and others. We dare not encourage the mob very much. They go crazy too quickly; and in such cases it is better to take ten ells from it than to allow it a hands-breadth, or even a fingers-breadth. And it is better for the tyrants to wrong them a hundred times than for the mob to treat the tyrant unjustly even once. If injustice is to be suffered, then it would be better for subjects to suffer it from their rulers than for the rulers to suffer it from their subjects. For the mob has no moderation and does not even know what moderation is. And in every mob there are more than five tyrants hiding. Now it is better to suffer injustice from one tyrant, that is, from the ruler, than to suffer injustice from unnumbered tyrants in a mob. …

A second question: "Suppose my lord were wrong in going to war?" I reply: If you know for sure that he is wrong, then you should fear and obey God more than men, Acts 5:29, and you should neither fight nor serve, for you cannot have a good conscience before God. "Yes," you say, "but my lord forces me to do it - he would take away my fief and refuse to give me my money, pay, and wages. In addition, I would be despised and shamed as a coward, even worse, as perjurer who deserted his lord in need." I answer: You must take that risk and, for God's sake, let whatever happens, happen. He can restore it to you a hundredfold, as he promises in the gospel, "Whoever leaves house, farm, wife, and property, will receive a hundredfold," etc. (Matthew 19:29).

You will also face this same danger in other occupations where the authorities compel you to act unjustly. But since God will have us leave even father and mother for his sake, we must certainly also leave lords for his sake. But if you do not know, or cannot find out, whether your lord is wrong, you should not weaken your obedience to conscience for the sake of an uncertain justice. Rather you should think the best of your lord, as is the way of love, for "love believes all things" and "does not think evil," 1 Corinthians 13:4–7. So, then, you are secure and can walk well before God. If they put you to shame or call you disloyal, it is better that God honors you as loyal and honest than for the world to call you loyal and honest. What good would it do you if the world thought of you as a Solomon or a Moses, when in God's judgment you were considered as bad as Saul or Ahab? …

Criticism of merchants and big business

It is not very well known that Luther also commented on economic issues. For a long time, his critical statements on this subject were considered completely outdated, but this could change. Referring to exclusion and inequality in the capitalist system, Pope Francis said in 2013, "Such an economy kills", daring to touch upon a taboo. Islam also denounces a monetary economy in which capital is increased purely by speculation. In 2015, the first bank in Germany was opened which operates according to Islamic principles, including the prohibition of charging interest for financial loans. For Luther, as for the Church of the Middle Ages, taking interest was unacceptable for the Christian faith. At that time, he sided with the conservatives in these matters. During the 16th century, a liberal attitude gained ground, first in the Roman Church and later among the Protestants as well, paving the way for modern capitalism.

As early as 1520, in his tract to the nobility, Luther had commented briefly on economic issues and attacked the Fuggers. In 1524, he turned to the subject again in a separate paper laying out the principles.

Martin Luther, Von Kaufhandlung und Wucher (1524):
WA, Vol. 15, pp. 293–322.
Translation: AL, Vol. 5, pp. 135–162.

The holy gospel, now that it has come to light, rebukes and reveals all the "works of darkness," as St. Paul calls them in Romans 13:12. For it is a brilliant light, which illumines the whole world and teaches how evil are the works of the world, and shows the true works we ought to do for God and our neighbor. As a result even some of the merchants have been awakened and become aware that in their trading many a wicked trick and hurtful financial practice is in use. It is to be feared that the words of Ecclesiasticus apply here, namely, that business people can hardly be without sin (Ecclesiasticus 26:29). Indeed, I think St. Paul's saying in the last chapter of the first epistle to Timothy fits the case, "The love of money is the root of all evil" (1 Timothy 6:10), and again, "Those who desire to be rich fall into the Devil's snare and into many useless and hurtful desires that plunge individuals into ruin and perdition" (1 Timothy 6:9). …

First. Among themselves business people have a common rule that is their chief maxim and the basis of all their sharp practices, where they say: "I may sell my goods as high as I can." They think this is their right. Thus occasion is given for avarice, and every window and door to hell is opened. What else does it mean but this: I care nothing about my neighbor; so long as I have my profit and satisfy my greed, of what concern is it to me if it injures my neighbor in ten ways at once? There you see how shamelessly this maxim flies squarely in the face not only of Christian love but also of natural law. How can there be anything good then in business? How can it be without sin when such injustice is the chief maxim and rule of the whole business? On such a basis trade can be nothing but robbing and stealing the property of others. …

The rule ought not to be, "I may sell my wares as dear as I can or will," but, "I may sell my wares as dear as I ought, or as is right and fair." For your selling ought not to be an act that is entirely within your own power and discretion, without law or limit, as though you were a god and beholden to no one. Because your selling is an act performed with your neighbor, it should rather be so governed by law and conscience that you do it without harm and injury to him, your concern being directed more toward doing him no injury than toward making money for yourself. But where are there such business people? How few merchants there would be, and how trade would decline, if they were to amend this evil rule and put things on a fair and Christian basis!

You ask, then, "How dear may I sell? How am I to arrive at what is fair and right so I do not take increase from neighbor or overcharge him?" Answer: That is something that will never be governed either by writing or speaking; nor has anyone ever undertaken to fix the value of every commodity, and to increase or lower prices accordingly. The reason is this: goods are not all alike; one is transported a greater distance than another and one involves greater outlay than another. In this respect, therefore, everything is and must remain uncertain, and no fixed determination can be made, any more than one can designate a certain city as the place from which all wares are to be brought, or establish a definite cost price for them. It may happen that the same wares, brought from the same city by the same road, cost vastly more in one year than they did the year before because the weather was worse, or the road, or because something else happened that increased the expense at one time over that at another time. Now it is fair and right that a merchant take as much profit on his wares as will reimburse him for their cost and compensate him for his trouble, his labor, and his risk. Even a farmhand must have food and pay for his labor. Who can serve or labor for nothing? The gospel says, "The laborer deserves his wages" (Luke 10:7).

But in order not to leave the question entirely unanswered, the best and safest way would be to have the political authorities appoint wise and honest men to compute the costs of all sorts of wares and accordingly set prices which would enable the merchant to get along and provide for him an adequate living, as is being done at certain places with respect to wine, fish, bread, and the like. But we Germans have too many other things to do; we are too busy drinking and dancing to provide for rules and regulations of this sort. Since this kind of ordinance therefore is not to be expected, the next best thing is to let goods be valued at the price for which they are bought and sold in the common market, or in the land generally. In this matter we can accept the proverb, "Follow the crowd and you won't get lost." Any profit made in this way I consider honest and proper, because here there is always the risk involved of having to suffer loss in wares and outlay, and excessive profits are scarcely possible. …

In determining how much profit you ought to take from your business and your labor, there is no better way to reckon it than by computing the amount of time and labor you have put into it, and comparing that with the effort of a day laborer who works at some other occupation and determine how much he earns in a day. On that basis figure how many days you have spent in getting your wares and bringing them to your place of business, and how much labor and risk was involved; for a great amount of labor and time ought to have a correspondingly greater return. That is the most accurate, the best, and the most definite advice and direction that can be given in this matter. Let those who dislike it, improve it themselves. I base my case (as I have said) on the gospel that the laborer deserves his wages (Luke 10:7); and Paul also says in 1 Corinthians 9:7, "He who tends the flock should get some of the milk. Who can go to war at his own expense?" If you have a better ground than that, you are welcome to it. …

We return now to the merchants' tricks. Some of them,

when they see that they cannot otherwise effect their selfish profiteering transactions and establish their monopolies because others have the same goods and wares, proceed to sell their goods so dirt cheap that the others cannot meet the competition, and are forced either to withhold their goods from sale, or to face ruin by selling them as cheaply as their competitors do. Thus, the greedy ones get their monopoly after all. Such fellows are not worthy to be called human beings or to live among people in a community; they are not even worth admonishing or instructing, for their envy and greed is so open and shameless that even at the cost of their own losses they cause loss to others, in order that they may have the whole place to themselves. The temporal authorities would do right if they took from such fellows everything they had, and drove them out of the country. It would scarcely have been necessary to tell of such practices, but I wanted to include them so that one might see what great villainy there is in trade and commerce, and to make evident to everyone what is going on in the world, in order that all may know how to protect themselves against such a dangerous class. …

On the trading companies I ought to say a good deal, but the whole subject is such a bottomless pit of avarice and wrongdoing that there is nothing in it that can be discussed with a good conscience. Who is so stupid that he cannot see that the trading companies are nothing but pure monopolies? Even the temporal laws of the heathen forbid them as openly harmful to the whole world, to say nothing of divine right and Christian law. They control all commodities, deal in them as they please, and practice without concealment all the tricks that have been mentioned. They raise or lower prices at their pleasure. They oppress and ruin all the small businessmen, like the pike, the little fish in the water, just as if they were lords over God's creatures and immune from all the laws of faith and love.

So it happens that all over the world spices must be bought at whatever price they choose to set, and they vary it from time to time. This year they raise the price of ginger, next year that of saffron, or vice versa; so that in the end it all comes out the same: they do not have to suffer any loss, injury, or risk. If the ginger spoils or they have to take a loss on it, they make it up on saffron, and vice versa, so that they make sure of their profit. All this is contrary to the natural order, not only of merchandise, but of all temporal goods, which God wills should be subject to risk and uncertainty. But they have found a way to make safe, certain, and continual profit out of unsafe, uncertain, and perishable goods; though because of it all the world must be sucked dry and all the money sink and swim in their gullets.

How could it ever be right and according to God's will that an individual in such a short time should grow so rich that he could buy out kings and emperors? They have brought things to such a pass that everybody else has to do business at the risk of loss, winning this year and losing next year, while they themselves can always win, making up their losses by increased profits. It is no wonder that they quickly appropriate the wealth of the whole world, for a pfennig that is permanent and sure is better than a gulden that is temporary and uncertain. But these companies are always dealing with permanent and sure gulden for our temporary and uncertain pfennigs. Is it any wonder that they become kings and we beggars?

Kings and princes ought to look into this matter and forbid them by strict laws. But I hear that they have a finger in it themselves, and the saying of Isaiah 1:23 is fulfilled, "Your princes have become companions of thieves." They hang thieves who have stolen a gulden or half a gulden, but do business with those who rob the whole world and steal more than all the rest, so that the proverb remains true, "Big thieves hang little thieves." As the Roman senator Cato said, "Simple thieves lie in dungeons and stocks; public thieves walk abroad in gold and silk." What will God say to this at last? He will do as he says through Ezekiel: princes and merchants, one thief with the other, he will melt together like lead and bronze (Ezekiel 22:20) as when a city burns to the ground, so that there shall be neither princes nor merchants anymore. That time, I fear, is already at the door. We do not think of amending our lives, no matter how great our sin and wrong. So, too, God cannot leave wrong unpunished.

This is why no one need ask how he may with a good conscience be a member of a trading company. My only advice is this: Get out; they will not change. If the trading companies are to stay, right and honesty must perish; if right and honesty are to stay, the trading companies must perish. The bed is too narrow, says Isaiah, one must fall out, the covering is too small, it will not cover both (Isaiah 28:20).

Luther says no to the peasants' revolt

As early as 1520, in his nobility tract, Luther had already held up the peasants as an example to the merchants: "I know full well that it would be a far godlier thing to increase agriculture and decrease commerce." A few years later, the peasants came forward with social demands. In their "Twelve Articles", a program that was printed and widely distributed, they demanded the abolition of serfdom, relief from taxes and the free election of pastors in village communities. The discontented peasants grouped together in "brotherly unions" and took up arms, first of all in Southern Germany, later in other regions, especially in Thuringia. They made attacks on castles and monasteries. The peasants wanted to take back by force the resources which had been taken from them. At first they proposed negotiations, but then they resorted to violence. The Peasants' War began in March 1525, and ended a few months later with a crushing defeat of the peasants. On several occasions, Luther made his opinion on the peasants' uprising known. When he heard of orgies of violence, he distanced himself from the peasants as well as from those in the Church who supported them, such as Thomas Müntzer, and called on the authorities to take violent action against the peasants and their accomplices. He was interested, on the one hand, in maintaining order and the sovereignty of the authorities, while on the other hand he was concerned that the Reformation could be discredited because of the outbreaks of violence. Nevertheless, he also repeated the proposal for negotiations and called for leniency with those who were merely followers of the movement.

Luther did not always prove to be peace–loving. On several occasions he called for the use of force, not only against the peasants, but also against the Jews, the Christian Anabaptists, the Turks, as well as against the pope and other representatives of the old church. This aspect of Luther was also reflected in illustrations that were published during his lifetime. Hans Holbein, a painter from Basel, depicted Luther in 1522 as Hercules Germanicus, the German Hercules. In ancient mythology, Hercules was a demigod who braved many dangers and killed several monsters. In Holbein's picture, Luther is decapitating medieval theologians. This was naturally meant symbolically, for they were already dead, and Luther was only using arguments to withstand them.

Martin Luther Wider die räuberischen und mörderischen Rotten der Bauern (1525): WA, Vol. 18, pp. 344–361.
Translation: LW, Vol. 46, pp. 45–55.

In my earlier book on this matter, I did not venture to judge the peasants, since they had offered to be corrected and to be instructed; and Christ in Matthew 7:1 commands us not to judge. But before I could even inspect the situation, they forgot their promise and violently took matters into their own hands and are robbing and raging like mad dogs. All this now makes it clear that they were trying to deceive us and that the assertions they made in their *Twelve Articles* were nothing but lies presented under the name of the gospel. To put it briefly, they are doing the devil's work. This is particularly the work of that archdevil who rules at Mühlhausen[8], and does nothing except stir up robbery, murder, and bloodshed; as Christ describes him in John 8:44, "He was a murderer from the beginning." Since these peasants and wretched people have now let themselves be misled and are acting differently than they promised, I, too, must write differently of them than I have written, and begin by setting their sin before them, as God commands Isa-

8 Thomas Müntzer, a former adherent of Luther, leader of the German peasant uprising in 1525.

iah (Isaiah 58:1) and Ezekiel (Ezekiel 2:7), on the chance that some of them may see themselves for what they are. Then I must instruct the rulers how they are to conduct themselves in these circumstances.

The peasants have taken upon themselves the burden of three terrible sins against God and man; by this they have abundantly merited death in body and soul. In the first place, they have sworn to be true and faithful, submissive and obedient, to their rulers, as Christ commands when he says, "Render to Caesar the things that are Caesar's" (Luke 20:25). And Romans 13:1 says, "Let every person be subject to the governing authorities." Since they are now deliberately and violently breaking this oath of obedience and setting themselves in opposition to their masters, they have forfeited body and soul, as faithless, perjured, lying, disobedient rascals and scoundrels usually do. St. Paul passed this judgment on them in Romans 13:2 when he said that those who resist the authorities will bring a judgment upon themselves. This saying will smite the peasants sooner or later, for God wants people to be loyal and to do their duty.

In the second place, they are starting a rebellion, and are violently robbing and plundering monasteries and castles which are not theirs; by this they have doubly deserved death in body and soul as highwaymen and murderers. Furthermore, anyone who can be proved to be a seditious person is an outlaw before God and the emperor; and whoever is the first to put him to death does right and well. For if a man is in open rebellion, everyone is both his judge and his executioner; just as when a fire starts, the first man who can put it out is the best man to do the job. For rebellion is not just simple murder; it is like a great fire, which attacks and devastates a whole land. Thus rebellion brings with it a land filled with murder and bloodshed; it makes widows and orphans, and turns everything upside down, like the worst disaster. Therefore let everyone who can, smite, slay, and stab, secretly or openly, remembering that nothing can be more poisonous, hurtful, or devilish than a rebel. It is just as when one must kill a mad dog; if you do not strike him, he will strike you, and a whole land with you.

In the third place, they cloak this terrible and horrible sin with the gospel, call themselves "Christian brethren," take oaths and submit to them, and compel people to go along with them in these abominations. Thus they become the worst blasphemers of God and slanderers of his holy name. Under the outward appearance of the gospel, they honor and serve the devil, thus deserving death in body and soul ten times over. I have never heard of a more hideous sin. I suspect that the devil feels that the Last Day is coming and therefore he undertakes such an unheard-of act, as though saying to himself, "This is the end, therefore it shall be the worst; I will stir up the dregs and knock out the bottom." God will guard us against him! See what a mighty prince the devil is, how he has the world in his hands and can throw everything into confusion, when he can so quickly catch so many thousands of peasants, deceive them, blind them, harden them, and throw them into revolt, and do with them whatever his raging fury undertakes.

It does not help the peasants when they pretend that according to Genesis 1 and 2, all things were created free and common, and that all of us alike have been baptized. For under the New Testament, Moses does not count; for there stands our Master, Christ, and subjects us, along with our bodies and our property, to the emperor and the law of this world, when he says, "Render to Caesar the things that are Caesar's" (Luke

20:25). Paul, too, speaking in Romans 13:1 to all baptized Christians, says, "Let every person be subject to the governing authorities." And Peter says, "Be subject to every ordinance of man" (1 Peter 2:13). We are bound to live according to this teaching of Christ, as the Father commands from heaven, saying, "This is my beloved Son, listen to him" (Matthew 17:5). For baptism does not make men free in body and property, but in soul; and the gospel does not make goods common, except in the case of those who, of their own free will, do what the apostles and disciples did in Acts 4:32–37. They did not demand, as do our insane peasants in their raging, that the goods of others - of Pilate and Herod - should be common, but only their own goods. Our peasants, however, want to make the goods of other men common, and keep their own for themselves. Fine Christians they are! I think there is not a devil left in hell; they have all gone into the peasants. Their raving has gone beyond all measure.

Now since the peasants have brought [the wrath of] both God and man down upon themselves and are already many times guilty of death in body and soul, and since they submit to no court and wait for no verdict, but only rage on, I must instruct the temporal authorities on how they may act with a clear conscience in this matter. First, I will not oppose a ruler who, even though he does not tolerate the gospel, will smite and punish these peasants without first offering to submit the case to judgment. He is within his rights, since the peasants are not contending any longer for the gospel, but have become faithless, perjured, disobedient, rebellious murderers, robbers, and blasphemers, whom even a heathen ruler has the right and authority to punish. Indeed, it is his duty to punish such scoundrels, for this is why he bears the sword and is "the servant of God to execute his wrath on the wrongdoer," Romans 13:4.

But if the ruler is a Christian and tolerates the gospel, so that the peasants have no appearance of a case against him, he should proceed with fear. First he must take the matter to God, confessing that we have deserved these things, and remembering that God may, perhaps, have thus aroused the devil as a punishment upon all Germany. Then he should humbly pray for help against the devil, for we are contending not only "against flesh and blood," but "against the spiritual hosts of wickedness in the air" (Ephesians 6:12; 2:2), which must be attacked with prayer. Then, when our hearts are so turned to God that we are ready to let his divine will be done, whether he will or will not have us to be princes and lords, we must go beyond our duty, and offer the mad peasants an opportunity to come to terms, even though they are not worthy of it. Finally, if that does not help, then swiftly take to the sword.

For in this case a prince and lord must remember that according to Romans 13:4, he is God's minister and the servant of his wrath and that the sword has been given him to use against such people. If he does not fulfil the duties of his office by punishing some and protecting others, he commits as great a sin before God as when someone who has not been given the sword commits murder. If he is able to punish and does not do it – even though he would have had to kill someone or shed blood – he becomes guilty of all the murder and evil that these people commit. For by deliberately disregarding God's command he permits such rascals to go about their wicked business, even though he was able to prevent it and it was his duty to do so. This is not a time to sleep. And there is no place for patience or mercy. This is the time of the sword, not the day of grace.

The rulers, then, should press on and take action in this matter with a good conscience as long as their hearts still beat. It is to the rulers' advantage that the peasants have a bad conscience and an unjust cause, and that any peasant who is killed is lost in body and soul and is eternally the devil's. But the rulers have a good conscience and a just cause; they can, therefore, say to God with all confidence of heart, "Behold, my God, you have appointed me prince or lord, of this I can have no doubt; and you have given me the sword to use against evildoers (Romans 13:4). It is your word, and it cannot lie, so I must fulfill the duties of my office, or forfeit your grace. It is also plain that these peasants have deserved death many times over, in your eyes and in the eyes of the world, and have been committed to me for punishment. If you will me to be slain by them, and let my authority be taken from me and destroyed, so be it: let your will be done. I shall be defeated and die because of your divine command and word and shall die while obeying your command and fulfilling the duties of my office. Therefore I will punish and smite as long as my heart beats. You will be the judge and make things right."

Thus, anyone who is killed fighting on the side of the rulers may be a true martyr in the eyes of God, if he fights with the kind of conscience I have just described, for he acts in obedience to God's word. On the other hand, anyone who perishes on the peasants' side is an eternal firebrand of hell, for he bears the sword against God's word and is disobedient to him, and is a member of the devil. And even if the peasants happen to gain the upper hand (God forbid!) – for to God all things are possible, and we do not know whether it may be his will, through the devil, to destroy all rule and order and cast the world upon a desolate heap, as a prelude to the Last Day, which cannot be far off – nevertheless, those who are found exercising the duties of their office can die without worry and go to the scaffold with a good conscience, and leave the kingdom of this world to the devil and take in exchange the everlasting kingdom. These are strange times, when a prince can win heaven with bloodshed better than other men with prayer!

Finally, there is another thing that ought to motivate the rulers. The peasants are not content with belonging to the devil themselves; they force and compel many good people to join their devilish league against their wills, and so make them partakers of all of their own wickedness and damnation. Anyone who consorts with them goes to the devil with them and is guilty of all the evil deeds that they commit, even though he has to do this because he is so weak in faith that he could not resist them. A pious Christian ought to suffer a hundred deaths rather than give a hairsbreadth of consent to the peasants' cause. O how many martyrs could now be made by the bloodthirsty peasants and the prophets of murder! Now the rulers ought to have mercy on these prisoners of the peasants, and if they had no other reason to use the sword with a good conscience against the peasants, and to risk their own lives and property in fighting them, this would be reason enough, and more than enough: they would be rescuing and helping these souls whom the peasants have forced into their devilish league and who, without willing it, are sinning so horribly and must be damned. For truly these souls are in purgatory; indeed, they are in the bonds of hell and the devil.

Therefore, dear lords, here is a place where you can release, rescue, help. Have mercy on these poor people! Let whoever can stab, smite, slay. If you die in doing it, good for you! A more blessed death can never be yours, for you die while obeying the divine word and commandment in Romans 13:1–7, and in loving service of your neighbor, whom you are rescuing from the bonds of hell and of the devil. And so I beg everyone who can to flee from the peasants as from the devil himself; those who do not flee, I pray that God will enlighten and convert. As for those who are not to be converted, God grant that they may have neither fortune nor success. To this let every pious Christian say, "Amen!" For this prayer is right and good, and pleases God; this I know. If anyone thinks this too harsh, let him remember that rebellion is intolerable and that the destruction of the world is to be expected every hour.

“Treat the Jews kindly!” (1523)

The farmers had set their hopes on the Reformation and were disappointed. In Germany, serfdom was not finally abolished until the 19th century. There were also other groups in the population who were disadvantaged and oppressed and had high expectations from the Reformation. This was especially true of the Jews, who had been subjected to persecution and expulsion in many cities of the Reich in the 15th century. There were no Jews in Wittenberg itself, for they had already been expelled in the early 14th century, so that Luther hardly had any personal contact with Jews. Nonetheless, he also dealt with this topic. Starting from his reflections on biblical theology, he adopted his own position on the Jewish issue in 1523 and made far–reaching proposals.

The reason why Luther came to write about Jesus’ Jewishness, and thus about the Jews, was that in 1523 the Roman Church had accused him of denying the virginity of Mary. His work on the Jews did not therefore have a missionary intention, and was not addressed to Jews, but it was also read by them.

Martin Luther, Dass Jesus Christus ein geborener Jude sei (1523):
WA, Vol. 11, pp. 307–336.
Translation: AL, Vol. 5, pp. 398–439.

A new lie about me is being circulated. I am supposed to have preached and written that Mary, the mother of God, was not a virgin either before or after the birth of Christ, but that she conceived Christ through Joseph, and had more children after that. …

But after all, it is such a poor miserable lie that I despise it and would rather not reply to it. In these past three years I have grown quite accustomed to hearing lies, even from our nearest neighbors. And they in turn have grown accustomed to the noble virtue of neither blushing nor feeling ashamed when they are publicly convicted of lying. They let themselves be chided as liars, yet continue their lying. Still they are the best Christians, striving with all that they have and are to devour the Turk and to extirpate all heresy.

Since for the sake of others, however, I am compelled to answer these lies, I thought I would also write something useful in addition, so that I do not vainly steal the reader's time with such dirty rotten business. Therefore, I will cite from Scripture the reasons that move me to believe that Christ was a Jew born of a virgin, that I might perhaps also win some Jews to the Christian faith. Our fools, the popes, bishops, sophists, and monks and nuns – the crude asses' heads – have hitherto so treated the Jews that anyone who wished to be a good Christian would almost have had to become a Jew. If I had been a Jew and had seen such dolts and blockheads govern and teach the Christian faith, I would sooner have become a hog than a Christian.

They have dealt with the Jews as if they were dogs rather than human beings; they have done little else than deride them and seize their property. When they baptize them they show them nothing of Christian doctrine or life, but only subject them to popishness and monkery. When the Jews then see that Judaism has such strong support in Scripture, and that Christianity has become a mere babble without reliance on Scripture, how can they possibly compose themselves and become right and good Christians? I have myself heard from pious baptized Jews that if they had not in our day heard the gospel they would have remained Jews under the cloak of Christianity for the rest of their days. For they acknowledge that they have never yet heard anything about Christ from those who baptized and taught them.

I hope that if one deals in a compassionate way with the Jews and instructs them carefully from Holy Scripture, many of them will become genuine Christians and turn again to the faith of their ancestors, the prophets and patriarchs. They will only be frightened further away from it if their Judaism is so utterly rejected that nothing is allowed to remain, and they are treated only with arrogance and scorn. If the apostles, who also were Jews, had dealt with us Gentiles as we Gentiles deal with the Jews, there would never have been a Christian among the Gentiles. Since they dealt with us Gentiles in such brotherly fashion, we in our turn ought to treat the Jews in a brotherly manner in order that we might convert some of them. For even we ourselves are not yet all very far along, not to speak of having arrived.

When we are inclined to boast of our position we should remember that we are but Gentiles, while the Jews are of the bloodline of Christ. We are aliens and in-laws; they are blood relatives, cousins, and brothers of our Lord. Therefore, if one is to boast of flesh and blood, the Jews are actually nearer to Christ than we are, as St. Paul says in Romans 9:5. God has also demonstrated this by God's own acts, for to no nation among the Gentiles has God granted so high an honor as to the Jews. For from among the Gentiles there have been raised up no patriarchs, no apostles, no prophets, indeed, very few genuine Christians either. And although the gospel has been proclaimed to all the world, yet God committed the Holy Scriptures, that is, the law and the prophets, to no nation except the Jews, as Paul says in Romans 3:2 and Psalm 147:19–20, "God declares the word to Jacob, God's statutes and ordinances to Israel. God has not dealt thus with any other nation; nor revealed God's ordinances to them."

Accordingly, I beg my dear papists, should they be growing weary of denouncing me as a heretic, to seize the opportunity of denouncing me as a Jew. Perhaps I may yet turn out to be also a Turk, or whatever else my fine gentlemen may wish. …

If the Jews should take offense because we confess our Jesus to be a man, and yet true God, we will deal forcefully with that from Scripture in due time. But this is too harsh for a beginning. Let them first be suckled with milk, and begin by recognizing this man Jesus as the true Messiah; after that they may drink wine, and learn also that he is true God. For they have been led astray so long and so far that one must deal gently with them, as people who have been all too strongly indoctrinated to believe that God cannot be human.

Therefore, I would request and advise that one deal gently with them and instruct them from Scripture; then some of them may come along. Instead of this we are trying only to drive them by force, slandering them, accusing them of having Christian blood if they don't stink, and I know not what other foolishness. So long as we thus treat them like dogs, how can we expect to work any good among them? Again, when we forbid them to labor and do business and have any human fellowship with us, thereby forcing them into usury, how is that supposed to do them any good?

If we really want to help them, we must be guided in our dealings with them not by papal law but by the law of Christian love. We must receive them cordially, and permit them to trade and work with us, that they may have occasion and opportunity to associate with us, hear our Christian teaching, and witness our Christian life. If some of them should prove stiff-necked, what of it? After all, we ourselves are not all good Christians either. Here I will let the matter rest for the present, until I see what I have accomplished. God grant us all his mercy. Amen

“We should set fire to the synagogues!” (1543)

In later years, Luther once again formed a fundamental opinion on the Jewish question. His two statements are twenty years apart – and worlds apart, as well. Unfortunately, he did not pursue the pro–Jewish, forward–looking ideas of 1523, but fell back into the hostile attitude he had known and adopted as a student and monk in Erfurt; this was based on his disappointment that the Jews, contrary to his expectations, were not prepared to recognize any testimony in the Old Testament that Jesus is the Messiah of Israel, and they did not want to convert to Christianity. In 1543, he published an anti–Jewish treatise which was later even quoted by the National Socialists: “On the Jews and Their Lies”. He went on to produce further texts and sermons in a similar vein. Luther did not even flinch from using the term “Saujuden” (“sow Jews”) either, calling the synagogues “sow schools” and their rabbis “swine”. Even his two very last sermons in February 1546 were directed against the Jews, demanding their expulsion. Mainly he accused them of hating Christians and practicing usury. But he also resorted to the stereotypical medieval allegations that Jews poisoned wells and murdered Christian children.

Martin Luther, Von den Juden und ihren Lügen (1543):
WA, Vol. 53, pp. 412–552.
Translation: AL, Vol. 5, pp. 572–576.

What shall we Christians do with this rejected and condemned people, the Jews? Since they live among us, we dare not tolerate their conduct, now that we are aware of their lying and reviling and blaspheming. If we do, we become sharers in their lies, cursing, and blasphemy. Thus we cannot extinguish the unquenchable fire of divine wrath, of which the prophets speak, nor can we convert the Jews. With prayer and the fear of God we must practice a tough mercy to see whether we might save at least a few from the glowing flames. We dare not avenge ourselves. Vengeance a thousand times worse than we could wish them already has them by the throat.

I shall give you my sincere advice: First, to set fire to their synagogues or schools and to bury and cover with dirt whatever will not burn, so that no one will ever again see a stone or cinder of them. This is to be done in honor of our Lord and of Christendom, so that God might see that we are Christians, and do not condone or knowingly tolerate such public lying, cursing, and blaspheming of his Son and of his Christians. For whatever we tolerated in the past unknowingly - and I myself was unaware of it - will be pardoned by God. But if we, now that we are informed, were to protect and shield such a house for the Jews, existing right before our very noses, in which they lie about, blaspheme, curse, vilify, and defame Christ and us (as was heard above), it would be the same as if we were doing all this and even worse ourselves, as we very well know.

In Deuteronomy 13:12 ff. Moses writes that any city that is given to idolatry shall be totally destroyed by fire, and nothing of it shall be preserved. If he were alive today, he would be the first to set fire to the synagogues and houses of the Jews. For in Deuteronomy 4:2 and 12:32 he commanded very explicitly that nothing was to be added to or subtracted from his law. And Samuel says in 1 Samuel 15:23 that disobedience to God is idolatry. Now the Jews' teaching at present is nothing but the ruminations of rabbis and the idolatry of disobedience, so that Moses has become entirely unknown among them (as we said before), just as in our own day the Bible became unknown under the papacy. So also, for Moses' sake, their schools cannot be tolerated; they defame him just as much as they do us. It is not necessary that they have their own free churches for this idolatry.

Second, I advise that their houses also be razed and destroyed. For they pursue in them the same aims as in their synagogues. Instead they might be lodged under a roof or in a barn, like the gypsies. This will bring home to them that they are not masters in our country, as they boast, but that they are living in exile and in captivity, as they incessantly wail and lament about us before God.

Third, I advise that all their prayer books and Talmudic writings, in which such idolatry, lies, curses, and blasphemy are taught, be taken from them.

Fourth, I advise that their rabbis be forbidden to teach henceforth on pain of loss of life and limb. For they have justly forfeited the right to such an office by holding the poor Jews captive with the saying of Moses (Deuteronomy 17:10 ff.) in which he commands them to obey their teachers on penalty of death, although Moses clearly adds: "what they teach you in accord with the law of the Lord." Those villains ignore that. They wantonly employ the poor people's obedience contrary to the law of the Lord and infuse them with this poison, cursing, and blasphemy. In the same way the pope also held us captive with the declaration in Matthew 16:18, "You are Peter," etc., inducing us to believe all the lies and deceptions that issued from his devilish mind. He did not teach in accord with the word of God, and therefore he forfeited the right to teach.

Fifth, I advise that safe conduct on the highways be abolished completely for the Jews. For they have no business in the countryside, since they are not lords, officials, tradesmen, or the like. Let them stay at home. I have heard it said that a rich

Jew is now traveling across the country with twelve horses – his ambition is to become a Kokhba[9] – devouring princes, lords, lands, and people with usury, so that the high lords view it with jealous eyes. If you great lords and princes will not forbid such usurers the highway legally, someday a mob may gather against them, when from this modest book they have learned the true nature of the Jews and how one should deal with them and not protect their doings. For you, too, must not and cannot protect them unless you wish to become participants in all their abominations in the sight of God. Consider carefully what good could come from this, and prevent it.

Sixth, I advise that usury be prohibited to them, and that all cash and treasure of silver and gold be taken from them and put aside for safekeeping. The reason for such a measure is that, as said above, they have no other means of earning a livelihood than usury, and by it they have stolen and robbed from us all they possess. Such funds should be used in no other way than the following: Whenever a Jew is sincerely converted, he should be handed one hundred, two hundred, or three hundred florins, as personal circumstances may suggest. With this he could set himself up in some occupation for the support of his poor wife and children, and the maintenance of the old or feeble. For such evil gains are cursed if they are not put to use with God's blessing in a good and worthy cause. …

Seventh, I recommend putting a flail, an ax, a hoe, a spade, a distaff, or a spindle into the hands of young, strong Jews and Jewesses, letting them earn their bread in the sweat of their brow, as was imposed on the children of Adam (Genesis 3:19).

---

9 Leader of a Jewish revolt against the Romans in the 2nd century.

For it is not fitting that they should let us accursed Goyim toil in the sweat of our faces while they, the holy people, idle away their time behind the stove, feasting and farting, and on top of all, boasting blasphemously of their lordship over the Christians because of our sweat. No, one should toss out these lazy rogues by the seat of their pants.

But if we are afraid that they might harm us or our wives, children, servants, cattle, etc., if they had to serve and work for us - for it is reasonable to assume that such noble lords of the world and venomous, bitter worms are not accustomed to working and would be very reluctant to humble themselves so deeply before the accursed Goyim - then let us emulate the common sense of other nations such as France, Spain, Bohemia, etc., compute with them how much their usury has extorted from us, divide this amicably, but then eject them forever from the country. For, as we have heard, God's anger with them is so intense that gentle mercy will only tend to make them worse and worse, while sharp mercy will reform them but little. Therefore, in any case, away with them! …

Turks, Mohammed, Islam, Koran

Luther commented not only on the Jews, but also on the Muslims on several occasions. He knew them mostly as Turks, whose armies advanced against the Empire from the south–east and besieged Vienna in 1529. Luther was familiar with the Koran and helped to ensure that it was printed for the first time in Latin in Basel in 1542/43 and thus made known to the West. Luther rejected Islam just as he did Judaism. In contrast to Judaism, however, Luther was able to discover in Muslims positive aspects of their religion and mentality.

Martin Luther, Eine Heerpredigt wider den Türken (1530):
WA, Vol. 30/2, pp. 149–197.
Translation: Neville Williamson.

Scripture prophesies that two cruel tyrants will devastate and destroy Christianity before the Day of Judgment, one of them in a spiritual manner, with cunning or false worship and teaching that contradicts the proper Christian faith and the gospel. Daniel 11:36 ff. describes how he will exalt himself above all gods and objects of worship, he whom Paul calls the Antichrist in 2 Thessalonians 2:4. This is the pope with his popery, of which we have written enough elsewhere. The other tyrant will act in the most beastly way, wielding the sword physically and bodily, as is abundantly prophesied in Daniel 7:7 f. and by Christ in Matthew 24:15, when he speaks of a tribulation such as has not yet been seen on earth. This is the Turk. Because the end of the world is at hand, the devil must first make a most dreadful attack on Christianity with his two mighty forces, dismissing us in the way that suits him before we rise to heaven.

Whoever will be a Christian at this time should take heart in Christ, no longer hoping for peace and good days. The time has come for the tribulation of this prophecy. Likewise, our hope and consolation for the future in Christ and our salvation is not far off, but will follow very quickly, as we will hear. Therefore, hold fast and be sure that the Turk is surely the devil's last and greatest fury against Christ, whereby he goes to the ultimate extreme; he will pour out his wrath upon Christ's kingdom and also bring the greatest punishment of God on earth against those ungrateful and ungodly people who despise and persecute Christ and his word, and doubtlessly also the prelude to hell and eternal punishment. For Daniel says that judgment and hell shall follow immediately after the Turk (Daniel 7:10). And events prove the truth of that, seeing the gruesome deeds of the Turk, who strangles, impales and massacres people - even women and children, young and old - who have done nothing to him, and acts as though he were the devil himself in his anger. For there has never been a kingdom that raged so murderously and furiously as his. ...

So now we have seen what we should think of the Turk and his Mohammedan kingdom in the light of the Holy Scriptures, namely that he is an enemy of God, blaspheming and persecuting Christ and his saints by sword and battle. He is intent upon waging war against Christ and his followers. For although other kings in former times persecuted Christians with the sword, their kingdom and rule had not been founded in order to blaspheme and make war on Christ, but it happened by chance, by abuse. If one king acted as a persecutor, a later king was good and stopped it again. So it was not the kingdoms or governments themselves that turned against Christ, but the people who were in government were sometimes evil. Yet Mohammed's sword and kingdom are directed against Christ, as though they had no other purpose, and could not be better employed than to blaspheme Christ and fight against him, as is proved by his Koran and the deeds he has done.

Knowing this, everyone can advise his conscience and be sure of his thoughts and behavior, should he be called to fight against the Turk. He should be in no doubt that he is fighting against the enemy of God and the blasphemer of Christ, indeed against the devil himself, when fighting against the Turk, if this war begins. If he kills a Turk, for example, he must not be worried that he is shedding innocent blood or killing a Christian, since he is most certainly killing an enemy of God and blasphemer of Christ, whom God himself has condemned to hellfire as an enemy of Christ and his saints in the book of Daniel 7. Therefore there cannot be any Christian or friend of God in the Turkish army, unless he denies Christ and will also become an enemy of God and his saints. Thus they all belong to the devil and are possessed by the devil, just like their master Mohammed and the Turkish emperor himself. …

Among the many other irritating things about the Turks, the most striking one is that their priests and clergy lead such serious, consistent, strict lives that one might think they were angels and not human beings. All our priests and monks in the papacy are a joke in comparison. The Turkish priests often go into a trance, even at table with other people, sitting there as though they were dead. Apart from that, they sometimes also do great miraculous signs. Who would not be amazed and impressed by this? But if you should meet such people, know and remember that they nonetheless have no knowledge or consideration for your creed or your Lord Jesus Christ. Therefore it must be false. For the devil can also be earnest, put on a stern face, fast a great deal, perform false miracles and delight his followers. But he cannot bear Jesus Christ or listen to him. Therefore be aware that these Turkish saints are saints of the devil, who want to become pious and blessed through their own great works and to help others without the one Savior, Jesus Christ. Thus they lead themselves astray, as well as all others who do not know or respect the faith in Jesus Christ, just as our monks wanted to help us get to heaven with their own holiness.

Secondly, you will also find that they often come together for prayer in their places of worship and pray with such discipline, quietude and beautiful gestures as you will not find anywhere in our churches. A special place there is set aside for the women, who are veiled so that no one can look at them. Our brothers who are imprisoned in Turkey even complain about our own people, because they do not behave and show themselves in our churches in such a quiet, orderly and spiritual way. Lo and behold, this could be another reason for you to think in your heart, "Truly, Christians do not behave and show themselves so well in their churches." In that case, press your thumb against one finger and think of Jesus Christ, whom they neither know nor respect. Then it is of no importance whether and how someone may behave, show himself or act. If they do not believe in Jesus Christ, be sure that God prefers eating and drinking in faith to fasting without faith. Better a few decent gestures in faith than many beautiful gestures without faith. Better a few prayers in faith than a multitude of prayers without faith. In the Gospel of Luke 7:39 ff., Christ judges that the poor sinner with her few gestures is more pious than Simon the leper with all his pomp. And the publican, a poor sinner, was better without fasting and religious exercises than the haughty

Pharisee with his fasting and all holiness (Luke 18:14). And speaking to the splendid, unbelieving Pharisees, Christ further said: "The publicans and harlots are going into the kingdom of God before you" (Matthew 21:31).

Thirdly, you will also find that pilgrimages are made there to the Turkish saints, who did not die believing in Christ, but sharing Mohammed's faith, as they confess and boast. The Turks make vows that they will visit them. They go there and invoke them, in the very same way that we have gone on our pilgrimages and called upon our saints. Many people find help, and many great signs take place, just as they did for us. We have written long and frequently about such false miracles which have ostensibly taken place in our country thanks to the saints, as we thought, and during the pilgrimages. The dead have been raised, the blind received their sight, the lame were able to walk, and so on. In Matthew 24:24, Christ proclaimed that the false Christs and false prophets would perform such miracles. Paul also said in 2 Thessalonians 2:9 that the elect would also be deceived. For it is no great matter for the devil to afflict a person so badly that this person, and everyone else, thinks he is blind, lame or dead. As soon as the devil has established idolatry in this way, driving people away from Christ and persuading them to call on the saints, in this case himself, then he will call a halt to the affliction, so that the person believes his saint has helped him. The devil is also artful enough to drive away real illnesses in some cases and heal real injuries. For he is a doctor above all medical doctors, and a prince of this world. Behold what miracles he performs with and through his magicians! What peculiar methods he uses to help them do unbelievable things. . . .

Fourthly, you will see that the Turks keep an outward appearance of being serious, strict and honorable. They drink no wine, they do not guzzle and gorge as we do. They do not dress so freely and loosely, build so magnificently, flaunt, swear and curse like us. They are highly obedient, disciplined and deferent to their emperor and lord. Their government is outwardly as orderly and efficient as we would like it to be in our German lands.

And though their law allows one man to have twelve wives and as many maidservants and concubines as he wishes in addition, whereby all his children share the inheritance equally, nonetheless they all hold their wives in great restraint and demand obedience from them. The husband seldom talks to one of his wives in front of other people or sits easily at her side or caresses her. Although such wives were married to their husbands by the priests, the men still retain the right and power to send away whomever they wish, regardless of whether she deserved such treatment or he loves her or is tired of her. In this way they keep their wives strictly under control. And although such a marriage is not a marriage before God, but more a pretense than a marriage, they still control their wives and ensure that they behave beautifully, so that there is none of this pertness, opulence and frivolity, none of this superfluous jewelry, luxury and splendor among those women as there is with us.

"No" to the council

In his tract to the nobility of 1520, Luther had called for a council to be convened in order to discuss and resolve the abuses within the Church. However, he always insisted that the council be "Christian" and "free". That meant that it should only accept the authority of the Bible and not be subordinate to the pope. Luther called for a council, but the popes had no intention of convening one, because they feared that it could represent a threat to themselves. This only changed in 1534 with the election of Pope Paul III, who was urged by the Emperor to look more closely into the idea of a council. He first issued a summons to a council in 1537, but it was not until 1545 that it really took place. The Protestants were forced to make a decision as to whether they should participate or not. Luther categorically refused to participate in the forthcoming council because it was not "Christian" and not "free". He addressed the subject in 1539 and at other times, criticizing the pope's procedure and questioning the sense of councils altogether. He also repeated, once again in vain, his proposal for a national council, which should be restricted to Germany and chaired by the emperor. When the papal Council of Trent gathered in 1545, no Protestants were present.

Martin Luther, Von den Konzilen und Kirchen (1539):
WA, Vol. 50, pp. 488–653.
Translation: AL, Vol. 3, pp. 324–443.

I often joined in the general laughter when I saw someone offer a morsel of bread on the tip of a knife to dogs and then, as they snapped at it, slap their snouts with the knife handle, so that the poor dogs not only lost the bread but also had to suffer pain. That is a good joke. It never occurred to me at that time that the devil could also play his jokes on us and consider us such wretched dogs, until I learned how the most holy father, the pope, with his bulls, books, and daily practices plays the same kind of a dog's joke on Christendom. But, Lord God, with what great harm to the soul and with what mockery of divine majesty! It is just what he is doing with the council now: the whole world has been waiting and clamoring for it; the good emperor and his whole empire have been working to attain it for nearly twenty years; and the pope has always made vain promises and put it off, offering the morsel of bread to the emperor, as to a dog, until, at the opportune moment, he slaps him on the snout while mocking him as his fool and dupe.

Now he is summoning the council for the third time; but he first sends his apostles into all lands to have kings and princes pledge their allegiance to the pope's doctrines. The bishops and their clergy concur in this strategy and absolutely refuse either to yield or to permit a reform, thus the course of the council is already determined, before it even convenes, namely, not to undertake any reforms, but to observe everything in accord with what has come to be present practice. Isn't that a splendid council? It has not yet convened, and already it has done what it was to do when it met, that is, to slap the emperor on the snout, and even more, to overtake the Holy Spirit and outstrip him by far! Yet I have feared, and often written and said, that they would not and could not hold a council unless they had first captured and controlled the emperor, kings, and princes, so as to have total freedom to decree whatever they pleased, to buttress their tyranny, and to oppress Christendom with far greater burdens than ever before.

In God's name, if you lords – emperor, kings, princes – like the way in which these accursed, damned people trample on your muzzles and rap your snouts, we have to let it happen and remember that they acted much worse in the past: they deposed kings and emperors, anathematized them, drove them out, betrayed them, murdered them, and vented their devilish malice on them, as history testifies; and they intend to go on doing that. Despite this, Christ will know how to find and preserve his Christendom, even against the gates of hell (Matthew 16:18), though emperors and kings neither would nor could help in any way. ...

In summary, put them all together, both fathers and councils, and you still will not be able to cull from them all the teachings of the Christian faith, even if you culled forever. If it had not been for Holy Scripture, the church, had it depended on the councils and fathers, would not have lasted long. And in proof of this: where do the fathers and councils get what they teach or deal with? Do you think that they first invented it in their own day, or that the Holy Spirit always inspired them with something new? How was the church preserved prior to these councils and fathers? Or were there no Christians before councils and fathers came up? That is why we must speak differently about the councils and fathers and look not at the letters but at the meaning. ...

We would have enough matters today that are sufficiently important and weighty to warrant the summoning of a council. For we poor, wretched Christians of small faith and, unfortunately, real *Misergi*, that is, Christians who hate work – those of us who are still left – would have to put the pope on trial ...

At this point we ask and cry for a council, requesting advice and help from all of Christendom against this arch-arsonist of churches and slayer of Christians ...

And even if other monarchs declined to do anything toward a principal council, Emperor Charles and the German princes could still hold a provincial council in Germany. Some think that this would result in a schism, but who knows? If we did our part in it and sincerely sought God's honor and the salvation of souls, God might yet touch and turn the hearts of the other monarchs so that they would, in time, approve and accept the judgment of this council. It could not happen suddenly; but if Germany were to accept it, it would also have an echo in other countries, whither it cannot or can hardly reach without a great preacher such as the council is, and without a strong voice heard from afar.

Well then, if we must despair of a council let us commend the matter to the true judge, our merciful God. …

“The Antichrist rules in Rome!”

In his “Address to the Christian Nobility” of 1520, Luther had already expressed his suspicion that the pope in Rome was the “beast from the sea” described in the Revelation of John (Revelation 13) and the “Antichrist” prophesied in 1 John 2:18, who would destroy the Church from within. Later, Luther repeatedly dealt with – and rejected – the pope’s claim to be the head of all Christians, which still obtains today. Furthermore, Luther energetically and polemically contradicted the infallibility, to which the pope already laid claim at that time, but which was not proclaimed as a dogma by the Roman Catholic Church until 1870. Also the pope’s exclusive claim to the “Apostolic See”, meaning the succession to the apostle Peter, was also denied by Luther. In 1545, in his fundamental and at the same time final work, he already designates the papacy in the title as “instituted by the devil”, not by Jesus or Peter.

Luther argues from the Bible and from history. He refers to the generally recognized church fathers of the 3rd, 4th and 5th centuries, Cyprian, Jerome and Augustine, as well as to a council that took place in Constantinople (not Chalcedon) in 680/81. In Gregory the Great, who served as Bishop of Rome from 590 to 604 and is also generally held in high esteem, Luther sees the last incumbent of this office who did not make excessive papal claims in connection with it. Boniface III, who reigned in 607, was for Luther the pope who started the ill–fated history of the papacy.

Luther’s life was rich in changes, and there are many discrepancies in his biography. This is also evident in the pictures that show Luther in different phases of his life. After 1525, the ascetic monk became a husband and family man who loved good food and abundant drink. The rebellious scholar full of innovative ideas became a sedate professor with a good salary. That is how Lucas Cranach the Younger portrayed him for the last time in 1546, shortly before his death. The last period of Luther’s life was also marked by disappointments and illnesses. This may also explain the polemical style of his later writings, which is almost unbearable for today's readers.

Martin Luther, Wider das Papsttum zu Rom,
vom Teufel gestiftet (1545): WA 54, pp. 195–299.
Translation: LW, Vol. 41, pp. 257–376.

It is very easy to prove that the pope is neither the commander or head of Christendom, nor lord of the world above emperor, councils, and everything, as he lies, blasphemes, curses, and raves in his decretals, to which the hellish Satan drives him. He himself knows full well – and it is as clear as the dear sun from all the decrees of the ancient councils, from all the histories, from the writings of the holy fathers, Jerome, Augustine, and Cyprian, and from all of Christendom before the first pope, who was called Boniface III – that the bishop of Rome was nothing more than a bishop and should still be that. St. Jerome dared to say freely, "All bishops are equal, all together they have inherited the throne of the apostles," and adds the example, "as the bishop of a small city – like Engubium and Rome, Regium and Constantinople, Thebes and Alexandria." He says that one is higher or lower than another because one bishopric is richer or poorer than the other. Other than this they are all equally the successors to the apostles, so he says. This (I say) the pope in Rome knows perfectly well, and he also knows that St. Jerome wrote this; and as proof, it is contained in the *Decretum*, as we read in C. XCIII. Still, the pope dares to lie so brazenly and blasphemously against it, and deceive the whole world.

In addition, St. Gregory, when it [the title "universal pope"] was offered to him by several great bishops, sharply refused it and writes that none of his predecessors had been so bold as to accept or wish to carry such a title, although the sixth council in Chalcedon had offered it to them; he closes by saying briefly and to the point that no one should call himself the highest bishop or head of the whole of Christendom, as many decrees also say, and furthermore, that the bishop of Rome too, though he is one of the greater ones, is nonetheless not to be called *universalis*, the head of "all" Christendom. This is the very plain truth, regardless of how he himself and his hypocrites martyr and crucify these words, for they are too clear and powerful. Thus their deeds are out in the open, for he has never had authority over the bishops in Africa, Greece, Asia, Egypt, Syria, Persia, etc., and never will have; indeed, at that time he did not have authority over the bishops in Italy either, especially those of Milan and Ravenna.

This St. Gregory was the last bishop of Rome, and the Roman church has not had another bishop since then, up to the present day, and will not get one either, unless a miraculous change should occur; instead, vain popes, who are masks of the devil (as you will hear), have ruled there and damaged all the churches physically and spiritually. It is certain, as was said, that at the time of St. Gregory there was no pope, and he himself, together with his predecessors, did not want to be pope; moreover, he condemned the papacy in many of his writings, although he had been painted with a papal crown and many lies have been made up about him. But he is not a pope and does not wish to be a pope, as his books testify to the disgrace of all the popes who have arisen after him and against him. …

Here we come to the really important points. It is now certain that the pope and his office is merely a figment of human imagination and invention, for as we have heard, he does not come from nor wish to come from the order of temporal authority. He does not and does not wish to come from the order of the church or the councils. Thus one knows for certain that not one letter of God's word will be found by him in Scripture; instead, he placed himself this high by his own arrogance, arbitrariness, and malice, then decorated himself with God's word, thereby blaspheming abominably and making an idol of himself. He filled Christendom with his horrible idolatry, he lied, cheated, and made those who believed and trusted this into damned idolaters, as though God had commanded it in his word; thus they were compelled to fear, honor, worship, and serve the devil in the name of God. There you have the pope, what he is, whence he comes, namely, a horror (as Christ says, Matthew 24:15) of all idolatry, brought forth by all the devils from the depths of hell.

"Yes," you say, "he really claims to come out of God's word and out of God, for in many decretals he quotes the passage in Matthew 16:18, 'You are Peter, and on this rock I will build my church. I will give thee the keys of the kingdom,' etc. That is as much as saying that the pope in Rome is lord over all Christendom." Truly, that might do it! Who could have missed such high reason in the most holy father? Someone really should have warned a poor fellow before he sinned so deeply and called the pope an ass, feel, idol, and devil. How fortunate for me that I tightened my belt; I was already getting a laughing fit from my shock over the pope's great reasoning and it might easily have happened, had I not been wearing trousers, that I would have made something people don't like to smell, so afraid and awed was I at such papal great wisdom! …

The Lord then says, "And I tell you, you are Peter, and on this rock will I build my church." In John 1:42, he calls him

Cephas, "You shall be called Cephas," *Keph* in Hebrew, *Kepha* in Chaldean, and *Petros* or *Petra* in Greek, *Rupes* in Latin, all of which mean *rock* in German – like the high rocks the castles are built on. Now the Lord wants to say, "You are Peter, that is, a man of rock. For you have recognized and named the right Man, who is the true rock, as Scripture names him, Christ. On this rock, that is, on me, Christ, I will build all of my Christendom, just as you and the other disciples are built on it through my Father in heaven, who revealed it to you." In plain German one would say, "You say (on behalf of all) that I am the Messiah or Christ, the Son of the living God; very well then, I say to you, you are a Christian, and I shall build my church on a Christian." For in German the word "Christ" means both the Lord himself, as one sings, "Christ the Lord is risen, Christ ascended to heaven," and he who believes in the Lord Christ, as one says, "You are a Christ." Thus Luke in Acts 11:26 says that the disciples in Antioch were first called Christians, which is why names have survived such as, "Christians, Christendom, Christian faith," etc. So here our Lord gives Simon, son of Jona, the name "man of rock" or "Christian" because he, from the Father, recognized the rock, or Christ, and praised him with his mouth on behalf of all the apostles.

From this it is clear enough that by the building of his church on the rock or on himself, Christ meant nothing else but (as was said above, from the apostles Peter and Paul) the common Christian faith, that whoever believes in Christ is built on this rock and will attain salvation, even against all the gates of hell; whoever does not believe in Christ is not built on this rock and must be damned, with all the gates of hell. This is the simple, single, certain understanding of these words, and there can be no other. This the words clearly and convincingly prove, and they agree with the words in Mark 16:16, "He who believes and is baptized will be saved," and with John 11:26, "Whoever believes in me shall never die." Yes, I say, remember well and mark diligently that the Lord in Matthew 16 does not speak of laws, Ten Commandments, or the works we should or could do, but of the Christian faith or the work of the Father, which he, with the Son and the Holy Spirit, performs in us, namely, that he spiritually builds us on the rock, his Son, and teaches us to believe in Christ, that we might become his house and dwelling, as is proven in 1 Peter 2:4–7 and Ephesians 2:19–22.

Further, "And I will give you the keys of the kingdom of heaven, and whatever you bind on earth shall be bound in heaven, and whatever you loose on earth shall be loosed in heaven" (Matthew 16:19). The Lord wants to provide well for his churches, built on him and believing in him. Because they should preach and confess the gospel before the whole world and govern on the basis that Christ Jesus is the Son of God, he wants to have their words honored and not scorned, as though he were speaking personally from heaven. Now he who hears the gospel from the apostles or churches and does not want to believe should be sentenced to be damned. Again, if he should fall after he has believed and will not convert back to faith, he should be sentenced in the same way – he should keep his sins and be damned. On the other hand, he who hears and believes the gospel, or turns from his sins back to faith, should have his sins forgiven and should attain salvation. And he will consider such a verdict in heaven as if he had spoken it himself. See, these are the keys of the kingdom of heaven and they should be used to give eternal retention and remission of sins in the church, not just at the time of baptism, or once in a lifetime, but continuously until the end - retention for the unrepentant and unbelievers, remission for the repentant and believers. …

Now if the pope could still stand stiffly and proudly, which he cannot, on the passage in Matthew 16, then we on the other hand stand even more proudly and stiffly on Matthew 18. It is not another Christ who speaks in Matthew 16 with St. Peter, and then in Matthew 18 with the other disciples, saying the same words and giving power to bind and loose sin. So let the pope go ahead with his St. Peter, binding and loosing what he can. We shall consider the power of the other apostles to bind and loosen to be the same as St. Peter's - even if a thousand St. Peters were one Peter, and the whole world were a pope, and, in addition, an angel from heaven were on his side! For we have here the Lord himself, over all angels and creatures, who says, "They shall all have the same power, keys, and office" - even two simple Christians assembled only in his name. The pope and all the devils shall not make a fool, liar, and drunkard out of this Lord for us; instead, we shall kick the pope with our feet and say he is a desperate liar, blasphemer, and idolatrous devil, who, in the name of St. Peter, has snatched the keys for himself, though Christ has given them to everyone in common, and who wants to make the Lord, in Matthew 16, a liar; indeed, this one should praise! …

The pope probably thinks the Holy Spirit is tied to Rome. If he could produce reliable seals and letters to prove it, he would have won. If he wants to be head of all the churches (which is impossible), then he must first prove to us that he and his descendants must, beyond a doubt, be the possessors, by inheritance, of the Holy Spirit, and cannot err. Yes, I would like to see those seals and briefs! For his allegation, based on Matthew 16:18, that the Roman church is built on the rock so that the gates of hell shall not overcome it has been clearly enough proven above to have been said of the whole of Christendom and not of the Roman papal see. And the summation is, as was said, that God sets no store in his realm by the great, high, powerful, many, wise, noble, etc., but, as Mary sings, "He has regarded the low estate of his handmaiden" (Luke 1:48). And as he says to his apostles in Matthew 18,3–4 and on many other occasions, "Whoever would be great among you must be the least, and whoever would be first among you must be your slave; even as I did not come to be served but to serve among you" (Matthew 20:26–28).

But in the papacy and all the decretals the main point is that he alone is the greatest, highest, and mightiest, to whom no one is equal, whom no one should condemn or judge, but to whom everyone should be subject, and by whom everyone should let himself be judged. And yet, at the same time, he claims to be a servant of all the servants of God – that is, in a Roman and popish way, lord of lords, king of kings, and set above all Christians, that is, above God, Christ, and the Holy Spirit, who lives and dwells in all Christians, John 15:4; 14:17, 23. It is he whom St. Paul calls in 2 Thessalonians 2:3, "The man of sin and the son of perdition," the Antichrist, who has rebelled against God and set himself up above him. Christendom has no head and can have none, except the only Son of God, Jesus Christ, who has seals and briefs so that he cannot err, and who is tied neither to Rome nor any other place. …

I must stop: I can no longer rummage in the blasphemous, hellish devil's filth and stench; someone else may read too. He who wants to hear God speak should read Holy Scripture. He who wants to hear the devil speak should read the pope's decretals and bulls. Oh, woe, woe, woe unto him who comes along and becomes pope or cardinal; it would be better for him if he had never been born (Matthew 26:24). Judas betrayed and killed the Lord, but the pope betrays and brings ruin upon the Christian church, which the Lord held more precious and dearer than himself or his blood, for he sacrificed himself for it. Woe unto you, pope!

"No fear of death!"

The Christian faith contains a hope beyond death. It also makes us ready for death and dying and is a consolation on the deathbed. In Luther's time, death was omnipresent. Many children died shortly after birth, many women died in childbed, countless lives were wiped out by epidemics. Between 1520 and 1530 Luther already reckoned with his imminent death. In 1519 he had written a short text in the way of a sermon intended to prepare Christians for dying and death.

In 1519, Luther's thinking is still quite traditional in many respects. The saints played a major role for him, and he still regarded the extreme unction – known nowadays as the Anointing of the Sick – as a valuable sacrament. But he also – already – emphasizes that faith alone is decisive. And in the question of predestination, he also already adopts the position that he later developed in his dispute with Erasmus: nobody should suffer uncertainty by worrying about divine election. Instead, the believer should hold on to God's promise of salvation.

Martin Luther, Ein Sermon von der Bereitung zum Sterben (1519):
WA, Vol. 2, pp. 680–697.
Translation: AL, Vol. 4, pp. 290–305.

First, since death marks a farewell from this world and all its activities, it is necessary that a man regulate his temporal goods properly or as he wishes to have them ordered, lest after his death there be occasion for squabbles, quarrels, or other misunderstanding among his surviving friends. This pertains to the physical or external departure from this world and to the surrender of our possessions.

Second, we must also take leave spiritually. That is, we must cheerfully and sincerely forgive, for God's sake, all men who have offended us. At the same time we must also, for God's sake, earnestly seek the forgiveness of all the people whom we undoubtedly have greatly offended by setting them a bad example or by bestowing too few of the kindnesses demanded by the law of Christian brotherly love. This is necessary lest the soul remain burdened by its actions here on earth.

Third, since everyone must depart, we must turn our eyes to God, to whom the path of death leads and directs us. Here we find the beginning of the narrow gate and of the straight path to life (Matthew 7:14). All must joyfully venture forth on this path, for though the gate is quite narrow, the path is not long. Just as an infant is born with peril and pain from the small abode of its mother's womb into this immense heaven and earth, that is, into this world, so man departs this life through the narrow gate of death. And although the heavens and the earth in which we dwell at present seem large and wide to us, they are nevertheless much narrower and smaller than the mother's womb in comparison with the future heaven. Therefore, the death of the dear saints is called a new birth, and their feast day is known in Latin as *natale*, that is, the day of their birth. However, the narrow passage of death makes us think of this life as expansive and the life beyond as confined. Therefore, we must believe this and learn a lesson from the physical birth of a child, as Christ declares, "When a woman is in travail she has sorrow; but when she has recovered, she no longer remembers the anguish, since a child is born by her into the world" (John 16:21). So it is that in dying we must bear this anguish and know that a large mansion and joy will follow.

Fourth, such preparation and readiness for this journey are accomplished first of all by providing ourselves with a sincere confession (of at least the greatest sins and those which by diligent search can be recalled by our memory), with the holy Christian sacrament of the holy and true body of Christ, and with the unction. If these can be had, one should devoutly desire them and receive them with great confidence. If they cannot be had, our longing and yearning for them should nevertheless be a comfort and we should not be too dismayed by this circumstance. Christ says, "All things are possible to him who believes" (Mark 9:23). The sacraments are nothing else than signs which help and incite us to faith, as we shall see. Without this faith they serve no purpose.

Fifth, we must earnestly, diligently, and highly esteem the holy sacraments, hold them in honor, freely and cheerfully rely on them, and so balance them against sin, death, and hell that they will outweigh these by far. We must occupy ourselves much more with the sacraments and their virtues than with our sins. However, we must know how to give them due honor and we must know what their virtues are. I show them due honor when I believe that I truly receive what the sacraments signify and all that God declares and indicates in them, so that I can say with Mary in firm faith, "Let it be to me according to your words and signs" (Luke 1:38). Since God himself here speaks and acts through the priest, we would do him in his Word and work no greater dishonor than to doubt whether it is true. And we can do him no greater honor than to believe that his Word and work are true and to firmly rely on them.

Sixth, to recognize the virtues of the sacraments, we must know the evils which they contend with and which we face. There are three such evils: first, the terrifying image of death; second, the awesomely manifold image of sin; third, the unbearable and unavoidable image of hell and eternal damnation.

Every other evil issues from these three and grows large and strong as a result of such mingling.

Death looms so large and is terrifying because our foolish and fainthearted nature has etched its image too vividly within itself and constantly fixes its gaze on it. Moreover, the devil presses man to look closely at the gruesome mien and image of death to add to his worry, timidity, and despair. Indeed, he conjures up before man's eyes all the kinds of sudden and terrible death ever seen, heard, or read by man. And then he also slyly suggests the wrath of God with which he [the devil] in days past now and then tormented and destroyed sinners. In that way he fills our foolish human nature with the dread of death while cultivating a love and concern for life, so that burdened with such thoughts man forgets God, flees and abhors death, and thus, in the end, is and remains disobedient to God.

We should familiarize ourselves with death during our lifetime, inviting death into our presence when it is still at a distance and not on the move. At the time of dying, however, this is hazardous and useless, for then death looms large of its own accord. In that hour we must put the thought of death out of mind and refuse to see it, as we shall hear. The power and might of death are rooted in the fearfulness of our nature and in our untimely and undue viewing and contemplating of it.

Seventh, sin also grows large and important when we dwell on it and brood over it too much. This is increased by the fearfulness of our conscience, which is ashamed before God and accuses itself terribly. That is the water that the devil has been seeking for his mill. He makes our sins seem large and numerous. He reminds us of all who have sinned and of the many who were damned for lesser sins than ours so as to make us despair or die reluctantly, thus forgetting God and being found disobedient in the hour of death. This is true especially since man feels that he should think of his sins at that time and that it is right and useful for him to engage in such contemplation. But he finds himself so unprepared and unfit that now even all his good works are turned into sins. As a result, this must lead to an unwillingness to die, disobedience to the will of God, and eternal damnation. That is not the fitting time to meditate on sin. That must be done during one's lifetime. Thus the evil spirit turns everything upside down for us. During our lifetime, when we should constantly have our eyes fixed on the image of death, sin, and hell – as we read in Psalm 51:3, "My sin is ever before me" – the devil closes our eyes and hides these images. But in the hour of death when our eyes should see only life, grace, and salvation, he at once opens our eyes and frightens us with these untimely images so that we shall not see the true ones.

Eighth, hell also looms large because of undue scrutiny and stern thought devoted to it out of season. This is increased immeasurably by our ignorance of God's counsel. The evil spirit prods the soul so that it burdens itself with all kinds of useless presumptions, especially with the most dangerous undertaking of delving into the mystery of God's will to ascertain whether one is "chosen" or not. Here the devil practices his ultimate, greatest, and most cunning art and power. By this he sets man above God, insofar as man seeks signs of God's will and becomes impatient because he is not supposed to know whether he is among the elect. Man looks with suspicion upon God, so that he soon desires a different God. In brief, the devil is determined to blast God's love from a man's mind and to arouse thoughts of God's wrath. The more docilely man follows the devil and accepts these thoughts, the more imperiled his position is. In the end he cannot save himself, and he falls prey to hatred and blasphemy of God. What is my desire to know whether I am chosen other than a presumption to know all that God knows and to be equal with him so that he will know no more than I do? Thus God is no longer God with a knowledge surpassing mine. Then the devil reminds us of the many heathen, Jews, and Christians who are lost, agitating such dangerous and pernicious thoughts so violently that man, who would otherwise gladly die, now becomes loath to depart this life. When man is assailed by thoughts regarding his election, he is being assailed by hell, as the psalms lament so much. He who surmounts this temptation has vanquished sin, hell, and death all in one.

Ninth, in this affair we must exercise all diligence not to open our homes to any of these images and not to paint the devil over the door. These foes will of themselves boldly rush in and seek to occupy the heart completely with their image, their arguments, and their signs. And when that happens man is doomed and God is entirely forgotten. The only thing to do with these pictures at that time is to combat and expel them. Indeed, where they are found alone and not in conjunction with other pictures, they belong nowhere else than in hell among the devils.

But he who wants to fight against them and drive them out will find that it is not enough just to wrestle and tussle and scuffle with them. They will prove too strong for him, and matters will go from bad to worse. The one and only approach is to drop them entirely and have nothing to do with them. But how is that done? It is done in this way: You must look at death while you are alive and see sin in the light of grace and hell in the light of heaven, permitting nothing to divert you from that view. Adhere to that even if all angels, all creatures, yes, even your own thoughts, depict God in a different light - something these will not do. It is only the evil spirit who lends that impression. What shall we do about that?

Tenth, you must not view or ponder death as such, not in yourself or in your nature, nor in those who were killed by God's wrath and were overcome by death. If you do that you will be lost and defeated with them. But you must resolutely turn your gaze, the thoughts of your heart, and all your senses away from this picture and look at death closely and untiringly only as seen in those who died in God's grace and who have overcome death, particularly in Christ and then also in all his saints. In such pictures death will not appear terrible and gruesome. No, it will seem contemptible and dead, slain and overcome in life. For Christ is nothing other than sheer life, as his saints are likewise. The more profoundly you impress that image upon your heart and gaze upon it, the more the image of death will pale and vanish of itself without struggle or battle. Thus your heart will be at peace and you will be able to die calmly in Christ and with Christ, as we read in Revelation 14:13, "Blessed are they who die in the Lord Christ." This was foreshown in Numbers 21:6-9, where we hear that when the children of Israel were bitten by fiery serpents they did not struggle with these serpents, but merely had to raise their eyes to the dead bronze serpent and the living ones dropped from them by themselves and perished. Thus you must concern yourself solely with the death of Christ and then you will find life. But if you look at death in any other way, it will kill you with great anxiety and anguish. This is why Christ says, "In the world - that is, in yourselves - you have unrest, but in me you will find peace" (John 16:33).

Eleventh, you must not look at sin in sinners, or in your conscience, or in those who abide in sin to the end and are damned. If you do, you will surely follow them and also be overcome. You must turn your thoughts away from that and look at sin only within the picture of grace. Engrave that picture in yourself with all your power and keep it before your eyes. The picture of grace is nothing else but that of Christ on the cross and of all his dear saints. …

Fifteenth, we now turn to the holy sacraments and their blessings to learn to know their benefits and how to use them. Anyone who is granted the time and the grace to confess, to be absolved, and to receive the sacrament and Extreme Unction before his death has great cause indeed to love, praise, and thank God and to die cheerfully, if he relies firmly on and believes in the sacraments, as we said earlier. In the sacraments your God, Christ himself, deals, speaks, and works with you through the priest. His are not the works and words of man. In the sacraments God himself grants you all the blessings we just mentioned in connection with Christ. God wants the sacraments to be a sign and testimony that Christ's life has taken your death, his obedience your sin, his love your hell, upon themselves and overcome them. Moreover, through the same sacraments you are included and made one with all the saints. You thereby enter into the true communion of saints so that they die with you in Christ, bear sin, and vanquish hell. It follows from this that the sacraments, that is, the external words of God as spoken by a priest, are a truly great comfort and at the same time a visible sign of divine intent. We must cling to them with a staunch faith as to the good staff which the patriarch Jacob used when crossing the Jordan (Genesis 32:10), or as to a lantern by which we must be guided, and carefully walk with open eyes the dark path of death, sin, and hell, as the prophet says, "Thy word is a light to my feet" (Psalm 119:105). St. Peter also declares, "And we have a sure word from God. You will do well to pay attention to it" (2 Peter 1:19). There is no other help in death's agonies, for everyone who is saved is saved only by that sign. It points to Christ and his image, enabling you to say when faced by the image of death, sin, and hell, "God promised and in his sacraments he gave me a sure sign of his grace that Christ's life overcame my death in his death, that his obedience blotted out my sin in his suffering, that his love destroyed my hell in his forsakenness. This sign and promise of my salvation will not lie to me or deceive me. It is God who has promised it, and he cannot lie either in words or in deeds." He who thus insists and relies on the sacraments will find that his election and predestination will turn out well without his worry and effort. …

Eighteenth, in the hour of his death no Christian should doubt that he is not alone. He can be certain, as the sacraments point out, that a great many eyes are upon him: first, the eyes of God and of Christ himself, for the Christian believes his words and clings to his sacraments; then also, the eyes of the dear angels, of the saints, and of all Christians. There is no doubt, as the Sacrament of the Altar indicates, that all of these in a body run to him as one of their own, help him overcome sin, death, and hell, and bear all things with him. In that hour the work of love and the communion of saints are seriously and mightily active. A Christian must see this for himself and have no doubt regarding it, for then he will be bold in death. He who doubts this does not believe in the most venerable Sacrament of the Body of Christ, in which are pointed out, promised, and pledged the communion, help, love, comfort, and support of all the saints in all times of need. If you believe in the signs and words of God, his eyes rest upon you, as he says in Psalm 32:8, "My eyes will constantly be upon you lest you perish." If God looks upon you, all the angels, saints, and all creatures will fix their eyes upon you. And if you remain in that faith, all of them will uphold you with their hands. And when your soul leaves your body, they will be on hand to receive it, and you cannot perish. This is borne out in the person of Elisha, who according to 2 Kings 6:16–17 said to his servant, "Fear not, for those who are with us are more than those who are with them." This he said although enemies had surrounded them and they could see nothing but these. The Lord opened the eyes of the young man, and they were surrounded by a huge mass of horses and chariots of fire. The same is true of everyone who trusts God. Then the words found in Psalm 34:7 apply, "The angel of the Lord will encamp around those who fear him, and deliver them." And in Psalm 125:1–2, "Those who trust in the Lord are like Mount Zion, which cannot be moved, but abides forever. As the mountains (that is, the angels) are round about Jerusalem, so the Lord is round about his people, from this time forth and forevermore." And in Psalm 91:11–16, "For he has charged his angels to bear you on their hands and to guard you wherever you go lest you dash your foot against a stone. You will tread on the lion and the adder, the young lion and the serpent you will trample under foot (this means that all the power and the cunning of the devil will be unable to harm you), because he has trusted in me and I will deliver him; I will protect him because he knows my name. When he calls to me, I will answer him; I will be with him in all his trials, I will rescue him and honor him. With eternal life will I satisfy him, and show him my eternal grace." Thus the Apostle also declares that the angels, whose number is legion, are all ministering spirits and are sent out for the sake of those who are to be saved (Hebrews 1:14).

These are all such great matters that who can believe them? Therefore, we must know that even though the works of God surpass human understanding, God yet effects all of this through such insignificant signs as the sacraments to teach us what a great thing a true faith in God really is.

Nineteenth, let no one presume to perform such things by his own power, but humbly ask God to create and preserve such faith in and such understanding of his holy sacraments in him. He must practice awe and humility in all this, lest he ascribe these works to himself instead of allowing God the glory. To this end he must call upon the holy angels, particularly his own angel, the Mother of God, and all the apostles and saints, especially since God has granted him exceptional zeal for this. However, he dare not doubt, but must believe that his prayer will be heard. He has two reasons for this. The first one is that he has just heard from the Scriptures how God commanded the angels to give love and help to all who believe and how the sacrament conveys this. We must hold this before them and remind them of it, not that the angels do not know this, or would otherwise not do it, but to make our faith and trust in them, and through them in God, stronger and bolder as we face death. The other reason is that God has enjoined us firmly to believe in the fulfillment of our prayer (Mark 11:24) and that it is truly an Amen. We must also bring this command of God to his attention and say, "My God, you have commanded me to pray and to believe that my prayer will be heard. For this reason I come to you in prayer and am assured that you will not forsake me but will grant me a genuine faith."

Moreover, we should implore God and his dear saints our whole life long for true faith in the last hour, as we sing so very fittingly on the day of Pentecost, "Now let us pray to the Holy Spirit for the true faith of all things the most, that in our last moments he may befriend us, and as home we go, he may tend us." When the hour of death is at hand we must offer this prayer to God and, in addition, remind him of his command and of his promise and not doubt that our prayer will be fulfilled. After all, if God commanded us to pray and to trust in prayer, and, furthermore, has granted us the grace to pray, why should we doubt that his purpose in this was also to hear and to fulfill it?

Twentieth, what more should God do to persuade you to accept death willingly and not to dread but to overcome it? In Christ he offers you the image of life, of grace, and of salvation so that you may not be horrified by the images of sin, death, and hell. Furthermore, he lays your sin, your death, and your hell on his dearest Son, vanquishes them, and renders them harmless for you. In addition, he lets the trials of sin, death, and hell that come to you also assail his Son and teaches you how to preserve yourself in the midst of these and how to make them harmless and bearable. And to relieve you of all doubt, he grants you a sure sign, namely, the holy sacraments. He commands his angels, all saints, all creatures to join him in watching over you, to be concerned about your soul, and to receive it. He commands you to ask him for this and to be assured of fulfillment. What more can or should he do? From this you can see that he is a true God and that he performs great, right, and divine works for you. Why, then, should he not impose something big upon you (such as dying), as long as he adds to it great benefits, help, and strength, and thereby wants to test the power of his grace. Thus we read in Psalm 111:2, "Great are the works of the Lord, selected according to his pleasure."

Therefore, we ought to thank him with a joyful heart for showing us such wonderful, rich, and immeasurable grace and mercy against death, hell, and sin, and to laud and love his grace rather than fearing death so greatly. Love and praise make dying very much easier, as God tells us through Isaiah, "For the sake of my praise I restrain it [wrath] for you, that I may not cut you off" (Isaiah 48:9). To that end may God help us. Amen.

Justus Jonas on Luther's last days and his death

By coincidence Luther died in Eisleben, the same town in which he had been born. Luther traveled there in winter 1545/46 to settle a dispute between the Mansfeld counts. He had already been ill on the way there, and he was not to recover. On 18 February 1546, he died in the presence of some friends and colleagues, among them Justus Jonas, a reformer in Halle an der Saale. He wrote of Luther's last days and hours in a report, and a drawing of Luther's face in death was also made. In this way, Luther's followers wanted to place it on record that he had died a peaceful and blessed death.

Luther died at a difficult time. The Council of Trent had met in 1545. However, the Protestants had refused to participate, as they did not consider it free and Christian. The emperor was outraged, war was in the offing. A few months after Luther's death, a religious war indeed began in Germany that had long been expected. The Protestants now had to go through difficult years without Luther until the Peace of Augsburg in 1555.

Justus Jonas, Doctor Martin Luthers abschied und sterben (1546): Christof Schubart (ed.): Die Berichte über Luthers Tod und Begräbnis. Texte und Untersuchungen, Weimar 1917, pp. 2–5. Translation: Neville Williamson

In Wittenberg and on the journey, the revered Doctor Martin Luther, dear father of us all in Christ, complained about his health and then, after his arrival in Eisleben, that he felt very weak. Nevertheless, in Eisleben, while we were discussing the business of the counts, he took lunch and dinner and ate and drank well. He also praised the food and drink and said that he greatly enjoyed the cooking in the place where he was born. He also slept well and peacefully every night.

His servant Ambrosius, I myself Doctor Jonas, his two little sons Martin and Paul and one or two other servants shared the chamber with him. Every evening we gave him the warmed pillows he was used to when putting him to bed; I often did this together with Magister Michael Celius, the preacher from Mansfeld. For three weeks he said good night to us every evening, often with these words: "Doctor Jonas and Master Michael, pray to our Lord that all will be well with his church and cause, because the Council in Trent is much enraged." Doctor Luther also sent to Wittenberg for sustaining food, water and brandy, such as he used to take at home. His wife also sent it here on her own initiative. So every two or three days during these three weeks, when negotiations were being held, he sat together with my most gracious lord, Prince Wolf of Anhalt, and Count Hans Heinrich of Schwarzburg.

But yesterday, on the Wednesday after Valentine's Day, 17 February, following the wishes of the Prince of Anhalt and Count Albrecht, and also on my request and advice, he remained in his room in the morning and did not go to the negotiations. But in his room he walked up and down without breeches, in an overgown, looking out of the window from time to time and praying; he prayed so loudly that we, who were with him in the room, could also hear it. But he was always cheerful. From time to time he addressed us directly and said: "Doctor Jonas and Master Michael! I was born and baptized here in Eisleben – what if I should remain here?"

But on that Wednesday he did not take his meal in his chamber, but downstairs in the big parlor, and at table he spoke a lot about beautiful Bible words. Once or twice, during the general conversation, he said: "Should I, God willing, reach an agreement among my dear rulers, the counts, so that the purpose of this journey is fulfilled, then I will go home and lay down to sleep in my coffin and let the worms feed on the body of a good fat doctor."

But before dinner on this very Wednesday, he began to complain that he had a feeling of pressure on his chest, but not in the region of the heart. He asked to be rubbed with warm towels. Afterwards he said that the pressure had eased a little. He took his meal in the big parlor, saying "It is no fun to be alone." At dinner he ate well and was cheerful, sometimes making jokes. After dinner he once again complained about the pressure on his chest, and asked for warm towels. Then the other gentlemen and we ourselves wanted to send for the doctors, a magister and a doctor, but he wouldn't have it, and then he slept for two and a half or maybe three and a half hours on the couch. We stayed by him until about half past ten o'clock: Master Michael Celius, I Jonas, the landlord and town clerk of Eisleben, the landlady and his two little sons. Afterwards, he said he would like to have the bed in his chamber warmed for him. This was done with great care, and then we put him to bed. Magister Celius also lay in the chamber as well as Luther's servant Ambrosius, who had come with him from Wittenberg. Apart from them, I myself, his two little sons and the servants were also lying with him in the chamber. About eleven o'clock he fell asleep and was at rest; his breathing was normal. Then at one o'clock at night he called his servant Ambrosius and me. First of all he told the servant: "Heat up the parlor!" The servant made haste to do so, and when the parlor was warm, for which preparations had already been made in the night, he said to me: "Oh, my God, Doctor Jonas, I feel so sick, I feel such a strong pressure on my chest. Oh, I am going to remain in Eisleben."

Meanwhile Ambrosius and all of us went over to him and helped him out of bed. After going down into the parlor, he walked around again, but then he wanted the warm towels. We quickly had both doctors in the town woken, the doctor and the magister, and they came straightaway. We also called for my most gracious Count Albrecht to be woken, and he soon arrived with the Countess. We tried caraway brandy and the doctor's own medicine and everything else. Then the doctor [Luther] began to pray: "My heavenly Father, eternal, merciful God! You have revealed to me your dear son, our Lord Jesus Christ. I have preached him, I have confessed him, I love and honor him as my dear savior and redeemer, who is persecuted, abhorred and scorned by the wicked. Now receive my soul." Then he said three times, in Latin: "Into your hand I commit my spirit, for you have redeemed me, God of truth" (Psalm 31:5), and added: "For God so loved the world..." (John 3:16). Despite our efforts to strengthen him with the help of the doctors, he began to get quieter, as though he were fading away, and he did not answer us, even when we called to him loudly and shook him. The countess and the doctors rubbed caraway brandy onto him. Then he began to reply to me and Master Michael Celius again with yes and no, but only very weakly. And when we spoke to him in a loud voice and asked, "Dearly beloved Father, you confess Christ, the Son of God, our Savior and Redeemer," he raised his voice again loud enough to be heard: "Yes". After this, his forehead and face turned cold, and no matter how loudly we shouted, shook him and called him by his baptismal name "Doctor Martin", he no longer answered. He breathed out softly and sighed, with his hands folded and clasped together, and thus he fell asleep in Christ sometime between two and three o'clock in the night before daybreak, causing us much grief with saddened hearts and many tears. Count Albrecht and our gracious lady, the countess, as well as my gracious Lords of Schwarzburg, were there in time, some of them just before the end. …

Index of Luther's writings quoted

Index of Luther editions used

WA	Martin Luther: Kritische Gesamtausgabe. Schriften, Vol. 1-65, Weimar 1883-1993.
WA.DB	Martin Luther: Kritische Gesamtausgabe. Die Deutsche Bibel 1522-1546, Vol. 1-12. Weimar 1906-1961.
WA.TR	Martin Luther: Kritische Gesamtausgabe. Tischreden 1531-1546, Vol. 1-6, Weimar 1912-1921.
LW	Luther's Works: The American Edition, Vol. 1-55, Concordia Publishing House / Fortress Press 1955-1986.
AL	The Annotated Luther, Vol. 1-6, Fortress Press 2015-2017.

Christine Axt-Piscalar
Andreas Ohlemacher
(Hrsg.)

Um des Evangeliums willen

Gesetz und Evangelium, Glaube und Werke, Alter und Neuer Bund, Verheißung und Erfüllung

Eine Handreichung für Predigerinnen und Prediger

84 pages | paperback
14,5 x 21,5 cm
ISBN 978-3-374-06903-3
EUR 9,80 [D]

Every week preachers face the challenge of exploring the biblical texts in their diversity. As an inner-biblical key to the understanding of these texts, the so-called duals of law and gospel, faith and good works, old and new covenant, promise and fulfillment have a long tradition in the Evangelical Lutheran Church as an approach for the understanding of the Bible. However, they can be misunderstood and particularly turned against Jewish theology. The handout deals with this danger consciously and openly by describing how the respective duals are to be understood – and thus also how they are not to be understood and must not be understood. It describes the different theological backgrounds of the duals and illuminates their respective existential power for the present and future.

EVANGELISCHE VERLAGSANSTALT
Leipzig www.eva-leipzig.de

Tel +49 (0) 341/ 7 11 41 -44 shop@eva-leipzig.de